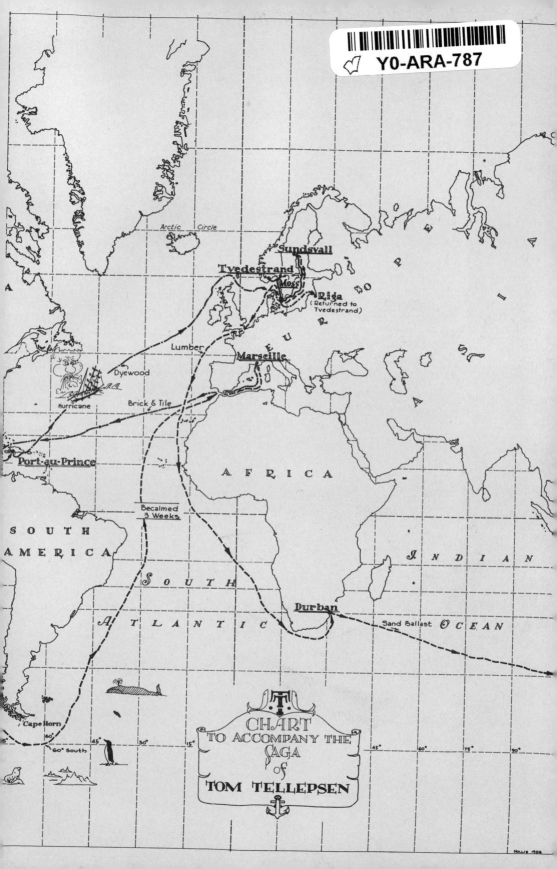

Arctic Circle

Sundsvall

Tvedestrand
Moss
Riga
(Returned to
Tvedestrand)

E U R O P E

Lumber

Marseille

Dyewood

Hurricane

Brick & Tile

Port-au-Prince

A F R I C A

Becalmed
3 Weeks

S O U T H

A M E R I C A

S O U T H

I N D I A N

Durban

A T L A N T I C

Sand Ballast O C E A N

Cape Horn

60° South

CHART
TO ACCOMPANY THE
SAGA
of
TOM TELLEPSEN

Hollis 1959

Tom Tellepsen

TOM TELLEPSEN
BUILDER & BELIEVER

A BIOGRAPHY

BY

ANDREA K. FLYNN

ILLUSTRATED

THE ANSON JONES PRESS

SALADO   TEXAS

M   C   M   L   V   I

Copyright 1956

by

Andrea K. Flynn

———

Library of Congress Card 57-6174

PRINTED AND BOUND IN TEXAS, UNITED STATES OF AMERICA

I N GRATITUDE TO GOD and the God-loving
country of America, I am thankful for
a full life on this continent: also for my
dear wife and three children, daughter-
in-law, two sons-in-law and ten grandchildren — to them I dedicate this book.

TOM TELLEPSEN

Preface

Tom Tellepsen is best known to his friends, his employees and his community as "Mr. Tom."

His is a title of esteem and respect. As *"Mister* Tom," he represents success — financially, in his business; personally, in his reputation as a self-made man, obscure immigrant to honored citizen; in the position of his household as a cultural and spiritual force in Houston.

As "Mr. *Tom,"* he represents the paternal kindness of every successful man who is humble before his God. The familiarity derives from affection which has that gentle, intimate humor of those who love as well as revere.

Mankind inclines to symbolism in judging their own, and "Mr. Tom" is symbolic of opportunity, the kind of opportunity which made it possible for a lad, shipping to sea at the age of fourteen, to find happiness, prosperity and self-fulfilment in a new country. Taking from his native Norway the attributes of industry, perseverance, belief in God and in himself, "Mr. Tom" joined to these the best qualities of the New World, of Texas — courage, ingenuity, the spirit to adventure. "Mr. Tom" is thus a character in the unending American story and has that rare privilege of becoming a tradition in his own lifetime.

An Introduction

THE SUBJECT'S POINT OF VIEW

Why chronicle the saga of Tom Tellepsen?

What persuaded Tom Tellepsen, a shy and modest man, to accept in his own mind the idea of telling his story?

Perhaps it began by the simple wish to relate the experiences of a lifetime for the benefit of his children and his children's children. Here is a thin strand of immortality to which we all wistfully cling.

But as the idea took shape, so did an underlying motive—as direct and uncomplicated as the man himself. "If I could come this far," Mr. Tom says to the reader, "so can you. Take the story of my life as encouragement that you, too, can achieve anything you put your mind and hand to, God willing."

So Tom Tellepsen considers the telling of his story as yet another way of serving his fellow men and of affirming his faith in God.

An Introduction

THE AUTHOR'S POINT OF VIEW

Why chronicle the saga of Tom Tellepsen?

An immigrant lad, he found in America the opportunity of achieving wealth and eminence, but this sort of success story has been written many times before, and others of equally modest beginnings have risen to even greater heights. Of little formal education, Tom Tellepsen began as an humble carpenter's apprentice to become the builder of beautiful modern buildings like The Shamrock: but there are many examples in our history of self-made, self-educated men. Born a poor boy, he recognized that the wealth he had acquired was a responsibility as well as a privilege, and he has been generous in helping others, but there are other philanthropists who have shared and endowed more spectacularly.

The saga of Tom Tellepsen is a bit of all three — the story of opportunity, of enterprise, of benevolence. Yet it is still more.

As a child Tom Tellepsen believed in himself because his mother believed in him, and he loved her. As he grew older he came to identify this confidence with God. He acknowledged His guidance, and in gratitude he did not only the best he could do, but the most he could do. He had ambition, and he dreamed his dreams with an intensity that would not tolerate doubt or discouragement. It is this simple and significant philosophy that makes the story of Tom Tellepsen unique.

The story is an inspiration — not only as evidence that wealth and success can be achieved from simple beginnings, but that self-confidence, hard work, faith and integrity are the ingredients for happiness and a full and vital life.

ix

The story of Tom Tellepsen is an answer to those who say there is no longer opportunity; frontiers will always exist to the dedicated mind and the determined will. The story of Tom Tellepsen is an answer to those who call religion self-deception, and condemn religion for the shortcomings of those who declare but do not abide.

Our generation has breathed the dry dust of pessimism, of cynicism. Therefore we have welcomed the soothing voices that tell us how to be forceful, how to be popular, how to be successful. Dazzled by these assurances, we too often forget that they alone are not enough. It is what we do about our every day life, how we meet day-by-day situations that determines how effective we become. The methods are old-fashioned and unglamorous. They require courage, tenacity, ingenuity, and above all, hard and willing labor. The world needs not so much the happy philosophies but the affirmative action, and the persistent, confident faith that is the wellspring of that action.

And this, in substance, is the saga of Tom Tellepsen.

Contents

Illustrations

Boyhood

Geography is a mirror held up to the countenance of the world. Reflected thus, the Scandinavian Peninsula is the skeleton of a giant, sprawled on its side. To the west, the ribbed walls of rock cleave sharply into the cold, blue water; on the east and south, the mountains break less steeply, and the fjords stretch themselves ten to twenty-five miles, with sloping rocky hills and forests levelling to the water's edge. Down the meandering fjords step gaunt islands towards the narrow, shallow mouth which forbids entrance and yet invites the inland wayfarer to distant, deep seas beyond.

On March 21, 1888, and the first day of an imperceptible spring, Torjus (Tom) Tellefsen, was born in the town of Tvedestrand in southeast Norway, at the head of such a fjord, the Fjord of Tvedestrand. He was, by the time he was sixteen to know geography intimately, to travel under sail from Europe at 62° north latitude to Africa and south to 60° south latitude, and around the world, through the Pacific islands, around the Horn, to the Mediterranean, back to the West Indies, again across the Atlantic bound for the Baltic Sea.

* * * * * * *

Tellef Halvorsen came to Tvedestrand as a young man. He was born at Treungen, district of Telemarken, in the interior. His forebears had been farmers. His father's farm, called Haugestöl, was not large enough to divide among Tellef, the youngest son, and his brothers, as was the custom in Norway. Besides, Tellef was different. He was restless and discontented. Even as a small boy he

1

would wander off into the mountains above the river and sit for hours, chin in hand, gazing at the horizon. His mother scolded him often for not hearing what she said to him. He was not exactly inattentive, but it was as if he were listening for a distant sound. Like surf and wind over water. He came to Tvedestrand to apprentice as a ships' carpenter, the only one of the brothers to learn a trade.

At this time, Tvedestrand was a town of about 1,200 inhabitants. Although ignored by many map makers who charted Risör to the north and Arendal to the south, Tvedestrand boasted a proud and salty tradition, having served as a port since the sixteenth century. Lumber and pig iron were its principal exports. A small shipbuilding industry was located here. Almost without exception, every townsman had either sailed the seven seas himself or was related to a sailor or shipowner. Tvedestrand was a logical place, therefore, for Tellef to learn his trade. Here he met and married Tora Björnevikhalsen whose father and brothers were seafaring men.

Not long after his first son, Halvor, was born, Tellef decided to follow the example of an older brother, Egild Halvorsen, who had gone to America in 1869. Tellef sailed for New York and found employment as a carpenter. The birth of a second son, Torjus (Tom), gave Tellef further incentive, and he proudly wrote Tora that he was now foreman of a crew building foundation forms for the Williamsburg bridge in New York City.

But Tellef was not to realize his dream of bringing his family to America. When Tom was only eighteen months old, word was received that his father had been killed in a construction accident. Details are not clear. A friend who roomed with Tellef reported that an emergency required someone to do a dangerous job and, as foreman, Tellef insisted on doing it himself. What was feared might happen, did happen, and a timber fell, crushing Tellef. He was buried in New York.

Tellef's most valuable possessions, his carpenter's tools, were shipped to Tora in Tvedestrand — a forlorn inheritance of a father's dream. Tora's background was such that she was not prepared to earn her own living, but she had courage and was devoted to her young sons. She sold the tools and with their proceeds bought a Singer knitting machine, learning the technique of operation in a matter of months. The rooms she had been renting from Mr. Dedekam when Tom was born were too small for two growing boys and her new "enterprise." She installed her family in a house on the main

The lake above Tvedestrand whose waters fed the **stream**
past Miller Master Larsen's mill.

Tvedestrand—The arrow points to the house where **Tom**
lived as a boy.

Tellef Halvorsen

Tora Halvorsen—and her knitting machine

Halvor, Tom and model steamboat

Tom, Halvor and cat

street of Tvedestrand and took orders for sweaters, socks, and knitted garments and pieces of all kinds.

In the life of Tom Tellefsen, the figure of his mother was to stand as a symbol and an enduring inspiration. Perhaps she was not a beautiful woman, in the strictest sense, but her face had the composure of decision and self assurance. Her large brown eyes were expressive of distance, yet the corners wrinkled and softened the austere appraisal. The thin lips held a straight line and indicated an indomitable spirit. The folk of Tvedestrand recognized in "Mother Tora" the strength of a good woman and the gentleness of an understanding mother. It has been said that she would, with energy and innocence, tell others what to do: what she told them they did and loved doing it!

To Tom, his mother was both good and beautiful. He recognized in her — in her character and in her life — the real meaning of religion: "She has God within her." From his admiration and unstinting devotion to her, Tora drew the courage and renewed confidence she must have needed in the difficult years to follow.

On the other hand, the knowledge of his mother's great love and faith in him was never absent from Tom's consciousness. It gave him strength in times of weakness, patience in times of heartache; sustained him in the face of hardship and temptation. Her teachings of what constituted right and wrong have been the basis of Tom's high principles throughout his life.

Tom remembers those early years with warmth and an almost photographic clearness. Their apartment consisted of two rooms and a kitchen on the second floor of a four-story house. Tvedestrand is built on a hill, so that the Halvorsens had two entrances at different levels. Underneath their living room was a butcher shop with entrance on the main street. Two casement windows of the living room looked out over this street. Tora placed her knitting machine in front of these windows so that she might look out and observe the comings and goings of her friends and neighbors. Proceeding up Main Street one came to the outside steps leading up to the vestibule that adjoined the living room. The kitchen on the other side of the house had a doorway which led up into the back yard. This arrangement conspired with the drifting snow so that at least on one occasion, Tom had to tunnel out the kitchen door to the street above! By the outhouse, Tom and Halvor built a lean-to for a varying succession of pets: rabbits, pigeons, and even a goat. There was a flower garden, too, in the upper back yard.

3

The exterior of the house was frame, and the interior walls were paneled in wood which was painted. The living room was papered with what was called tapestry. Tora had a gift for creating beauty from simple things, and Tom describes his home with pleasure in the flowers growing year round in the window boxes inside the windows, the dainty white curtains, the shelves with their colorful souvenirs from faraway places. Even the sleek cat who invariably sat by the knitting machine and observed Tora's skillful fingers with lazy eyes added to a distinct memory lovely as a Chardin painting.

Perishables were stored in the cellar. Kerosene lamps provided illumination. Early in 1900, electricity was made available to the townsfolk. When Tom came home in 1912, his mother was cooking with electricity. But, when Tom was a boy, the wood-burning cook stove and the stove which heated bedroom and living room required kindling and firewood. In the summer, Tom would go with his little wagon and gather the chips and shavings that remained when trees were felled in the forest — enough to supply his mother's cooking needs. In the wintertime, they would buy firewood — oak and birch.

Tora Halvorsen was a very religious woman. No matter to what good purpose the coins could have been put in her own household, more than the tithe was set aside for the collection plate. She was active in church affairs and for fifteen years headed the China mission. The state church in Norway is the Evangelical Lutheran church. Tora helped establish the "free" church in Tvedestrand. This church was organized roughly along the lines of the Presbyterian church as adapted from Scotland. Prayer meetings were held in her home every week up until the time of her death. The boys accompanied her to Sunday school and church every Sunday. Tom would sometimes fidget if the sermon was long, and he would mentally count off the seconds. "One minute gone," he would say to himself.

Measured by income, Tom was poor, but his environment was better than average. One neighbor, Carl Bech, was a prosperous shipowner. Children recognize few economic or social differences. Frank as they may be in judging each other, children can be just as generous in ignoring adult prejudices. Tom's friends loved Mother Tora as they admired Tom's spunk. To Tom's friend, Birger Jorkjend, she was "Dear Mother Tora." Another boyhood friend, Carl Gundersen, remembers her as a sincerely religious woman whom he always looked up to and respected.

4

It was typical of Tora that Tom's birthday parties would include all his friends who enjoyed the pastry and the hot chocolate with whipped cream. They crowded around his mother for the stories she would tell. He, in turn, attended their birthday parties, exchanged presents with them and was considered their equal.

From the time he was five, Tom had contributed to the household accounts and as he grew older, he became the main provider. He was under contract to several store owners to sweep the cobblestone streets in front of their establishments. He unloaded brick and tile from the harbor barges. He delivered the knitwear to his mother's clients and this required making collections. Sometimes it meant his going back again and again. Though a bitter experience for one so young, this contact with human nature taught a valuable lesson in patience, tact and perseverance.

After Tora's death, Birger Jorkjend wrote Tom that among his mother's other belongings was found the suit of clothes Tom had worn to clean the boiler of the steamboat that plied back and forth from the mouth of the fjord to the harbor. Tom well remembers these occasions:

Tom squirmed through the manhole into the boiler. The prospect of ten kroner (about $2.10 in those days) performed alchemy: the ugly odor of grease, slime and salt water became the most exquisite of perfumes. He worked as fast as he could. First he scraped the flues with a sharp knife, the corroded particles spewing before the quick blade. Then he used a stiff brush to insure the smoothness of the surface. It was hot and stuffy inside the boiler. Tom worked in a cramped position. He grimaced as he struggled to reach the undermost parts. Only a very small boy could even wiggle to each extremity of flue. Only a boy with strong arms could apply the needed pressure to knife and brush.

For several years, now, Tom had done this; it was one of his most dependable contracts and at a handsome return.

"It is more than this," thought Tom. "It is the job that *I* can do best — only I — because I am small and strong and Mr. Dedekam knows I will do a thorough cleaning." Tom gave an extra push to the brush. "Mother understands this pride I have. That is why she saves the same clothing year after year for me to wear when I clean the boiler — because they have become my uniform, and she is proud, too."

Tom sold and delivered papers (there were three newspapers in Tvedestrand at that time). He sawed and chopped wood. He ran errands. When a large ship carrying mail and passengers would cast anchor outside Tvedestrand Fjord, the steam packet boat would ferry the passengers and cargo to the village. Visiting salesmen needed boys to carry their sample cases and luggage, and Tom was a favorite, partly because he could jump the farthest — from wharf to gunwale — and therefore was able to contact his prospect before the other boys! His compensation ranged from twenty-five öre to a krone.

There were two banks in Tvedestrand, and the largest, a savings bank, gave Tom employment as bank runner when their regular employee was absent or on vacation. Also, Tom often worked at one of the grocery stores, scooping up the rice, flour and sugar onto the scales, weighing and sacking the merchandise. Tom was a perfectionist, even then, in making a neat and emphatic fold of the sack top. None of the precious contents ever seeped out of Tom's well fastened packages. The white apron he wore so proudly was, to him, the noblest of uniforms. In Tom's opinion, he was really somebody when he could clerk at the grocery.

Because he was so deserving, always willing and ingenious in his talents, Tom was asked to do many unusual tasks. One he will never forget:

Tom edged himself gingerly out the limb of the plum tree. The plums were particularly large this year, some almost purple in their fullness. "It is no wonder," thought Tom, "that Mrs. Torvildsen wants every one" before they fell of their own weight and ripeness and bruised their plump sides on the ground some twenty feet below. Tom teetered precariously on his airy perch. He liked it here. It gave him the same feeling of height and distance as did the cliffs, except that looking down from the mountain, you imagined what you saw, and here you could see what it was you imagined!

6

There was his house down the winding road — a corner of the dovecote was visible, the one he and Halvor had built. Tom wondered if the beautiful blue pigeon, their most recent possession, would roost there tonight, or fly home, as was his wont, to his former owner, Mr. Johan Holm. "Now rabbits," Tom thought to himself, "are soft and cuddly pets and even make mother laugh with their bright eyes and inquiring noses." Yet, the rabbits were domestic folk and stayed close to home. But the pigeons, they loved their freedom and would fly away — always to return. "Not I," said Tom, "if I were a pigeon I would fly up out over the fjord to the mouth and over the Skagerrak and to the world beyond."

The swaying of the branch brought Tom abruptly back to the plum orchard. He shifted slightly to see if he could somehow sight Birger's house, but it was obscured by the solid structure of Mrs. Torvildsen's home and a thicket of apple and pear trees. Birger was Mrs. Torvildsen's nephew, and Tom's good friend, and he had promised to come by that afternoon and let Tom drop the fruit to him instead of having to inch the basket along the branch ahead of him. The tree had already been plucked of its accessible plums, and it was Tom's task only to get the plums off the ends of the branches — so he had done for many summers now, light and agile as he was.

The late summer sun, the height and the heady fragrance of the fruit prolonged the daydream into which the boy had fallen. He and Birger had talked so much lately about what they would do when they were out of school and old enough to go to sea . . . . "to go to sea," that tantalizing thought. Tom swung himself erect for a better glimpse of the harbor and the twisting fjord. As he did so, there was a brittle crack, the branch bent suddenly, catapulting the basket of plums to the ground. Tom grasped wildly for a second hold, lost balance and fell. A thud, a quick agonizing pain in his shoulder, and the summer afternoon was blotted into darkness.

The sound of the surf and the oceans Tom had dreamed about was in his ears when he regained consciousness three days later. He awoke to find himself in his bed with Dr. Erick Ericksen bending over him — his mother a blur at the foot of the bed. His broken arm was bandaged and in a sling. His head ached; his eyes hurt. Slowly the familiar room became clear, and the doctor's words penetrated.

"How do you feel, Torjus?" he asked.

Tom's mother walked around the bed and knelt. In the warmth of her embrace, Tom knew that he was all right. "That was a bad fall, my son, but God has heard my prayers."

Although he rebelled at the inactivity — there was work to be done, and Halvor would scurry off with messages and errands to do for his younger brother — Tom found being an invalid was somewhat of an adventure. There was a steady stream of visitors into the bedroom: Fritz and Abba Bech; Carl, Hans, Sander and Ola Gundersen; Birger Jorkjend; Louis Nævestad; Nils Gutormsen; and Alf Holst — all appeared, somewhat embarrassed in their sympathy, but promising all sorts of activity once he was out of bed.

Aunt Teresie brought her brown basket of sweets. "For you alone," she said, offering a piece of Napoleon cake. She chided him, "This time you needn't cough as a hint that you'd like to sample the contents of my basket. Nor can you disappear when I have given them to you. You'll stay where I can see and talk to you."

His mother, too, would come and sit by his bed and tell him stories of her childhood and her hopes for him. "Three times before this you have broken your arm, Torjus," she said. "The sea has no trees: we will have to put you on a ship." "Masts are trees of the sea, Mother," Tom reminded her. Tora smiled knowingly, "But you will be the captain, Torjus."

For a flagging appetite, Tora brought up from the cellar a jar of strawberry jam, made from the wild ones, small but sweet, that Tom had gathered in the woods. Meat, prepared usually only on Sunday, appeared on his tray nearly every day: succulent roast of horsemeat and meat balls in a savory sauce with mealy potatoes shaken with melted butter and parsley. Wild cranberries served as a garnish.

One afternoon, rousing from his nap, he heard in the next room the familiar and awesome voice of his principal, Mr. Taraldsen. Dignified, with his long white beard, Mr. Taraldsen was indeed a personage in the community. "It is an honor," his mother whispered, "that Mr. Taraldsen has come to see you — he says you are a fine boy and a good pupil. I am proud."

Tom's muttered expression of gratitude and Mr. Taraldsen's remarks of encouragement and good will were diverted by an offer of coffee and pastries in the living room with

Mrs. Carl Bech and Mrs. Johan Wrolsen, for whom Tom sawed and chopped wood in the fall. Tom listened to his mother making preparations in the kitchen and idly turned his head towards the living room door.

Mr. Taraldsen's words came to him faintly. "What a pity the boy is not a member of the Lutheran Church."

"Well," thought Tom impishly, "I wonder if mother would be proud of that!"

Everyone has a favorite uncle, and Uncle Jörgen was Tom's. Jörgen was Tora's brother and a ship's carpenter. This was a reputable and well paid occupation; the wage being comparable to that of a first mate. Jörgen would sign on for two or three years at sea, and his visits home were memorable for the two boys, Tom and Halvor, who were his favorites. Jörgen had a name for Tom: from the Norwegian it would translate roughly as "lightning" reflecting Tom's faculty for being straight and quick. Tom loved his uncle very much, and the feeling was mutual. Not so strange then, that when Tom's family visited in Tvedestrand in 1922, Tom's son, ten-year old Howard, should find a kindred spirit in Uncle Jörgen. When Howard returned home, he immediately set up a work bench *a la* Uncle Jörgen — meticulously hanging up his tools and keeping everything in its proper place. The example of Uncle Jörgen made a deep impression.

Uncle Jörgen brought Tom and Halvor many unusual and interesting gifts from the distant places his ship would visit. His lively stories did much to further Tom's not-too-secret determination to go to sea. The two were often together and they loved to go fishing. When Tom was still very young he insisted on carrying home the codfish Jörgen caught, even though it meant dragging them down the street.

Jörgen's wife, Teresie, was also loved by the boys, particularly for her culinary treats. Tom would often visit his aunt when his uncle was at sea, and his patience won him many a slice of bread with sugar or that particularly delectable dessert, a kind of jello with cream, which is still a favorite today.

Tom was also very fond of his mother's sister, Lisa — "Aunt Lisa" as she was known to the neighborhood children. Thomas, the elder brother, went down with his ship somewhere off the Cape of Good Hope. The four — Thomas, Jörgen, Lisa and Tora, were devoted to their father, Torjus Torjusen Björnevikhalsen, who lived so long alone in his home with the fjord in his front yard. It could be reached only by boat or by a long trip over the mountain. It was here Tom's mother had been born on June 27, 1861. Retired from the sea, this quiet, stately old gentleman worked in his shop, hewing oars by hand from the timbers he cut in the forest. To Tom often fell the task of straightening the bent nails which were carefully kept and reused. When age made it necessary for Björnevikhalsen to live with Jörgen in Tvedestrand, he would insist on rowing to his workshop every day. Grandfather Torjus bequeathed to his children and his children's children courage and independence of mind and spirit. Integrity, patience and perseverance were the lessons he taught, and Tom was an apt pupil.

Tom had another Uncle Jörgen — his father's brother, Jörgen Halvorsen Goderstad. Jörgen's farm was located ten miles up in the mountains from Tvedestrand. Each summer from the time Tom was seven, he and Halvor would walk up to the farm and spend their vacation helping in the harvest fields, along with the two Goderstad boys and three Goderstad girls. They would arise at three in the morning and do the chores, spending the daylight hours harvesting the oats and barley, cutting and turning the hay to dry and later bundling it and tossing the bundles into the waiting wagon. What fun it was to ride high on the well stacked load — what fun to jump into the hay when it was safely put away in the loft in the barn!

When the steaming bowl of rice was brought to the table, and the family crowded around, Tom did not hold back. This was his favorite dish — dotted with butter, its hot goodness accentuated by the cinnamon and sugar topping and cooled but slightly by the white ribbon of rich, fresh cream. This delicacy of rice boiled with milk was the main course at the dinner celebrating the end of the harvest.

Tom liked to turn the grindstone used in sharpening the sickles, and, when he was very young, this required standing on tip

---

The way in which surnames were derived in Norway is interesting and also confusing. A son's surname was taken from his father's first name, i.e. Tom, as the son of Tellef Halvoren, was "Torjus Tellefsen." In rural communities, groups of farms or homes in an area had a geographic name which was their mailing address. In addition, an individual farm or home was designated by a name which had descended through generations from the time of the original owner who had established the farm or home. This name was then appended to a man's surname when he took over a farm, thus Tellef Halvorsen's brother was called "Jorgen Halvorsen Goderstad" — Goderstad being the name of his farm.

toe. Often he would go with the dog to bring in the cows who were allowed to graze in the meadow. The two horses were used in the fields, but on Sunday Uncle Jörgen might be persuaded to saddle them and the boys would ride.

The farm was largely self-sufficient. The women mostly cared for the chickens and the vegetable garden and did the milking. Tom and Halvor helped and observed. It was educational for the two coast-town children, and the exercise and hardy fare sent them back to Tora, brown and healthy.

Free schooling in Norway to the seventh grade was provided by the State. Reading, writing, arithmetic, geography, nature study and history were the principal subjects. There was also the requirement that no one be permitted to leave school until he was fourteen. Since Tom did not have the tuition to go on to the middle school, and he was not yet fourteen, he found it necessary to repeat the seventh grade. This was a fortunate circumstance for him, however, because the girl who sat across the aisle from him in that second year of the seventh grade was none other than Ingeborg Larsen, the girl he was later to marry!

Ingeborg was the miller's daughter. Her father was called Miller Master Ole Hendrik Larsen. Ingeborg was blonde, fair and high-spirited as a miller's daughter must rightly be, according to ballad and fairy tale. The name, Ingeborg, is to be found in the sagas. For Tom, it was love at first sight. He then and there chose Ingeborg to be his bride. It would be ten years before anyone except Tom would know of his intentions, but the dream of love is as much a part of love as is its declaration. And the secret, so close to his heart, must have given Tom comfort and solace, renewed courage and determination.

Miller Master Larsen's mill was located on a stream that skirted the mountain and drained from a lake into the fjord. Here he ground the grain the farmers brought him. He even imported unhusked corn from the United States which was made into corn meal. The display of corn husks he had in his office was of great interest to the school children. In conjunction with the mill, Miller Larsen kept a kind of store, stocked with staples which the farmers might take in exchange for their grain.

The Gundersen home adjoined the mill. Tom as a boy walked through the water wheel and envied the miller his private pond where trout were wont to slant their silver sides against the barrier of the dam. In the fall when the waters rushed faster after

11

the rains, eels were caught in a net across the dam, and the neighborhood shared in the bounty.

Below the Gundersens, the stream was dammed a second time to provide power for a factory making wooden shoes. Thus the Gundersen children had access to a small lake in their back yard — perfect for floating the sailboats, the barges, and other craft that children love so well.

Never idle, if Tom was not working or in school, he was always building something. The model steamboat with which Halvor and Tom posed so proudly for their photograph is an example of the ingenuity of their young minds. An old alarm clock, placed strategically inside the boat, was connected to the propeller shaft. She was launched with suitable ceremony in Gundersen's Lake.

Thus it was not all work and no play, and Tom was by no means a dull boy. His friends were numerous and playtime was eventful. Perhaps because his father had come to America; perhaps because the epic of America held the ring of adventure, the children read American Indian tales and played their counterpart in the mountains and forests above Tvedestrand. They made tomahawks, spears, bows and arrows and built lookout platforms in the trees. They fought tribal battles, took prisoners and sometimes inflicted real wounds, accidentally! Fritz Bech was the eldest and bore the title of chief; Tom was called "Little Tor."

The long winter months offered opportunity for many sports:

Tom felt elated. He had won second place in the ski jump with a leap of ninety feet. He was eleven years old. Halvor and Leif Kristofersen pounded on his shoulder and threw their caps in the air. "Hurrah for Torjus," they shouted.

The boys were much too excited to go home immediately from the ski run, although Tom looked forward to seeing the way his mother's face would light up with affectionate pride as he told her. Tom hadn't too much time to train for feats of physical prowess; he was always much too busy with his jobs and his experiments. Besides, he was a small boy, although wiry, and strong of hand, wrist and forearm.

"Let's ski a while," said Leif.

It didn't require a great deal of coaxing, and Tom took off on his skis, leading Halvor and Leif across the mountain slopes. The snow was deep, but with Tom breaking their path and packing the snow, the boys made easy progress.

Approaching downward toward the brook, Tom made a left turn onto the road which paralleled the stream. He coasted to a stop, watching Halvor and Leif as they took the decline. "Halvor's going too fast," thought Tom. Halvor shot past the road and into a snow drift, wildly waving his arms and sputtering in the snow.

Tom anxiously turned his eyes upward to the advancing figure of Leif. Leif was older and heavier than either of the brothers, and was not too apt a skier. "Brake it," shouted Tom, but in vain. Leif literally seemed to fly across the gully of the road. Over and over he went: two and three times he somersaulted, his skis like chips from the chopping block.

Halvor and Tom hastened out to the frozen face of the brook where Leif had finally come to a halt — on his head. His form was still. Between them, the two boys carried Leif down the road to the village. The concussion caused Lief to be hospitalized, unconscious for three weeks.

The boys agreed together, much later, that they had more than one reason to remember the day "Torjus came in second."

Besides the skiing, there was skating on the lake above Tvedestrand and on the fjord which sometimes froze over in spite of plowing operations to keep it open to the packet boat. The snow and ice afforded much valuable ammunition to boys intent on converting barriers of frigidity into fortresses. The Indians of the summer became warriors with hard snow balls, more accurate than arrows! Snow, like hay, made wonderful jumping-into, and the boys would shovel huge heaps of the feathery stuff, close to a building or platform. Tom was reputed to have made the leap from the highest level. Birger's father happened by one day — and this diversion came to a halt!

Tom and Halvor managed to save enough of their earnings to buy a sailboat. The boats of the fjords have the characteristic long and pointed appearance of the old viking craft. Children learn to swim and sail at an early age, and boating was a principal pastime. A picnic party to the islands or down the fjord by boat was an event and inspired Tom's still wistful ambition to some day return to Tvedestrand and buy or rent a house on an island and entertain all his old friends.

Fishing, too, was great fun and a rewarding sport; Tom on one memorable afternoon caught over fifty mackerel with rod and reel just off the wharf at the end of the fjord. They measured seven to eight inches in length. Small shrimp seined in the shallows were used as bait.

Swimming in the fjord was of necessity an energetic sport, considering the temperature of the water. Tom has reason to remember one swimming experience with regret — it was the cause of one of the two times his mother ever gave him a spanking. Yielding to persuasion and in disobedience of his mother's wishes, he went off with the other boys one Sunday morning and returned too late to go to church. The other occasion for punishment resulted from another boyish impulse. Each year a circus came to Tvedestrand. Proper citizens avoided the troupe, considering their entertainment sinful. Children were forbidden to attend. Curious, Tom and some of the other boys climbed up the mountain above the valley where the circus performers were encamped and watched them from a distance. Tom was punished for his disobedience.

Tom recalls another stranger who caused a flurry of excitement among Tom's friends. One day a Negro sailor came to Tvedestrand. He had signed on a Norwegian vessel in a foreign port, and since the owner of the ship lived in Tvedestrand, he had come here for his pay! The boys marveled at his dark skin and followed him all over town, but at a respectful distance.

As in every other household in Norway, Christmas at the Halvorsens was a very special occasion. Working at her knitting machine from early morning to late at night, Tora nevertheless took time to prepare for Christmas. She would send Tom and Halvor off on skis to cut down their Christmas fir. One time Tom wandered so far in search of just the right tree that snowblindness overcame him.

The tree was decorated mostly with ornaments made by the children themselves. Colorful paper baskets held nuts and raisins. The candles were clipped to the boughs and required constant watching; but sentry duty had its rewards: the candles cast such a lovely, flickering glow. The sweets and delicacies prepared even two months before Christmas caused small mouths to water. The famous *fattigmand* was rolled thin, cut into diamond shapes and fried in deep fat — the delicate flavor of cardamon and the crisp goodness retained by storing in tins in the cellar until their appearance on the holiday table.

Another Yuletide assignment for the boys was to bind the sheaves of oats and barley and tie them on a pedestal in front of the windows so that the winter-hungry birds might also share in the bounty of God's blessings.

In Norway, elves traditionally bring the presents which are opened after five o'clock on Christmas eve, at which time the church bells toll the beginning of the holidays.

Tora was held in high regard by the people of Tvedestrand, and they displayed their affection by remembering her young sons at Christmas:

"So kind they are," said Tom to his mother. He was only nine, yet wise for his years.

"I have saved the best for last," and his mother brought out from its hiding place an oblong package. "From Mr. Olesen," she said. Mr. Olesen was the shoemaker. Tom lost no time in opening the present, protesting at the same time that the best was his mother's gift, a box of the necessary tools and materials so that Halvor and he might build the model steamboat they had been planning.

From the wrappings Tom drew forth a beautiful soldier's uniform, scaled down to his own slight dimensions. He pulled it on over his clothes, exclaiming with delight and promising to give those American Indians in their war bonnets next spring a real tussle with an officer in the Norwegian Army.

May 17 is a holiday in Norway. It commemorates the separation from coalition with Denmark which had existed from 1397. The three Scandinavian countries had at one time been ruled by one king, although each retained a certain degree of autonomy. Sweden had made the break in the late fifteenth century. The association with Denmark had through the years involved Norway in European affairs and European wars. The Treaty of Kiel in 1814 gave sanction of the chief European powers to the separation of Denmark and Norway but substituted at the same time a proposal that Norway be ceded to Sweden — a scheme agreed upon between Russia

15

and Sweden when the latter yielded Finland to Russia. After considerable negotiation, however, Charles XIII of Sweden consented to recognize the independence of Norway and to govern the country in accordance with the constitution dated May 17, 1814, drawn up at Eidsvold.

On the morning of May 17 the children of Tvedestrand paraded through the streets carrying flags. In the afternoon, the adults would promenade, the band leading the procession and concluding festivities with a band concert at the park. It was the custom of Tom and his friends to provide their own particular brand of noise making. Going up into the mountains they would drill holes in the rock, fill the holes with gun powder, provide a fuse and, blocking the charge with a wooden plug, light the fuse and scamper for a safe distance to watch the rock explode. These were very satisfactory fireworks until tragedy intervened. One year a splinter from a wooden plug flew into the eye of Sander Gundersen, blinding him.

Another day of celebration was June 21, the first day of summer, St. Hans Aften:

For weeks now, the boys of Tvedestrand had been collecting old crates and odds and ends of waste lumber. Tomorrow, in observance of the first day of summer, a huge bonfire would be built out on the island in Tvedestrand Fjord. It was a small island, some thirty feet in diameter and barren of any vegetation. This was a civic affair, and the local committee had been active, making the necessary arrangements.

Tom rode out with the Bech boys to tow the bathhouse and anchor it away from the island during the festivities. It was here Tom had learned to swim when he was barely six years old. For Tom, it had been a case of sink or swim as the older boys had merely tossed him into the water, shouting encouragement and standing by to help if necessary. It wasn't necessary. Tom swam.

The shed-like structure had slatted sides below the water level, and similar slats likewise ran the length and width on the bottom, under water, giving the children ample room, however, to dive and swim. The roof afforded shelter from the weather.

"Torjus," said Fritz Bech, "come out with us in the boat tomorrow night instead of going up the mountain to watch

16

the bonfire — most of the boys are coming — Hans, Carl and maybe Birger." Tom considered briefly. "If it's all right with Mother, I'd like to," he said.

Later he told Tora their plans. She looked up from her machine and smiled at Tom. "Go, Torjus," she said. "I must finish this work for Mrs. Svendsen by day after tomorrow."

June 21 was a clear night, and as the boys rowed towards the island, the cone of fire had already taken shape, and the sound of voices singing came across the water with a mellow and undulant rhythm. Tom sat next to Carl in the stern and watched recede into the night the hulk of the old Nes Ironworks warehouse and wharf with its stack of pig iron, awaiting shipment. The other boats, in loose circles around the island, looked like tiny bugs fallen onto the surface of water. The faces of the singers were lit by the firelight, and their waving arms, as they hailed newly arrived acquaintances, cast weird shadows. Above, against the star-flecked sky, the mountains seemed to hover benignly. It was an unforgetable experience — the brilliant fire, the pleasant roll of the fjord, the soft singing, the feeling of closeness to God. Tom was content.

Of all his boyhood friends, Tom came to blows with only one, Louis Nævestad. There seems to have existed some slight sense of antagonism between the two boys. Once Tom sought entrance to a show in Louis' woodshed. The youngsters had written and rehearsed their own performance. For some reason, Louis barred Tom. Fisticuffs followed. Tom saw the show. He was nine at the time.

On another occasion when Tom was much younger, Louis dared him to put his finger on a chopping block. Louis' father was owner of a hardware store, and Louis' brother, Haakon, had a brand-new hatchet. Not one to dodge a dare, Tom extended his hand, and the blow, by accident, severed Tom's forefinger at the joint, leaving it dangling on a thread of flesh. Tom's mother was called, and wrapping the bloody hand in a towel, she carried him to Dr. Ericksen who stitched the finger together but warned that the digit would undoubtedly be stiff. Today there is a scar, but the finger is perfectly normal. Tom can vividly remember his mother's earnest prayers, and his sense of confidence that his mother and God in partnership would make his finger whole again. A child's religious belief is not only in a mystic deity, but in the faith and piety of those who pray for him.

Why do we remember what we first remember? Is it fear, pain, pleasure? Tom remembers the time when he was three years old and he had gone with the older boys on a hike up the mountain. They had suddenly encountered the gypsy, Griffenfeld. Tom's companions were frightened into flight, deserting him. Trying to run away, Tom stumbled into a pond. A Miss Larsen, friend of Tora's, heard his frantic cries, rescued him and brought him home. Which is the stronger memory — the fear, or the wonderful, warm happiness of being in his mother's arms?

Of all Tom's boyhood experiences, there is one that would seem most significant:

Tom put his hand on Halvor's shoulder. "It is three thirty, Halvor." He cautioned him, "Be quiet; don't wake mother."

Tom's mother stirred in the next bed. She was fully awake, but it was part of this early Easter morning adventure that the boys should rise, dress themselves, make their own preparations and steal away unnoticed.

Tom pulled his sweater over his head and glanced affectionately towards his mother. It was his favorite, and he had admired it so much when she was knitting it, "on order from Mrs. Gundersen," she had said, knowing all along it was a Christmas surprise for him.

Their woolen knit stockings pulled up to their knees, Tom and Halvor walked carefully into the kitchen before putting on their heavy walking shoes. The dim light from the kerosene lamp cast eerie shadows as they packed their pastries in a scarf. It was Tom's turn to carry the coffee kettle; the other boys were bringing the provisions. Nils Gutormsen's muffled knock almost coincided with their turning down the lamp. Nils was the son of the landlord and lived upstairs.

The three set off together down the road toward Bech's. Beside Fritz and Abba Bech and the four Gundersen boys, they would be joined by Louis Nævestad, Birger Jorkjend and Alf Holst. From here they would set up the mountain four miles to their rendezvous with the sunrise. As long as Tom could remember, the boys of Tvedestrand had made this trek on Easter morning. From the time he was eight, Tom had gone with them.

The moonlight made a path of tarnished silver out of the familiar road and the footpath that branched to the high part of the mountain. The snow was bruised and melting — hiding in the shadowed crevices of rock and under the lower boughs of the fir trees. The pines loomed large against the grotesque and naked branches of the birch and oak. Sounds out of sight echoed strangely, and the boys would wager, "Maybe it's a fox? A bear? Probably an early-rising rabbit or squirrel?"

Sometimes they sang, but mostly the boys walked arm in arm, in pairs or threes, going single file as they climbed to the summit. Each year they came to the same clear place — facing east — high over the valley and looking out over the fjord. They built their fire of branches and shavings and set the kettle to boiling.

"What is better than coffee at five o'clock in the morning on Easter, and high on the mountains behind Tvedestrand," whispered Birger to Tom, who was fumbling with his knapsack.

"A piece of Mr. Broms' pastry," answered Tom as he broke off a sugared morsel and thrust it into Birger's mouth. Both boys laughed happily.

Strangely, no one spoke loudly here. Even the hymns were softly sung. It was almost like being in church — in a vast, domeless arena, full of mystery, reverence and beauty. The boys fell silent. Light was creeping among them, and dawn seemed to bring the distances closer. The Skagerrak lay glistening beyond the mouth of the fjord. This was the rim of their world. Beyond lay the lands they read about, dreamed about, which they all hoped some day to visit. From the harbors of Norway have come the best navigators, the best sea captains in all the world. The children of the fjords, therefore, are bent to the sea, and their imaginations are colored by the tales and the exotic trinkets their seafaring relatives bring home.

The light intensified almost imperceptibly, but the sun was not yet visible. Tom moved away from the group. This was the time he liked the best. It was this moment of promise, of impending grandeur, that set his thoughts towards the future. He was filled with a longing and a purpose — a longing to understand the majesty of the rugged scene that lay before him, to relate this physical universe, which is God, to the parables and precepts of the Bible, which are God's teachings; and a purpose:

19

to do, to succeed, to become, to learn, to live, to serve. This is a child's prayer — the humility of wonder in the face of Nature and the mysteries of God and Man, and the unflinching dedication of self to the future. These dreams, these visions, these vistas of ambition — not for material reward, for that unhappily is purely an adult interpretation — but for self-fulfilment, for doing the best of what one is fitted to do — with honor, with success, with generosity, with meaning.

This is the prayer of innocents — purer and finer than supplication. Here on the mountain ledge, Tom found companionship with God and his fellow man.

The semicircle of the sun expanded until its brightness dissolved the distant boundary of the Skagerrak and with it, the dreams. Some of the boys started chucking rocks into the pool below. Tom still stood apart. The sound of the rocks falling into water echoed roundly. In his mind, he heard a clock chime, and he was again in the front room of Grandfather Björnevikhalsen's house on the fjord. The pendulum clock on the wall was a magnificent instrument, and in quiet moments today Tom can remember its beautiful tone. Looking out over the fjord, the young boy had dreamed his dream of the future — a part of the dream, a part of the vision, a part of the prayer that here on Easter morning filled his thoughts.

"Torjus," said Birger, "come down to earth." Tom turned towards him. "We'd better start back. I have to change clothes before going to church. Don't you?"

The journey down to Tvedestrand was hilarious. The older boys outdistanced the younger with war cries and broad jumps across the declining snow banks. Spring flowers were bravely venturing. There was the *comvaler* (our Lily of the Valley), a cream colored flower with delicate bells on a fragile stem. The white *hvitveis* had a lovely sister, *blåveis* (our anemones), and the latter's iridescent blue petals spread a bit of color in the shallow snow. Tom chose a bouquet for his mother. As they approached the town, the church bells started to toll. Tom and Halvor hastened their steps. The Easter morning adventure was over. They ran through the streets and breathlessly plunged down the steps to their kitchen door. Mother Tora was waiting, and she kissed them both.

"Hurry," she said, "let's not be late to church."

The Sea

Tom Kelly Butler is seventeen years old. He is a tall lad, over six feet, with a modern teenager's interest in sports, in automobiles, in all things mechanical. He is an Eagle Scout, a good student, and a grandson of whom to be proud. Tom Kelly has travelled by car and in his father's plane throughout the United States and is no doubt nonchalantly aware that ships now cross the Atlantic in six days, scheduled passenger planes span the same distance in twelve hours, and the human voice can bridge the gap of Old and New World in a matter of seconds.

Fifty-two years ago, Tom Kelly's maternal grandfather, Torjus Tellefsen, entered his seventeenth year in Riga, Latvia. On his fourteenth birthday and with his mother's consent, he had shipped out as cabin boy on a sailing ship. It had taken him two years to go around the world and return to Baltic waters. These were bewildering and exciting years for a lad, who before this, had never ventured beyond the mountains, the valleys, the nearby fjords of southeast Norway.

*　*　*　*　*　*

The *Imacos* owned by the Bech Company (Tom's neighbor), was berthed at Moss in the Oslo Fjord. The one-hundred mile trip by steamboat up the coast of Norway was, to Tom, reminiscent of Tvedestrand. Out of Moss, Tom found a new world — a world that moved endlessly in a pace and rhythm akin to breathing. The slurring sound of wake, the hollow gulp as sail caught wind, the high-pitched singsong of the sailors' calls — these sounds replaced the rumble of cartwheels on the cobblestones, the chiming of the church bell, the shout of newsboys and the peddler's cry.

The *Imacos* captured Tom's fancy from the very first glance. Her strange and foreign-sounding name was merely the composite of the first initials of the older Bech children, whom Tom had known, namely: *I*nger, *M*argareth, *A*lexander, *C*hristiane, *O*lga and *S*alve. The *Imacos* was, by classification, a bark, considered by many the peer of sailing craft. She carried three masts, two square-rigged and the mizzenmast fore-and-aft rigged. The foremast and mainmast each carried a complement of five sails: the foresail or mainsail (collectively called courses); the lower topsail; the upper topsail; the topgallant and the royal. In addition, there were headsails that bowed out along the thirty-foot bowsprit, and staysails that could be mounted between masts. In over-all length she measured some one hundred and seventy-five feet. Her maximum speed was said to be twelve knots, and to wide-eyed Tom she appeared a veritable jungle of canvas, lines, pin-rails, chocks and metal cleats for belaying lines.

Tom soon learned the jargon of the sailor: the rope ladders that swayed dizzily were shrouds, the rope rungs of the ladders being called ratlines; the cross bars that seemed like arms raised aloft to implore favorable winds, were yards, to which the sails were taken in and furled when not in use. Certain sails were reefed when winds blew hard. Making sail when the ship was clean meant setting the sails beginning with the lower topsails, followed by upper topsails, head sails, mizzen, courses and remainder of the square sails; a lengthy process with so small a crew. The climate of the winds would determine *how* she sailed (which sails and how they would be braced). All the square sails had to be loosed and lashed by individual sailors, going aloft, but the fore-and-aft sails could be handled from the deck. It was necessary to learn the location of each of the many lines of her running rigging so they could be instantly found on a dark night. Maneuvering or tacking required the entire crew to man the braces for adjusting sails to the wind. The bark was steered by wheel (the wheel turned opposite to those of today — port your helm would bring the boat to starboard). All of this Tom learned, since his duties, besides that of cabin boy, included taking his watch and his hour's trick at the wheel and helping to make and adjust sail. There was much to learn, as the sailing of a ship is complicated, and each sailor must of necessity be alert, quick and sure of his assignment.

As cabin boy, Tom cleaned the sailors' quarters in the forecastle where he also slept. He washed the dishes for the sailors' mess. Even the cleaning of the spittoons was his task. On deck, Tom was a member of the crew and took orders only from Captain Araldsen and the mates. But in the confines of their quarters, the sailors, too, were his superiors and he did their bidding. They were kind but firm, as all had apprenticed in such a way as Tom, and they knew the importance of discipline on shipboard and the value of following instructions closely and promptly.

For all these services, Tom received twenty kroner, or in terms of today's currency, about three dollars a month.

There were fourteen on board: the captain, two mates, the crew of eight including the two cabin boys, and the steward, sail-maker and carpenter. The latter two had their own shops and devoted full time to repairing or replacing sails or rigging, blocks, woodwork, etc. The other cabin boy was two years older than Tom, but Tom's agility and his earnest insistence on learning and doing his job well, often sent him to the other's rescue. The boy's name was Arnold Bakkeli, and he was the captain's nephew.

The *Imacos* was bound for Sundsvall in northeast Sweden to load lumber for South Africa. Shortly after leaving Moss and moving into the open waters of the Skagerrak, Tom became seasick:

Tom felt he could not endure that endless turmoil within him. He pushed open the forecastle door and went on deck. He grasped the shrouds with trembling fingers. "Shrouds," he thought, "what a fitting name." Immediately he *was* sick.

There was a hand on his shoulder. It was Gustav, the first mate. Cold perspiration stood on Tom's forehead as he rallied to stand erect. He felt weak and drained of every ounce of strength.

Gustav kept up a rambling conversation, diverting Tom's thoughts from his torture. "The year I sailed out of Bergen for Leith," he said, "I was scarcely six months older than you, Torjus. I remember very well that I knew the North Sea was waiting for me alone — to teach me I was not meant to be a sailor. It blustered and rolled and roared at me, and I was dizzy and sick. But there was a sailor on board who cured me. It's a drastic remedy, Torjus, but do you want to try?"

"Anything," groaned Tom. "Nothing could be as bad as this."

Gustav disappeared into the forecastle. Tom looked up at the cloud-flecked sky. The clouds were stationary, Tom felt, he alone was moving — he and the ship — ceaselessly. "If only I could be still *one* moment," thought Tom, "I'd be all right."

Gustav came toward him holding in his hand a sizable hunk of salt pork. Tom's eyes and stomach reacted. Throwing an arm about Tom's shoulders, Gustav held him firmly and quickly before Tom grasped his intentions, ground the slimy stuff into Tom's nostrils, into his mouth. Tom gasped for air. The revolting taste, the strong smell, the suffocating feel of grease, and Tom clawed at the gag that threatened to choke him. As it was released, Tom felt himself literally exploding. He vomited — again and again. Never had he known such agony. The retching continued until nothing, absolutely nothing, remained in his stomach. Tom slumped to the deck. The sky, the clouds, the sails merged into a blur.

Tom felt a cool, damp towel across his forehead. He propped himself weakly on one elbow. Miraculously, the nausea was gone. He sat up unsteadily and looked up at Gustav who stood over his bunk. "Good boy, Torjus," he said, and Tom grinned weakly. "You'll sleep now." And Tom slept.

It might have been the memory of long, white fingers stitching his garments, as he tried clumsily to mend the tear in his shirt, but by the time the *Imacos* reached the straits between Denmark and Sweden, Tom was the victim of another sickness — homesickness. The nights he lay in his narrow bunk, he was sleepless — he who had always been able to sleep. The nights he was on deck were even more painful — across that dark and rolling water, the wake made a shimmering path in the moonlight — a path that led back to his mother in Tvedestrand. Tom became morose; he was listless. The discerning eye of the captain was sympathetic, but he made no comment. Because the straits were narrow and hazardous, the *Imacos* took on a pilot who would guide her through the treacherous waters. Tom made up his mind, and when the pilot disembarked at Copenhagen, he carried with him Tom's letter to his mother, begging her to have him released and let him come home.

Strange is the perversity of man! In writing his letter, Tom seemed to empty himself of his doubts and his nostalgia. Perhaps homesickness and seasickness are not too unlike after all. The sailors had accepted Tom. They teased him but with a comradely affection, never referring to that none-too-secret letter. Daily, he followed his schedule of duties, and before Tom knew it, the prospect of leaving the ship became as unbearable as had the prospect of staying on board.

A letter awaited Tom in Sundsvall. Tora had secured Carl Bech's permission for Tom to leave the boat, and she had arranged passage for him back to Tvedestrand. Tom's second letter home was a source of both pride and disappointment to Tora. Her motherly anxiety for Tom's welfare had outweighed her ambition for him, and she was looking forward to his return. On the other hand, his determination to stay out his contract pleased her.

The *Imacos* loaded her cargo in record time and headed down the coast of Sweden and through the Kattegat and Skagerrak into the North Sea. Several days were required to navigate the English Channel. Tacking with the winds against them and through the choppy waters, it took about six hours to make the diagonal crossing from England to France, and vice versa. All of the crew were needed to maneuver the *Imacos*. Traffic was heavier here and fogs hampered visibility. Tom learned to turn the fog horn.

Once out into the Atlantic, life on board settled down to a pleasant routine. Tom was happy and contented. He now had the feel of the ship, and the next three months' sailing made him a veteran. He spoke the language of the sailor and had learned to take his watch and to steer in any kind of weather. It was his job to man the main royal and he began to have almost a proprietary feeling towards this particular sail.

His training was not without its painful moments. One day Tom stood watch on the forecastle head. It was a sleepy day and Tom yawned, slanting half-closed eyes to starboard. All was quiet. The slight, monotonous motion of the ship added to his drowsiness. He closed his eyes. "I'll rest them for a moment," he thought to himself, and fell asleep, standing up. The next he knew, a torrent of cold water drenched him. He gasped and staggered under the shock. The first mate roared with the laughter of anger and ridicule. The feeling of chagrin that engulfed Tom was almost as chilling as the cold water. Needless to say, he never slept on watch again.

Tom's studies in geography stood him in good stead, and he was not one to hang back when he had a question to ask. He kept his own chart and knew when they approached the Canary Islands, passing to the east of them.

As this was their first time to cross the Equator, Tom and Arne knew they would be initiated as subjects of Neptune, God of the Sea. This Tom had read about. Sometimes, the neophytes would be tarred and feathered, and Tom was apprehensive. As Neptune rose from the sea over the side of the *Imacos* where the ship's ladder was hung, Tom recognized the mop-beareded face and the twinkling eyes of the first mate. The other sailors sat around, grinning. The boys stood rather sheepishly and listened to the royal commandments. With anxious voices, pitched high to be heard over the rush of the water against the sides of the *Imacos,* they swore their undying allegiance.

Days later Gustav called Tom to the upper deck to point out animals swimming at a distance from the *Imacos.* "Sea lions," he said. Tom watched the bobbing heads and idly rolling bodies until they were out of sight.

Approaching the Cape of Good Hope, where his uncle had lost his life, Tom pondered the dangers of seafaring:

The mate's voice was urgent. "Torjus," he shouted, "help Arne make fast the main royal."

It was night, and the wind was rising. No moon nor stars were visible. Above him, Tom could barely detect Arne, struggling with the royal.

Tom made his way to the royal yard. The sail was loose but the pitching of the *Imacos* and the strong wind made the canvas seem a thing alive. Tom gestured to Arne to go starboard, indicating that he would go to the lee side of the yard to try to draw in the bulk of the flapping canvas, since the pressure of the wind had its weight unevenly distributed. Arne moved along the footropes and Tom busied himself, fisting in the stubborn sail. His fingers grew stiff in his effort to pull the canvas up to the yard and secure the gaskets. So occupied, it was several moments before Tom turned towards Arne to signal his progress. A chill swept through Tom. Arne was nowhere to be seen. A muffled scream brought Tom's glance downward. There, dangling by a rope, was Arne. He had fallen headfirst into the extended belly of the topgallant sail beneath him. The canvas had yielded

26

to his body to break his fall; his wildly grasping fingers had seized a buntline of the topgallant sail. He pulled himself up to the yard and straddling it, inched over to the mast.

On watch below, the mate sensed what had happened and dispatched one of the sailors to the royal yard, recalling the now well-frightened boys.

Easing up the east coast of Africa, the *Imacos* reached her destination — Durban. It was a short time after the conclusion of the Boer War, and South Africa was booming. Durban was a thriving port. It boasted an excellent harbor, in beautiful surroundings, a productive hinterland with coal fields in the vicinity. Docking facilities were inadequate. Captain Araldsen found that to berth he must make fast to a width of boats — his cargo to be passed over their decks to the wharf. It was a clumsy arrangement, and the sailors were vociferous in their complaints.

Tom stood on deck, looking towards the town. The controversy mattered little to him; it was all an adventure. To a lad, born and reared in a small Norwegian town, the glimpses that he had had of Durban excited him. The dark-skinned natives, clad only in loin cloths, were slim and sinewy, with close-cropped, woolly hair. They had watched the *Imacos* secure to the next boat. "What creatures are these?" Tom wondered. Their glances seemed to go past and through him. He had felt uncomfortable.

Little did Tom realize that he was to be singled out for further discomfort:

Captain Araldsen had just come aboard after a visit to the port authorities. "It's the best we can do." Tom overheard him talking to the first mate. "Tomorrow we will start unloading, using the Kafirs to help us. Tonight, post watch and let the crew go ashore."

Somewhere in the distance a bell sounded. "A long-tongued bell," thought Tom, so mellow and so melancholy its tone.

Captain Araldsen assembled his men on the deck. "The bell sounds when the Kafirs are called to their compound," he said. "There has been some trouble here, and the local officials segregate most of the natives at night. The Kafirs are proud and intelligent and once ruled most of this coast. I tell you this because they will work for and with us tomorrow. You must do nothing to offend them. Tonight you may go ashore, but remember, Durban is crowded and disorderly. Be careful."

It was good to set foot on solid ground. Tom found that it made him a little dizzy. Gustav walked beside him. The lights, the loud music blaring from open windows in the bars, made him dizzier still. Down the street came a fantastic apparition. Tom halted in dismay. It resembled an enormous bird with scarlet wings and a protruding beak. Coming closer, Tom could see that it was a Kafir in a sheath of feathers, pulling a small cart in which two English sailors sat, bumping over uneven ground and shouting to the passers-by. Behind them, what must have been a native's version of a bull — horns slightly awry — came charging, cart nearly overturning.

It was all so strange. Tom left Gustav, who wished to sample the wares of the bars, and wandered alone about Durban, coming upon the monument to Vasco da Gama, who is credited with having explored the Natal Coast in 1497. On the hill above the harbor could be seen the lights of the mansions where lived the town's notables and the governing dignitaries.

It was late when Tom returned to the *Imacos*. Making his way through a maze of bow, stern and spring lines, he had to step over sleeping sailors, so mild this August evening, their bed rolls had sprouted like untidy mushrooms.

Tom was aware of activity on board long before the breakfast plates and cups were put away. He was eager to join the crew.

"Torjus," Gustav was giving instructions, "you stand here at the gunwale and take the planks from the native here who will hand them to you from the hold. You pass them on to the next boat."

Tom took his place, and the unloading began. The powerfully built Kafir fed Tom heavy boards as if they were toothpicks. It was hard work, even for Tom, who mostly acted as fulcrum in swinging the timbers on to outstretched hands.

Towards the end of the day, Tom noticed that the native seemed to be tiring. He would slide the plank upward and leisurely prod it on deck. Tom started toward the opening to offer to change places with the Kafir. The dark head appeared at the level of the deck, and the native, surprised at Tom's proximity, stepped backward — gave a shrill cry, and disappeared. Tom looked anxiously downward. The man lay sprawled with a timber on top of him. The crew heard the cry, and the mate came running. Fortunately a hank of rope had broken the fall, and the blow from the plank was the major injury. But never had Tom heard such a torrent of incomprehensible gibberish — the Kafir gestured and shouted, his eyes flashing in anger. Captain Araldsen finally got him ashore, but the day's work was at an end.

That night Tom apprehensively noted the approach of the harbor patrol boat, and he found himself the center of an incident. The native was of noble birth and the tribe was aroused. They had made formal complaint to the police authorities, and the latter had come to investigate.

Tom explained as best he could just how the accident had happened, denying vehemently that he had pushed the man. Captain Araldsen backed him up without hesitation. "And he is a minor," he reminded the port officer. No charge was filed, but Tom was advised to stay on board ship and out of sight.

At first the Kafirs refused to return to the *Imacos,* but were finally persuaded. Tom busied himself below and had to be content with the filtered sound of the natives' chanting, and the sailors' boisterous encouragement.

One day Tom became aware that another craft was being made fast to the harbor side of the *Imacos.* He poked his head out the forecastle door for a better look. It was a harbor dredge, and the deck swarmed with Kafirs. Tom noticed a huge iron kettle amidships and was curious as to its purpose. As evening wore on, large quantities of rice were prepared in the kettle, and the natives gathered round, devouring it by fistfuls. When their meal was concluded, certain of the Kafirs started a humming, soon taken up by all on board until the swelling sound resembled distant drums; to this accompaniment, the natives slowly began their tribal dance. Faster and faster they moved, in perfect rhythm, their naked bodies and their motions tortuous, the muted tones throbbing with emotion. Tom watched and wondered. A world away from Tvedestrand. A very different world.

Loading sand for ballast, the *Imacos* headed for the Society Islands and Tahiti. The course took them far to the south — below

Australia and almost to 60° south latitude. En route, the ship passed numerous islands thickly populated with penguins, whose raucous cries were deafening, so continuous and shrill that the sailors could hardly hear each other. Sometimes the mountainous islands were so densely covered by these strange birds who could not fly, that the rocks were not visible.

As the *Imacos* approached the 180° meridian and crossed from east to west longitude, Captain Araldsen declared the dividend Monday "a spun yarn Sunday" and thus a second day of rest.

Tahiti — mountainous residue of volcanic wrath! Tahiti— glamor spot of the South Seas! Tahiti — queen island of the Society group, named by Commodore Cook for the Royal Society of Great Britain. Tahiti — subject of the haunting landscapes of Paul Gauguin!

Papeete was the destination of the *Imacos*. Watching the dugout approach from shore, carrying a native pilot, Tom sensed in its slow but steady progress the amiable pace of life in the islands.

The Polynesian is a handsome race — its skin the amber color of muted bronze. The natives are well built, with regal carriage. Tom took great delight in watching their festivals. On these gala occasions, the boys and girls would parade single file through the town. The girls wore large and fragrant blossoms to pin back their long hair. The perfume of these exotic flowers could be sensed for blocks away. The boys were dressed only in loin cloths, the girls in bright-hued, sarong-like garments that fell loosely to their knees. In the shrub-skirted square before the temple, the procession broke into formation and the rhythmic hula was performed, every movement symbolic. At the conclusion of the dance, the promenade back began — as gracefully as the unwinding of a lariat.

Here at Papeete, Tom tasted tropical fruits for the first time. Of them all, he liked watermelon best.

The *Imacos* unloaded its ballast and began filling its hold with copra, dried meat of the coconut. Copra was valuable as a food-stuff and as the basis of copra oil used in making soap and candles. In order to compress more into a limited space, the shelled meat was chopped with huge *machetes,* and Tom's wrists and forearms ached from the strenuous downward thrust required. He was one of the best choppers.

The supply of copra at Tahiti was not sufficient to make full cargo for the *Imacos,* and after talking with French officials, Captain Araldsen decided to cross the Society group to Raiatéa where there was known to be a quantity of coconuts. Theirs would be the second ship ever to approach this island. The Society Islands, once a French protectorate, were now considered a French colony. Raiatéa had been the last of the islands to submit. In fact, its chief had been captured by the French and interned in a French fortress on the island of Tasmania for ten years. Released, he awaited transportation from Papeete to his people. Captain Araldsen agreed to take him to Raiatéa:

Tom watched the tall native come aboard. He knew that he was a chieftain and that he would sleep in the sailmaker's shop and share the sailors' mess.

To Tom, his brown eyes smiled with a friendly dignity that could not be denied. Speaking no common language, the sailors nevertheless communicated with their guest by repeating the few Kanaka words they had learned at Papeete, augmented by vigorous and descriptive gestures. It soon became apparent that the high rank of their companion did not keep him from taking his share of those duties on board which he was qualified to do. He even supervised the preparation of a yam pudding for dinner the second night out. He was particularly fond of Tom, whose air of respect seemed to please him, and he laughed unrestrainedly at Tom's faltering "Ayta mayta wye-ennia" (wholly phonetic spelling) which meant "pretty girls."

The trip to the island of Raiatéa took two weeks. Winds were fitful and their progress slow. Sharks were sighted, and the sailors made a game of catching them. A rope dragging a big iron hook, baited with meat, was thrown out when a shark broke water near the boat. The shark would slyly approach the lure, bouncing idly in a lazy wake. Tom watched the white throat, as the fish turned and struck upwards with its ugly mouth. Tom found interesting the small sucker fish which attached to the shark and went along for a free ride. He also observed the pilot fish which accompanied the shark, some say to find food for him, others say as an uninvited guest once the shark has struck and killed its prey. Tom watched the sailors heave a carcass overboard and the pilot fish swam downward following the sinking hulk of flesh. One shark, cut open, revealed the cans the steward had dumped astern days previous.

One morning Tom heard the mate call preparations for taking in the lagging sails. That meant the island was in sight. He ran on deck. The ship rode listlessly, her sails slack. The island lay in front of them — green tranquillity on a quiet sea.

"The current is running against us. We'll have to carry out the anchor and drop it into the coral reefs; then kedge our way into the channel." Captain Araldsen called out his instructions.

The chief stood apart, his expressive eyes alight with the joy of his homecoming. He cried out and pointed towards a side-rigged dugout moving out from shore. The sailors could see a number of natives running out from the fringe of trees. In a matter of moments, the dugout was alongside. There were glad cries as the chief embraced the old man who climbed aboard. It was a moving sight — the excitement, and the childlike, boisterous happiness of the reunion. The chief then took ceremonious leave of Captain Araldsen.

Now came the task of bringing the ship into anchorage. The lifeboat carried the anchor ahead of the ship and it was tossed overboard. The coral held, and the windlass was put into action, pulling the ship to the anchor's position. So they proceeded. Later, it was found necessary for natives to dive from the lifeboat and hook the anchor among coral fingers strong enough to hold against the tugging of the cable.

At the end of the second day after their arrival, the crew was surprised to see a small armada of boats coming towards them. They were loaded with fruits and flowers. There were gifts of wild pig, roasted over a slow-burning fire, huge baskets of yams and root vegetables. The natives wore gala attire — their finest, and they sang their favorite songs, paddles swinging to the rhythm of the music, the clear drops of water spraying from the strokes like crystal pebbles. The young boys dived for coins or other treasure — sometimes diving from the surface on one side of the *Imacos* and coming up on the other. They would go out of sight completely, with the swift agility of fish.

The chief was tireless in making all arrangements, and the *Imacos* was soon riding low in the water with a full load of copra. It was hard to leave the island. Even Captain Araldsen seemed relaxed and jovial in his role as benefactor. Once the hold was loaded to capacity, however, departure was inevitable. Again the *Imacos* inched her way; the canoes accompanying her into open water, taking aboard the divers who had set the heavy anchor to engage in coral reefs. The lifeboat was brought in.

The natives shouted and waved farewell as the gentle breezes filled the sails and the *Imacos* moved away. Standing on deck, Tom watched the island become a distant line against the wake. The memory of Raiatéa was to remain with him all his life.

Marseilles was half a world away but their next destination. Their course lay east across the Pacific, and as the prevailing westerlies (called by the old clippers the roaring forties) took over, their pace accelerated. One time, Tom was lashed to the wheel in order to maintain course, so powerful were the fair winds that blew. The water washed over the ship's stern, so vigorous the push forward that even the *Imacos* could not keep pace. The pleasant stay in the islands, their rapid progress exhilarated the crew. They were happy.

At Papeete, three of the crew had jumped ship. Captain Araldsen merely shrugged his shoulders and signed on three new hands. One, a Frenchman, was an amateur magician, nimble of wit and finger. Impromptu demonstrations were the order of the off-watch, and Tom was particularly intrigued with the shoes which would turn over upon command, the knife from which water could be squeezed, the table that mysteriously moved.

Tom's wardrobe, meager as it was to start with, was by now almost depleted. He learned to sew a fine seam and did wonders in mending his threadbare garments. He made a new sailor hat, of which he was very proud, and indeed it was a neat and professional bit of stitching for a fifteen-year-old boy.

Tom utilized some of his leisure time to make a model of the *Imacos*. It was about eighteen inches long and was an exact replica. Every mast and yard, every block, every line had its small-size counterpart. Tiny holes were drilled in the blocks with a pin. Through these were threaded the lines that led from deck to yard. No sails were added but the rigging was otherwise fully complete. It was a beauty and Tom was understandably proud of it. Even the Captain complimented his painstaking efforts. This encouraged Tom to make an even smaller copy of the ship — in a bottle. First he inserted putty and made ridges to resemble waves. These he painted a sea blue — with white caps. Next came the tiny hull. The miniature masts lay flat but would rise like puppets when the proper string was pulled. The tiny yards turned. Tom made several of these delicate masterpieces, a time-consuming, exacting labor of love for boats and the sea. Tom was already thinking of his return. His determination

33

to some day be captain of a ship began to crystallize on the watches at night, when the stars and moon seemed so close, and the ship rode proudly, like a queen, through the hurrying water.

Approaching South America, the *Imacos* turned south, headed for the Horn. Whales, almost as big as the ship, made an inquiring appearance and would follow like porpoises. One sailor designed a triangular net which was baited with meat scraps. Trailing this net in the water, he trapped a huge wandering albatross by its crooked beak. The clumsy bird sprawled helpless on deck. The little dog, pet of the second mate, barked furiously at the unwieldly creature. One sweep of a powerful wing was enough to enforce a respectful silence. The dog ran cowering to Tom. Three or four albatross were caught. These were not edible, but the sailors made wallets out of the leather-like skin of the webbed feet. They plucked the feathers and made pillows. From the beak they fashioned various ornaments.

A smaller triangular net trapped other sea birds. One in particular was the size of a pigeon, with beautiful blue feathers. Most of the smaller birds could be eaten.

It must have been that no one of the crew had ever read or heard of Coleridge's *The Rime of the Ancient Mariner*. Eerily enough, had they been familiar with this classic, their similarly becoming becalmed near the Equator might have caused greater anxiety. There are many superstitions of the sea and punishment for the killing of sea birds is one.

Near 60° south latitude, the coldness intensified. Here the wild seacoast was dangerous and they stayed away from land. Constant lookout for half-submerged icebergs kept the men alert on their turn at watch. Some icebergs seemed as large as mountains and they breathed upon the *Imacos* with frigid breath. But rounding the Horn was uneventful. The crew congratulated themselves on a record run northward in the Atlantic. Approaching the Equator, Nature seemed to rouse herself to the over-confidence of man. Suddenly the wind died down. The Atlantic spread out to meet a cloudless sky. The heat was terrific and was to become more so during the three weeks the *Imacos* lay becalmed. Water was rationed. The supply of yams and produce from the islands ran out, and canned food became unbelievably monotonous. There was little work for the crew or cook, and the inactivity only added to the mounting tension of frustration. When they were almost out of water, Nature relented. She breathed gently. Sail and sailor took heart. That night a light rain fell. Every container on board was held aloft, and with their water supply meagerly replenished, the nightmare seemed a thing of the past.

The *Imacos* was running free, and trade winds carried the ship in the direction of the West Indies. Captain Araldsen then tacked eastward towards Gibraltar. Some one thousand miles out, an Italian tramp steamer was sighted. The crew of the *Imacos* immediately hoisted flags to the mastheads to signal need of food and water. The *Imacos* was given permission to approach and put out a lifeboat. They took on potatoes and other vegetables. The Italian crew brought forth a keg of chianti, and all toasted a successful run, each other, and the fortunes of the sea.

Tacking through the Straits of Gibraltar, Tom looked up at the threatening gun emplacements, like huge warlike gargoyles.

One hundred and forty days from the islands, the *Imacos* sailed into the harbor at Marseilles. The sailors lost no time in going ashore and promptly went berserk. Tom wondered if any of them would be in condition to load brick and tile for Havana.

Mail from home brought messages for his fifteenth birthday, now almost six months past, and a new sweater Tora had knitted. Tom felt not a twinge of homesickness, but "It is good to get letters," he thought. He took pleasure, therefore, in describing to Tora his impressions of Marseilles, really the first metropolitan city in which he had ever been. The huge plate glass windows caught his immediate attention. The lights of a theater entrance beckoned him inside. He sat in the balcony and watched the figures on stage move through symbolic ritual. Whether he was so far removed, or the play done in pantomime, Tom remembers nothing of a spoken dialogue.

Back across a peaceful Atlantic, and Tom was occupied with his regular chores, new patches on his trousers and another model of the *Imacos*. His straw mattress had shown increasing signs of wear. Tom threw it overboard, and from this point on, slept on the boards and slept soundly too. He recalled the way the Kafirs stretched out on their backs with a stone beneath their necks as a pillow.

The half-submerged hulk of the scuttled *Maine* was Tom's first impression of Havana harbor — that and the fortress at the harbor entrance. It was late summer in 1903 and the heat and humidity, coupled with brick dust from the cargo, brought about a painful rash all over Tom's body. Ignoring the discomfort, Tom went ashore and toured the city. The famous cemetery with its ancient monuments, the Spanish architecture of the balconied houses, each with its walled-in garden, the gay music of the calypso, all intrigued him.

Port-Au-Prince in the Haitian Republic was the next port of call: object — to load logwood, a red dye wood. On watch on the run between Cuba and Haiti, Tom caught sight of a number of huge sea turtles. In the distance they looked like tiny barren islands, but as the ship approached they suddenly disappeared.

In contrast to the blacks of South Africa, Tom found the citizens of Haiti friendly, although independent and self-assured. Wandering one day, he found himself swept along in a funeral procession. At the services he was impressed by the large and audible chorus of weeping females, whose wails had a tempo and expression as if they had been rehearsed. And this proved to be true. The chorus had been hired, according to custom, by the family of the deceased.

Tom was delighted with the appearance of the Army of the Republic. The sturdy black soldiers wore musical comedy uniforms, complete with towering paper hats.

Captain Araldsen sent Tom with two other members of the crew to secure fresh water. The men maneuvered the life boat across the reef at the mouth of the river and rowed upstream. Lazy alligators poked mud-stained snouts in their direction. The men located a spring up an inlet and filled the kegs they had brought along. Tom wandered away a distance to a pineapple field. He had never before seen the fruit growing. Boylike, he couldn't resist picking a pineapple from out of a cluster of spiked leaves. The shout of an overseer sent him scurrying back to the boat.

The *Imacos* set sail for Riga in Latvia, running between Cuba and Haiti and near the coast of Florida. Here a hurricane struck. This was one of the most terrifying experiences of Tom's sea voyage, in fact, of his whole life:

It was twilight.

The sky was the color of ashes as Tom felt his way along the footropes — the yard pressed hard against his body. He had been sent aloft to secure some of the dangling lines. Already the ship heeled at such an angle that Tom felt he could almost reach out and touch the water. As he made his way down through the rigging, the rising wind had a hollow, ominous sound.

The crew were busy preparing for the blow. Every movable object was secured, and the hatches battened down. Sails had been furled and the poles of the *Imacos* looked naked and forlorn, twitching nervously. A gust of wind snatched at the lower topsail on the mainmast which had been left up as a storm sail. It was ripped loose, like a mere scrap of paper.

Not until now had Tom had time to be apprehensive, but suddenly anxiety engulfed him. His hands began to tremble. His heart pounded in a seeming void.

Captain Araldsen gave instructions to pour all remaining stores of oil upon the water. It did little good. There was danger that the forecastle might be torn loose, and the crew, clad in slickers and rain hats fastened under their chins, stationed themselves as best they could on deck. They had to be constantly alert for damage to the ship and to keep their own balance and firm hold. As the ship shifted, so did they — scrambling up the heaving deck for a safe position out of the water that would swamp the lower gunwale. The ship rolled so deeply, the yards dipped into the sea.

The wheel spun, and the mate reluctantly lashed it down. They were no longer able to control the direction or the behavior of the ship. They were at the complete mercy of the storm, rolling in the troughs of gigantic waves.

The rain, which began fitfully and which soon was indistinguishable from the salty spray, now whipped down with painful intensity. Nostrils breathed brackish water; eyeballs ached from the sting of tiny pellets of cold fury. The sound of thunder was lost in the tumult of the wind and water thrust against the ship, but the terrifying glare of lightning broke the gloom of gray water and gray light and added to the eerie sense of having departed from reality. Tom's shoulders throbbed as he bent his body against the wind; his thighs and legs were numb with the effort to brace against the bolting of the ship.

The shouts of the mate left no doubt as to the urgency of his summons. Tom soon found out why. The spare mast the *Imacos* carried lashed to the deck had come loose. Its thrashing might do greater harm to the ship than waves or wind. The sailors, with superhuman effort, dropped full length upon it. Finally they succeeded in making it fast.

The storm intensified. Mountains of water attacked the vessel. For two days and two nights the convulsion of the

37

ship was such that no one dared even try to reach food or drink. It was a delirium of gray and black, of constant movement without slack or rest, of thirst and hunger, of wet and chill. Tom was numb with terror. He knew they would be drowned. He knew they would never reach land. He knew he would never see his mother again. He prayed silently and sometimes called aloud to a God who did not seem to hear.

Tom felt warmth upon his cold cheek. He realized suddenly that he was crying bitterly, wildly. His throat ached with the pent up agony of his emotions. The ship's carpenter crouched beside him. A quiet and reserved man in his forties, he had been a seaman since his youth. Tom had always admired him. "Torjus," his voice was hoarse with heavy breathing, "don't despair. I've seen it just as bad as this many a time. We'll get through, mark my words." Tom felt calm. Suddenly the weariness, the panic, the grief left him. The assurance was short-lived.

Tom cried out in horror. He had seen Arne stumble to the forecastle door and enter. A huge wave slapped at the ship, and water poured through the open door and into the forecastle which became, in truth, a fishbowl, with Arne struggling and gasping for air. The ship righted itself, and as it rolled, the water drained out the door with a mad rush, carrying Arne with it; he floundered and went over the side into the sea. The men heard a fragment only of his terrified screaming, the sound choked by the wind and the splashing of the water. They stared hopelessly into the black expanse of ocean. The ship again slipped down from the crest of a tremendous wave and became again momentarily erect, and they saw, unbelieving, clinging to the foremast shrouds the limp figure of Arne. Miraculously, as the fore yard slipped upward out of the water, he had clutched the ratlines and come up with it. Eager hands helped him as he half-descended, half-fell. His hat and coat and shirt were gone, and his body was cold with fear and the shock of of the dousing.

The lurching began to ease the second night, and the crew took anxious stock of damages. Everything had been tied down except the heavy grindstone that was stored in the prow. It weighed about one hundred and fifty pounds and measured a good three feet in diameter. It had disappeared.

Calm after the storm. Tom understood now the meaning of this phrase. He marveled at the way the sailors quietly went about their work of salvaging, repairing, putting the *Imacos* back into condition. As their actions had been stoic under the stress of the hurricane, so their joy at the safe outcome was subdued. To Tom, the sunshine was pure gold; the softened sea breeze touched his cheek with benediction. He felt a surge of exaltation. This was the last destination, short of home. In a few months he would be sixteen, his contract up, and he would again walk the streets of Tvedestrand and see his mother.

But danger had not completely deserted the *Imacos*. Crossing the Atlantic she encountered heavy fog. This was more than usually perilous because she was running in the passenger lanes. Tom was on watch. The fog horn was operated by hand, and Tom kept turning and listening. By varying the blasts, he warned any nearby craft of their position and their course. He heard an answering horn, and again repeated the warning. Suddenly, out of the vagueness of the fog, appeared a white hulk of a liner, so close that Tom could actually see people through the portholes. The boats passed without collision, but it was a very close call, and Tom's knees were not exactly steady as he resumed his signals.

Riga — capital city of a disputed land. Its various occupations by Russian, German, Polish and even Swedish forces are expressed in the contrasts of architecture and the mixture of language. Tom helped unload logwood at the quay. Wood-products fabricating, manufacture of paints and textiles, were leading industries in Riga.

Tom spent his sixteenth birthday wandering about Old Riga, admiring the thirteenth and fourteenth century cathedrals, the old gabled and turreted buildings, now mostly museums and showing the German influence of the days of the Hanseatic League.

When he returned to the *Imacos* that evening, he found Captain Araldsen awaiting him with a proposition:

"Torjus," he said, "I have a new job for you, and I will pay you forty kroner a month for our return trip to Tvedestrand."

Tom had a good idea what the captain was talking about. The steward had months ago confided to Tom his intention to leave the ship at Riga.

"Captain Araldsen," Tom protested, "thank you, sir, for the opportunity, but I haven't had any experience as a cook, and besides I don't think I'd like it. I wash enough dishes now as it is."

The captain laughed. "Now, Torjus, I wonder which is the real reason. You think about it. The mate can watch out over you and it isn't for long. We won't expect anything fancy."

Tom had saved for his mother the greater part of his wages, and the prospect of adding to this sum by doubling his pay on the return to Tvedestrand convinced Tom to try to stomach the job of catering to stomachs. It wasn't as bad as he had expected. The crew teased him unmercifully at first, but when he pointed out, with reason, that they would be the ones to suffer if they goaded him too far, the salty and uncomplimentary references to his first meal of brown bean rocks were hushed. After all, how did he know that you couldn't cook the beans the same morning you put them on to soak? Tom made his own yeast and baked sometimes seventeen loaves of bread in one day. He learned fast, and his specialty was a kind of bread pudding. Praise by the captain partially compensated for the fact that he still didn't like cooking a bit better!

As the *Imacos* approached the coast of Norway, Tom's excitement and impatience increased. Before leaving Denmark, Captain Araldsen had telegraphed ahead to Tvedestrand requesting that a pilot stand by to bring the *Imacos* into Tvedestrand Fjord. Even before land was sighted, the small boat carrying their pilot came into view. There were only two occupants, a man and a young boy about ten years of age. The sea was rough, and Tom wondered how they would board the pilot. After several unsuccessful attempts to bring the smaller boat alongside, the man shouted for a line. This he tied around his waist and jumped overboard. Thrashing like a huge jewfish, he was pulled up to the deck of the *Imacos*. The youngster waved good-bye and turned his craft about and headed in the direction whence he had come. Tom watched the boat move away and set to thinking. He was happy to be so nearly home, but at the same time, now that disembarking was only a matter of hours, he was regretful. By necessity and by character, Tom had always been more mature than his years. The usual painful transition of adolescence from boy to man had not existed for Tom. In the crucible of a sailing ship, the traits of manhood had been tempered and tested.

The *Imacos* tacked gracefully through the islands and came to berth before Tvedestrand. Throwing his bag over his shoulder, Tom set out up the familiar cobblestone street. It was almost dark. The light from the lamp on the table next to his mother's knitting machine cast a faint glow. Tom stopped a moment across the street and looked up at the window. His mother sat at her machine, her movements occasionally breaking the shaft of light. Suddenly, Tom's heart beat faster; a lump rose to his throat. He was up the steps, running like a child. He threw open the door, and in a moment his mother was in his arms.

It was late that night before Tom fell into an unaccustomed bed. At first he could not sleep. The bed seemed too rigid. He hunched his body, seeking the rhythm of the sea.

He would never forget this reunion. Not ordinarily talkative, he had run on continually, between mouthfuls of all his favorite foods, his mother's smiling eyes never leaving his tanned face.

"I'm going to study navigation and become a captain," he told her, and it summed up in a bold resolution all the experiences of the past two years. She impulsively crossed the room and hugged his shoulders.

"You can and will do anything you put your mind and heart to, Torjus." Her words had the ring of prophecy.

As if time were indeed precious, the next morning Tom set out to make the necessary arrangements. He must study and take an examination to be held at Arendal at a time scarcely six months away. There were two other applicants from Tvedestrand. Both were studying with Thomas Svensen, an elderly relative of Tora's who had a private school in navigation in Tvedestrand. Tom enrolled and paid his tuition.

At first Tom was handicapped by his lack of background in higher mathematics. The hours of study were long, and Tom struggled with unfamiliar terms and concepts. Even the snowballs, fashioned from the newly fallen snow, which broke against the classroom windows distracted him but slightly, and that only because he knew that one of the throwers was Ingeborg, pert and lovely, with her merry laugh that even today has the crystal sound of clear water over the wheel by her father's mill. It was a wonderful "remembrance" to Tom. The few evenings he stole from his studies might find him down on the skating pond, scowling at each rival who swung Ingeborg on his arm, gliding in long smooth circles. Once he helped her fasten her skates, and he claimed for his reward a turn about the pond.

The day of examination arrived. The three boys presented themselves at Arendal. The examining professor looked severe in his dark coat. "His eyes are friendly," thought Tom. The papers were spread out, and Tom put his mind to the problems. They were not easy, but as Tom progressed he felt he was doing fairly well — except for the problem in astronomy — how did one go about calculating — Tom raised his head at the staccato tapping of a pencil on the front desk. "Papers please." He gathered the sheaf and surrendered it. As he descended the steps he had the unreal feeling of being in a dream. He sat out on a bench in the little park by the school. Then it came to him. *That* was how to do it. Now he could see it. And he had missed the problem. He was heartsick because now that he knew the proper approach, he could have solved the problem correctly. For hours he walked the quiet streets, berating himself. Suddenly he came to a decision. He would go to the professor and tell him exactly how he had made his mistake, how to correct it, and what the proper procedure should have been. He hastened back to the school. Forestalling any objection, Tom burst forth into a none too coherent explanation, but his obvious sincerity and desperation made a deep impression on the teacher. The next day Tom learned that he had passed and would get his certificate.

Tom and his mother sat in the living room, talking. Finances were discussed, and Tom realized that with what his mother needed and his expenses during the past six months, he was broke. It was customary to buy stock in a shipping company if you hoped to captain one of their ships. He had no such funds to invest.

Then it dawned on him. He would come to America, land of opportunity, and make his fortune so that he might return to Tvedestrand to seek his fame.

Little did he suspect that America held for Torjus Tellefsen both fortune and fame.

Wandering

Tom sailed from Liverpool on the *SS Teutonic,* a White Star Liner. Steamship lines were competing for passengers by cutting fares, and this rate war favored Tom's meager resources. Steerage cost him only twenty dollars.

This crossing of the Atlantic was different. He was on his own, a paying guest, not a member of the crew. Typically, he did not consider the loss of that security the latter status had given him. He thought only ahead; his enthusiasm and optimism had no room for insecurity. He had something he must do, and now he was on his way to doing it.

"God bless and keep you," his mother had said, and because her benediction was the basis of his faith, he never doubted that God, too, was within him, guiding his footsteps, heeding his prayers. Worshiping God, to Tom, was believing in His goodness and obeying one's own conscience, which was God. "In doubting ourselves, we deny Him" . . so his mother had taught him. She had never permitted him to believe that fear motivated life. Punishment and Hell fire never entered his mind. He worshiped God affirmatively by accepting his life and determining to achieve self-fulfilment in honor, in success and in service to others. "What you do for others," his mother said, "you do for yourself."

As he watched the endless water, his thoughts must have dwelt on all of this — his mother, his childhood, his ideas of life and God. But Tom was not reflective by nature, and you can be sure that his dreams of the future were uppermost. He was impatient, as he has always been, to put his hands and mind to work. Idleness is not to be endured. The days seemed longer than on the *Imacos.*

He landed on Ellis Island on April 25, 1905, with the sum of twelve dollars in his pockets. Showing passers-by the address Tora had written out for him, he found his way to Mrs. Knutsen's boarding house in Brooklyn. The Knutsen family had come to New York from Tvedestrand some three or four years previous. It was good to hear Norwegian spoken, good to taste Norwegian dishes. The Knutsens had no lodging for Tom, but agreed to give him his meals. They helped him find a cubby-hole of a room which measured only four by eight feet and had no windows. "What mind," thought Tom, "it's only for sleeping. I will be working every daylight hour."

At the Knutsen's congenial board, Tom met John Reiersen, whom he had also known in Tvedestrand many years ago. Reiersen gave Tom encouragement in telling of his experiences in America. "I've been less than five years, Torjus," he said, "and I'm already foreman of my crew. I tell you all you need to get along is spirit and the will to work." Reiersen referred to his job with a demolishing company then engaged in moving buildings out of the Flatbush area so that the Pennsylvania Railroad station might be built.

Better even than these words, Reiersen got Tom a job, as a member of his crew. He earned less than $1.50 a day but it was a start. "All things start some place," grinned Tom, "and it's best if it's at the bottom; then you can go no way but up!"

He knew little English, and his pat rejoinder to a remark made to him was "I can't understand," but he learned phrases quickly and soon was able to make himself understood. He found American habits and customs confusing and marvelled at his fellow Italian workers who each ate a loaf of white bread for lunch.

Reiersen moved on, but Tom stayed in New York. He hoped to be a carpenter, and his purpose was to earn enough money at odd jobs to buy his tools. Job hunting took him mostly along the extended waterfront, the East River and the area along the Hudson River mouth. Such was his enthusiasm, he was determined not to be downhearted.

At last he got a break. He was hired at $1.50 a day for eight hours' work, clearing debris from a wharf on the Hudson River. He worked along with older boys of Italian descent. The job would last two weeks, and Tom put his heart and soul into his work. The other boys jeered his conscientious labor, but the latter did not go unnoticed, and when this job was over he was directed to go to New Jersey for similar work. He was elated until he was made to understand that although he would receive the same wage, he would be required to work nine hours instead of eight. Then a typical trait of Tom's asserted itself. He felt the offer belittled his good efforts and his abilities. He quit!

Three jobless weeks followed, and Tom's funds were running low. His unfailing optimism was shaken, and his step slowed. One afternoon he chanced to walk by a dock builder's warehouse and plant in Hoboken. The gate to the yard was open, and Tom could see a man inside checking equipment. On impulse, Tom went inside, introduced himself and haltingly explained his need of work.

The man seemed startled. "What part of Norway are you from?" he asked. "Tvedestrand — southeast Norway — on the coast," Tom replied.

This information transformed the man's grudging attention. He exclaimed aloud and grabbed Tom by the arm, speaking rapidly in Norwegian. This was the same person who had befriended Tellef, had in fact roomed with him. It was he who notified Tora of Tellef's accident and had sent the tools to her.

"Torjus Tellefsen," he cried, "this is a coincidence indeed. Your father and I were the very best of friends, and I would be most happy to help you, his son." And he told Tom the whole story. They had dinner together that night in a little cafe whose Spanish food reminded Tom of the West Indies. They talked and talked. Tom had already forgotten his temporary depression.

The next day Tom went to the owner of the plant with a note from his new friend, and he was given work immediately. He would have to go to New Haven, however, and this meant borrowing money from his friend, but this was gladly lent.

There Tom worked on a coal bunker plant, doing rough carpentry. Again coincidence recalled his father. The superintendent here was the same one who had been in charge at the time of his father's accident. The wages of $2.25 a day soon provided Tom with his own tools, and he wrote Tora that now he was on his way. And so he was. His hard work was rewarded by an increase to $2.75 a day. He stayed in New Haven for four months, when the job was completed.

Although Tom boarded well, his appetite had grown with his good prospects, and he would think nothing of consuming several pieces of apple pie and a quart of milk in the summer evenings after he had wandered about the streets of New Haven.

He bought a bicycle and toured the surrounding countryside. He loved the hills and the well-kept farms, which reminded

45

him of Norway. Sunday morning would often find him far from New Haven, and as he pedaled, he dreamed again his dream of the future. His mother seemed very close to him then. To her, in imagination, he confided his ambitions and determination to make good. These thoughts and the deepened sense he always had of her love and faith gave him added incentive to learn what he could about his trade, his new environment and the people with whom he worked. A letter from Tora, forwarded from the boarding house in Brooklyn, forced a decision. Captain Araldsen had paid her a visit, asking her to write to Tom that he would like to have him as his second mate. "He says," she wrote, "that you will make a good success of whatever you do." Tom pondered, but there was no turning back now. This America was his future. The sea had lost its great appeal. His hands and mind were eager now for new assignments, new tasks, and some day he would build great buildings, and do great things. He refused Captain Araldsen's offer, but he was proud that he had been asked.

Tom returned to New York and took a job on a pile driver in the East River. This he considered temporary because of his newly reached decision to learn to build, but it was work he could do, and milk and free lunch at the waterfront cafes cost him only five cents. Working on the pile driver was not dull by any means. One time the line holding the driver fast to the wharf was cast off by mistake and the equipment set adrift. Tom jumped overboard to make it secure and the dousing in the cold and murky water brought back memories of his seafaring days. He left his pile driving to build concession stands on Coney Island. There followed odd jobs such as scraping paint off boats in dry dock, a day's work now and then as a carpenter.

A housing project at Hawthorne, near White Plains, New York, came to Tom's attention. While here employed, he lived in a tent pitched near a corn field. It was informal and fun, and Tom admits he knows of nothing as delicious as corn, freshly picked, boiled in a paint bucket and served with plenty of butter and salt!

Tom was willing and worked hard. He learned fast, but he had little experience in the more exacting tasks of house building, such as cabinet work. As the project neared completion he was laid off. Always cautious with his wages and conservative in his needs, he had enough money to buy another bicycle, and he set off to find other employment. This time he was not alone. He had met a Norwegian ex-sailor, Ole Olesen, who had come to the United

States some years previous. He was a man in his forties, and he and Tom discovered that they had something more in common than language and present occupation; they came from the same general region in Norway. Tom had thought the man vaguely familiar and, concentrating, he remembered seeing the sailor implicated in a street brawl in Tvedestrand when Tom was a young boy! Together they toured likely building projects in the area from White Plains northward past West Point. One day at Garrison they stopped for lunch, and here Ole read in a paper that the Federal Government was advertising for construction men to go to Panama to work on the canal — for five dollars a day.

"Tom," he said, for by now the friendly Americans had anglicized the "Torjus" and even Ole called him "Tom." Tom spelled it "Thom." "Why don't we have a try at this? We can earn and save enough in a year to come back and get established here or maybe in the southwest which they say is expanding. Texas, perhaps."

Tom considered. He had heard other men discussing the pros and cons of going into Central America. He remembered, too, when one of the crew of the *Imacos* had contracted malaria when they were in the West Indies. "There's a lot of that in Panama," he told Ole, "and yellow fever too."

But the prospect of high wages persuaded Tom. He was strong and sturdy and any kind of illness seemed remote. With his expenses paid and his immediate future assured, he could send his mother the some $500-$600 that remained of his savings. This would make it possible for her to rent the larger and more comfortable apartment on the third floor of the Gutormsen house. Being now a woman of means, she need not work at her knitting machine for such long hours.

The two applied at the United States Employment Office in New York City, were accepted and soon were bound for Panama. There was a motley assortment of men on board the ship. Some were Americans and others were English and North Europeans. Ole and Tom were the only Norwegians. Tom particularly enjoyed the antics of a little rotund German whose jolly laugh made Kriss Kringle seem quite believable! One day the purser canvassed the passengers to recruit a band. "Do any of you play anything?" he asked the group including Tom, Ole and the German. "Ya," replied the latter, "I play pinochle." They all laughed, even the purser.

The boat docked at Colon, twelve days out of New York. Cristobal, on the American side, had no docking facilities as yet.

Tom's destination was Gatun, some six miles inland from Colon. He would work with the crew now making preparations for the Gatun locks.

At this time, in 1906, Congress had just adopted the lock-canal type in preference to the sea level canal, as had been started by Ferdinand de Lesseps. Work plans were somewhat disorganized, and living and working conditions in the area were poor and highly unsanitary. The United States had taken over the project under difficulties. They had purchased the old machinery and the little excavation accomplished by De Lesseps. The odor of his financial fiasco remained. Colombia failed to ratify the treaty granting the United States perpetual control over the land needed to build the Canal. The situation was somewhat improved when Panama seceded from Colombia and, in return for a cash payment and a yearly fee, gave the United States right to the land in perpetuity. The Canal Zone came into being and work was begun to make the some forty miles of isthmus into a canal for inter-oceanic shipping.

Tom's construction outfit was put to building barracks, commissaries, etc. In the meantime they lived and ate in tents. The mosquitoes came in hordes, and Tom didn't care whether they were members of the fifty known or ten unknown varieties. It was damp and hot, although the trade winds brought some relief. It showered every day. Everything mildewed — even the soles of his shoes, sometimes overnight. Malaria was prevalent. It was estimated in 1906 that eight out of every ten men engaged in the Canal project had malaria. Quinine was a breakfast food. Tom was an early victim, and he can remember taking as much as fourteen grains of quinine at a time during an attack.

The construction men moved into the barracks as they were finished and went on to build more to accommodate the engineering crews expected soon when the cut was ready for installation of the three sets of locks.

Tom was once reported dead of malaria:

Tom's bed appeared to him to be a hammock. He felt like he was swaying dizzily in several directions at once. Or maybe it was the room, going around and around. The voices of the poker players in their "friendly" game echoed unpleasantly. Their laughter hurt his ears.

48

Sweat poured from every gland, and yet he was cold. He pulled the blanket around his hunched body. Vaguely, he remembered the hospital in Cristobal where he had spent a week not too long ago — the white walls, the white sheets, all so white it pained his eyes to look at them. But the nurses were kind and their touch and medication were cooling. Tom groaned as he remembered.

Jerry stood over him. "How are you, Tom?" His voice was anxious. But you never sympathized with Tom, and you didn't let him know if you were worried. "Have you taken your quinine?" Tom nodded wearily. Jerry thrust a glass of cool water into Tom's hand and urged him to drink. The effort was exhausting, and Tom sank back.

He slept fitfully but by morning was better and could stand. He dressed against the advice of his roommate. Jerry was impatient. "Tom, stay here today. I'll tell McKinley. You can't work when you're so weak; look at your hands tremble, and your eyes are bloodshot and feverish yet. Wait till the attack passes. I'll check in on you at noon."

Tom was insistent. "I can work. You go on. Don't worry. I'll be all right." The men left and Tom struggled with a rising dizziness to pull on his shoes. He mustered his strength and reached the doorway. The barracks had long verandas where the men sat at night if the mosquitoes permitted their being out of doors. Old battered rocking chairs and camp stools stood aimlessly about. Tom barely made the first rocker and collapsed, slumped into a half-conscious delirium. He couldn't move. He couldn't call out. It seemed as if he were suspended in an almost inanimate state. There was light and there was shadow, but nothing took recognizable shape.

It was noon when Jerry, ahead of the other men, ran up the steps and found Tom, still unconscious and doubled up in the rocker. Tom was taken to the tent hospital. There was not a train to Cristobal until the next day. The camp doctor did not conceal his concern. "Tell McKinley Tellefsen's a goner for sure," he advised.

That night Tom awoke. It was dark within the tent. The fever had passed. He felt faint but very calm. Reaching for his clothes, he dressed himself slowly and walked back to his room. No poker game that night and the room was empty. He fell upon his bed and slept.

49

When Tom reported to work the next morning, he caused a near riot. News of his supposed death had reached McKinley, the superintendent, and he came running. "Is it really *you?*" he exclaimed. And Tom assured him that if a lion could indeed turn into a mouse, so feeble he was, he *was* yet himself.

Tom's ingenuity recommended him for some variety in jobs. He spent several months in Ancon on the Pacific side working on the floors of the new Tivoli Hotel. On three different occasions he was called upon in an emergency to run one of the steam shovels working on the cut at Gatun. The general foreman, Murphy, and Goddard, an operating engineer, lived on the same floor in the barracks with Tom. They took a brotherly interest in him. By using Tom on the shovel they hoped to advance him to a higher paying job. It was a good intention, but somehow the red tape of governmental personnel records never caught up with the situation, and Tom was never paid for his work on the shovel, but was indeed docked for every bit of time away from his job as carpenter! So he gave up this sort of "advancement" and devoted himself to learning what he could of construction. Methods were crude. None of the lumber was precut, and they had no machines for the purpose. This meant sawing and planing by hand all lumber for the trim around windows, doors, etc. It took a strong arm and a ready will. Tom had both.

There was little diversion for the men. Tom stayed out of the poker games held nightly in his room. He had never been much of a hunter. However, one day he borrowed a .22 rifle and decided to try his luck in the jungle. And as his luck would have it, he did shoot a bird — purely by accident, he claims. It was a parrakeet. He sent a wing home to his mother, little dreaming she would keep this memento until she died.

Tom's curiosity, enthusiasm and enterprise have always made him susceptible to promoters with ideas to exploit. Murphy hit on a plan to establish a fish business in Panama and spent many hours trying to convince Tom. Tom's indecision, fortunately, finally turned Murphy to another prospective partner.

It was late 1907 and President Theodore Roosevelt and his administration became alarmed at the high cost of the Canal to

50

date. A commission was sent to investigate and the canal was put under the Department of the Army. Colonel George W. Goethals became Chief Engineer and Colonel William C. Gorgas became Chief Sanitary Engineer. The latter were successful in improving health conditions. Clean water was piped from reservoirs; crude oil was spread on mosquito-bearing swamps.

The Army demanded better housing than had the civilian staff. Tom was sent to work on the residence of Colonel R. E. Woods (General Woods of Sears-Roebuck). As conditions changed for the better, and more publicity was given to the canal project, work became more desirable and the number of applicants increased. United States citizens began to complain against the number of foreigners employed. It became a requirement that all workers have their naturalization papers. Tom decided he should return to the United States and take out his papers and then head back for Panama. But his superintendent was loath to let him go. Tom was one of the last non-citizens to be released and upon arrival in the United States, he found the naturalization law had been revised. To become a citizen, he would first have to state his intentions, and it would then be necessary to wait five years before final papers could be had.

Tom now knows that it was God's will that he return to the United States to stay. He was keenly disappointed at first that he could not go back to the Canal Zone. It seemed to Tom that he was being thwarted in his purposes. Thus often does Fate work subtle benefits although those benefited feel frustrated and downhearted. Faith, the kind Tom had, bolstered the spirit. "What happens is God's will, and there is a reason." So thought Tom and took renewed courage in his prayerful thoughts. He came back to New York City late in the year 1908:

It was winter and the city streets were chill and bleak. Tom was visiting Halvor who also had come to America and settled on Staten Island with his wife and child.

Tom filed his intention papers on December 28, in Richmond County Court, State of New York, but nevertheless he was restless. Into his memory came the prophetic remarks of Ole, years before — why not the south? Why not Texas?

Tom fingered idly the brochure he had picked up that morning. The prospectus of the Terre Haute Home Seekers

51

Colony spoke in glowing terms of the Gulf Coast, a country where the birds never stopped singing, where flowers blossomed year round, and oranges grew in the gardens.

Tom had saved between three and four thousand dollars in the Canal Zone. His resolution to come to Texas was as impulsive and as decisive as was his coming to America. He put his money into three one-thousand dollar bills which he carried in his wallet. He bought a one-way ticket for Terre Haute, bid his brother and family good-bye, and was gone.

The coach that carried the hopefuls to Houston (at the land company's expense) changed at St. Louis. To Tom the Union Depot was a sprawling jigsaw of gleaming rails. Tom stopped to buy a supply of Havana cigars. Mr. Jones, (no kin to Jesse H. Jones) president of the Terre Haute Home Seekers Colony, stood at his elbow. He seemed to find Tom's company most desirable. Tom was embarrassed by his fawning attentions. He wished Jones wouldn't follow him about the way he did. His sly glances made Tom nervous. Tom fingered his wallet.

The Katy would be hours late into Houston. Tom talked to a Mrs. Brown, a well-dressed lady of middle age who also had succumbed to the utopian descriptions of the Gulf Coast area and who hoped to find there her dream of leisurely and gracious living.

It was almost dark as their train pulled into the Katy depot. The view out of the window had not been impressive. The buildings which were downtown Houston huddled across the gash made by Buffalo Bayou, which in the fading light looked clay-colored and sluggish.

Tom assisted his companion with her luggage, and they descended to the platform. The sound of billowing steam mingled with high-pitched voices. Mrs. Brown turned to Tom in sudden anxiety. He offered her his arm, and together they walked up the long and narrow steps and out onto Main Street.

Texas

Daylight waited. The bleak sky, like an inverted bowl of granite, barricaded the Texas landscape from sunshine and warmth. This was no storm, instead an all-engulfing heaviness of cold. The scrubby mesquite, sculptured by the prevailing south winds to lean away from the Gulf, now creaked uncomfortably as winds from the north bent them unnaturally upward. The somber chill made yellow grasses seem brittle under foot. Leaves and broken branches yielded to sudden gusts and tumbled before the wind. All else was still in the ominous quiet of a blue norther.

* * * * * * *

Tom stirred and opened his eyes. He pulled the cotton blanket closer about him. In the dimness of the room, he could see the finger-wide cracks in the vertical boards which made up the walls. The batten pieces had shrunk in weathering. The sounds outside were disquieting — the rubbing of the chinaberry tree against the siding, the impact of rolling things caught up by the wind and hurled against the building, the blatting of air in crevices, shrill music played by a ghostly hand. Tom struggled into his clothes and looked into the clouded mirror above the wash stand. The water in the bowl was ice.

Tom's thoughts went back over the last four days. Horse-drawn vehicles — hacks they were called — took Mr. Jones' party across the Milam Street bridge into town where they registered at the Rice Hotel. Next morning, automobiles had called for them. Houston boasted the latest models, and Tom rode wonderingly in a White Steamer. Each of the party was presented with a red rose at the Katy city passenger office at 513 Main Street. These mementos were donated by progressive public citizens to the some two thousand home seekers gathered in Houston.

Then they toured the city. Main Street was paved with creosoted wooden blocks, Crawford being the only street paved with brick. The main object of their tour lead the caravan out Harrisburg Boulevard in the direction of Pasadena. Here the tourists were escorted into the garden of a modest but beautifully landscaped home and were shown the ultimate of their promises — oranges growing in January! Tom made a guess at some dozen oranges visible among the gray-green foliage. It was rather disappointing. But it was true — citrus fruit *did* grow in Houston in the winter time!

The land Mr. Jones wanted Tom to see was in Mc-Mullen County, and next day, Tom, Mrs. Brown and several others left by train for Alice. Here they spent the night in an ancient, wooden hotel. They set out next morning to see the acreage. It was a day's jogging journey by horse and buggy to the ranch house. Mr. Jones apologized for their accommodations. "We'll be just camping," he said. It didn't matter; the sun was warm and the prairie around them seemed unaware of January — tiny blue flowers bloomed by the side of the trail.

Towards late afternoon Tom noticed a change in the sky, "and there is more sky in Texas than anywhere else," he thought. A lid of black clouds was rising in the north and moving relentlessly over the horizon. They were not like ordinary storm clouds, turbulent and swirling; they came instead in an even line as if being spread by a broad-bladed knife. A north wind stirred. Before the party reached the sprawling ranch house, the temperature had fallen some thirty degrees, and Mrs. Brown was shivering in her chiffon dress, her shawl and Tom's coat about her shoulders. Mr. Jones was uneasy. This was not the way he would have planned to launch any prospect; Tom listened idly to assurances that northers were only very temporary. And regardless of the weather, the price of $15.00 an acre seemed very reasonable.

* * * * * * *

A knock on the door interrupted Tom's thoughts. It was Mr. Jones with word about breakfast and their return. Tom did not commit himself on buying the land, but Jones was persistent. Later that day when they were back in Alice, Jones made a dramatic gesture. He offered the land to Tom for $10 an acre. It was too good a bargain to ignore. Tom agreed to buy one hundred and sixty acres and to give Mr. Jones as earnest money, half of the sales price or eight hundred dollars.

Much later Tom learned that comparable land at that time might have been purchased for fifty cents an acre, but, not knowing, he was proud and elated. "We are land owners, Mother," he wrote Tora that night just before train time. It was an important step for an immigrant lad of twenty: the rooting of an intention for permanence. His mother would understand. As Tom looked out the window at the monotonous landscape — level plains and patches of underbrush, his thoughts were far away. Even Mr. Jones did not presume to disturb him.

The deal was closed after Tom returned to Houston. He took a room in a boarding house facing Sam Houston Park. Tom discovered that his landlord, Tipps, had been a county clerk in East Texas, and he asked Tipps to go with him to Tilden, county seat of McMullen County, where he filed his deed. At that time, all one hundred and sixty acres were in McMullen County, but later when the boundary between Duval and McMullen counties was resurveyed, part of Tom's acreage fell in Duval County.

It would be a year before Tom would be furnished with an abstract and the sale be final. Laws and procedures concerning land ownership in Texas were confusing, to say the least. Tom, alien and newcomer, did not realize that the abstract had not been brought up to date, or that his title to the land was not a clear one. He had not been told that the American National Insurance Co. of Galveston held a mortgage against the entire ranch. C. W. Hall Co. had borrowed the money to buy the land and subdivide it. Tom's deed was recorded and he regularly paid taxes. Tom was notified later that the mortgage was foreclosed. Surprised and dismayed, he took the matter to his friend, Judge George W. Tharp who happened to know the attorney for the American National. The latter assured Tharp that he would look into Tom's case and clarify ownership. Tharp so advised Tom and the matter was dropped. Years later when the abstract was finally brought up to date, Tom learned that no rectification had ever been made, and that his property legally belonged to the insurance company. After some negotiation, Tom received a quitclaim deed from the American National who retained one half of the mineral rights. Tom's half interest in these rights has repaid the cost of the land threefold in the four times the land has been leased to oil companies. In addition, the assumption of ownership of the land stood him in good stead as collateral when he needed capital to proceed in the path that God was overseeing — strange His ways, but undeviating!

Houston, Texas, in January of 1909 had an estimated population of sixty-five thousand. H. B. Rice, the esteemed mayor of Houston, was receiving petitions for a bond election to raise $2,000,000 so that the ship channel might be dredged to twenty-five feet.

Houstonians were chuckling at the antics of the Hooligans, the Katzenjammer Kids, Buster Brown and Mary Jane in the *Houston Chronicle*, which boasted a circulation "larger than any paper in Houston or South Texas." And in the *Chronicle* Sunday section, Mrs. Cholly Knickerbocker described her latest fad of embroidering furs with jewels.

The phone number *2 4* would put you in contact with the Jesse Jones Lumber Co. Mr. Jones was also president of the Southern Loan and Investment Co.

Magnolia Park was beginning its residential construction and Houston Heights was already well established. Harrisburg was an incorporated community.

Ducks were hunted in the vicinity of Montrose Place, and river boats took eager fishermen from the docks at the foot of Main Street up the channel to Morgan's Point near La Porte. Others, like Tom and Richard Krupp, who kept his skiff moored near Harrisburg, preferred tributary waters such as Green's Bayou, where they could camp and fish.

Mosehart & Keller advertised the latest in gasoline powered automobiles — the E.M.F. and the White Steamer in the $2,000 class, complete with gas lamps, horns, gas tanks and crankshafts. The Houston Motor Co., Cadillac agency, also featured Columbus Electrics at $1,700 to $2,500, guaranteeing current for fifty miles a day and offering to keep the machines in working order, store, pick up and deliver daily for twenty-five dollars a month.

Butter could be purchased at the Great Atlantic & Pacific Co. for thirty-three cents a pound; sugar sold twenty-one and a half pounds for one dollar and two pounds of coffee cost fifty-five cents. Levy Bros. Dry Goods Co. advertised gingham for eight and one-third cents a yard, and six pairs of hose could be bought for two dollars. Undermuslins were included in the January White Sale. Krupp & Tuffly appealed to "dapper young dressers who want the limit in shoe style" and proudly presented a man's tan Russian calf for four dollars a pair. Other names over the store fronts included Foley Bros., Leopold & Price, James Bute, Thos. Goggan & Bros., Peden Iron & Steel, Henke & Pillot. In this month of January, 1909, Gimbel's in the Stowers Building were "sacrificing imported fur turbans for ladies, seven dollars and fifty cent values for three dollars and ninety-five cents."

At the Prince Theater (admission fifty cents to one dollar and fifty cents), a New York cast produced *The Clansman;* their European tour had been postponed. The billboard of the Majestic Theater on the corner of Congress and Austin, announced "always advanced vaudeville." Audiences at the Bijou on San Jacinto between Prairie Avenue and Preston hissed the villain, cheered the hero and wept with the heroine in *The Girl and the Outlaw.*

The day after his return from Alice, Tom opened an account in a bank on lower Main Street. Picture, if you can, the extreme astonishment of the teller in receiving from this unimpressively dressed stranger — three — one thousand dollar bills! Astonishment became respect, and he ushered Tom into the office of the president and introduced him to the other officials of the bank. Mr. Tom has long considered one's character to be as good as one's bank account, and surely that day, Tom's landed with both feet! Perhaps here was germinated that interest in banking that has become a source of pleasure and gratification in later life.

Tom was content to acquaint himself with Houston and spent the next few weeks wandering about and observing. On one of these occasions, he chanced to see a familiar face —a Mr. Alexander he had known in Panama. The two exchanged experiences, and it developed that Alexander was looking for backing in a new venture — making ice cream. He owned two mules and a wagon, and his partner had had experience in manufacturing ice cream. Tom went in with them, furnishing the money to buy the machinery and rent a building on Caroline between Texas and Prairie. They were known as the Artic Ice Cream Company.

Tom liked to eat at the White Kitchen on Main Street. It was run by a friendly, volatile Italian by the name of Mike Genora. Tom liked, too, the Chinese restaurant at Travis and Congress. Food gave Tom an idea. Since he had such ready access to ice cream, he would open up a small cafe of his own, a kind of ice cream parlor, with hamburgers added for more substantial fare. It was located on San Jacinto between Prairie and Texas, not far from the Bijou Theater, whose patrons and entertainers became Tom's customers. Tom built the counters himself and hired a cook. The hamburgers were merely meat and bread — the revolutionary Texas 'burger of the present day had yet to be concocted!

Occasionally, Tom went to the Bijou's performances.

The audience was hushed by the darkening of the theater. The curtains parted and Professor Émile appeared before them. A black cape was thrown nonchalantly over his shoulders.

"May I have a subject?" he asked.

There was a slight pause and a man came hesitantly forward and walked up the center steps to the stage. Tom gasped and chuckled. It was Joe, the driver of the truck that brought ice to the cafe.

"Now my good man," said the professor, "are you willing for me to hypnotize you. This is not against your will?"

Joe was awed by the bright lights and the applause and laughter which came from the vast dark chasm of the auditorium.

"Yes, sir — I mean, no, sir — your honor," he stammered.

The professor placed Joe in a chair, center stage, in full view of everyone. Slowly he began to talk in a singsong, "You are sleepy, you are going to sleep. It is so nice to go to sleep," and he turned in his hand a crystal ball whose slanted facets sent shafts of sharp light out even into the audience.

Joe was motionless. The Professor stopped his chanting and looked long into Joe's eyes. He bowed to the audience and cautioned them to be quiet. Turning to his assistant, he gave her a signal.

Into his hands she placed a long cane fishing pole. This he handed to Joe. "You are now sitting on the edge of a lake. You are going fishing. When I tell you to pull up, you will have a fish."

Joe stirred in excitement. He took the pole and threw the line out into the audience, holding it carefully and with an expectant hunch of his shoulders.

"Wait," said the Professor, "I think you have a bite."

Joe pulled violently. "No, no," said the Professor, not yet. Now you have scared him away."

The audience could contain itself no longer. It broke into merriment. Tom laughed until his sides ached. Joe seemed unaware of the noise. He poised the pole again. The assistant, now in the audience, fumbled with the end of the line, hidden by the skirt of the stage.

"Now, now," cried the Professor, and Joe heaved mightily to throw upon the stage a small rubber mouse. Again the audience reacted with loud laughs and catcalls. The Professor shook Joe by the shoulder, snapping his fingers with a decisive sound. Joe straightened. He looked at the Professor and again, sheepishly, at the pole in his hands. All applauded, and Joe grinned as he came back into the audience clutching a bill in his hands.

Six months of indifferent success, and the ice cream venture lapsed into failure. It was a keen disappointment to Tom because he was again broke. However, he felt he had now become a part of this city of Houston, and as he had learned something of small business practices, all was not in vain. He returned to carpentering, and this was God's will. Tom had learned a valuable lesson and one that, sooner or later, almost every successful man has had to learn: however glamorous or potentially fertile those distant greener pastures may appear, still you are more likely to be successful in a line of endeavor in which you have had some training and experience, however limited the horizon may seem at the moment. The rise to riches is a stairway proposition, not an elevator. Tom had basic experience in building, and his dreams on the hills of Connecticut would not be denied. He knew this, too: that however necessary it would be to work for someone else, it was temporary. He must be on his own. Eventually he would do for himself. Thus he could best fulfill his ambitions; thus he could best realize his dream to serve God in his own way.

Tom had several times noticed a sign on a decorating and upholstery shop on Travis Street — Jantzen. The name had a Scandinavian sound, and one day Tom went in and introduced himself. Mr. Jantzen was Danish and had spent some time in Norway. He was delighted to meet Tom and lent a sympathetic ear to his experiences. For once Tom lost his shyness. They became lifelong friends, as did Tom and Mr. Jantzen's son, Julian. Later on in the summer of 1911, Tom was to room with Mr. and Mrs. Julian Jantzen and here he brought his bride.

August is a hot month in Houston. It is still hurricane season, and the barometer receives as much attention as the thermometer. Tom went to work constructing forms for the first section of the Chronicle Building. One day soon after he started, a man in a seersucker suit approached him:

"Tom Tellefsen?" he asked. Tom arose, brushing the sawdust from his overalls.

"I am Tom Tellefsen," he said.

"This is a union job, Tellefsen," the man informed him. "You will have to apply for a union card — membership in the carpenters' local."

Tom took the application form. This was his first direct contact with unions. Knocking about as he had done, he had heard them discussed. It was rather hard for him to understand. All his life he had considered merit as the only basis for work. He deemed it unnecessary that men should band together to achieve fair treatment. Tom had won such treatment by hard work. But he knew it was an accepted practice, and he filled out the form.

The next day Tom again saw the union official approaching him, and he expected to receive his card.

"I'm sorry, Tellefsen," the man avoided Tom's eyes. "You've been blackballed. The Union won't take you."

"But why?" Tom's voice was unbelieving.

"Well," said the official apologetically, "you're what they call a snow bird and the men think the job can be handled by one of them."

"What is a snow bird?"

60

"A man who comes from the north." His voice became a bit edgy in the face of Tom's complete disbelief.

"But this is America," and Tom turned away to hide sudden tears. He didn't give way to his deep disappointment until he had walked away from the job and was back at Tipps' boarding house. It has often been said there is nothing so moving as a strong man crying. But of his own admission, Tom cried like a baby. Tom was too alert, too intent on his mission to get ahead, too vital and aggressive to ever have paid any attention to discrimination. He ignored it. Now it faced him. He hated not the injustice to him only, but the whole fallacy, the misconception by human beings of God's teachings.

Tom lost no time in finding another job. The McAshan Apartment on Main Street was under construction and Superintendent Timmerman hired Tom to build the staircase. The need for concentration in the exact fitting and trimming was good for Tom, and his determination revived.

The stairway was almost completed, and Tom was rightfully proud of his handiwork, when Olsen, the business agent of a carpenters' union, came to see him. Olsen knew of the blackballing incident and recognized the unfairness in Tom's case. He had talked to the men and came to offer Tom membership in the union.

Tom did not return to the Chronicle Building. Instead, he took a job in Pearland. After Pearland, Tom went to South Houston to work on a girls' boarding school for the firm of Castle & Podd, general contractors. Tom had a reputation as a "whiz" at laying floors. He did all the floors in the building and averaged sixteen hundred square feet of floor a day. This was something of a record. "A whiz — more like a whirlwind," was Ernie Podd's comment. Ernie was Tom's boss on this job. Tom thought it not remarkable. After all, he always did as much work as he could. "There's no satisfaction in doing anything short of your best," so Tom believed.

While in South Houston, which was just being developed, Tom bought a lot which he still owns and on which he pays taxes but hasn't seen since 1909! In the winter evenings he drew sketches of house plans and completed one for a bungalow which he hoped to build on his lot. He insists it was for speculation, but one wonders if the cards and letters he had been exchanging with Ingeborg Larsen after leaving Norway might not have implied a more romantic reason?

Castle & Podd obtained a contract for another school, the first to be built in Pasadena (The Oscar Kruse School, now known as the South Shaver Elementary School). Tom was made straw boss or working foreman. He boarded with a German family, the Pomeroys, and he wrote Tora in glowing terms of their kindness in making him, literally, one of the family. The cooking of Frau Pomeroy was not only palate-satisfying, but generous as well, and there were jolly evenings with the Pomeroy children and their friends.

Almost every Saturday afternoon Tom would walk into Harrisburg and take the streetcar to Houston. Often he visited the Podds but would always be back in Pasadena to go to Sunday evening services at the Baptist Church, the only church in Pasadena at that time. Although Tom found the service very different from what he remembered of his church in Tvedestrand, he learned then that regardless of the difference of creed, true Christianity has the same goals, the same basic precepts, the same standards. Facing the altar, Tom came to an awareness of the God he had known on the mountain top in Tvedestrand, sailing the calm waters of the Atlantic after the hurricane, sitting in the lamplit living room of his mother's house.

There were parties, too, and Tom especially enjoyed the hayrides on summer evenings. They went as far as La Porte, their singing given unexpected modulation by the bumps in the road. The lazy horse was no critic whatsoever and never varied his idling pace. Tom found the company of Miss Ethel Miller very pleasing. She played the organ at church and had a provoking preference for tall, slim men with slick black hair parted in the middle and plastered down. Her father was a truck farmer, and she and her mother raised strawberries. The some three to four hundred residents of Pasadena made their livelihood by growing vegetables and the luscious berries Tom found so different from the wild ones he used to pick in Norway.

Tom was twenty-two. Strong and straight, with his direct glance, Tom found favor with adults. Yet still he was liked by the younger set, who admired his modest manner and laughed at the twinkle in his eyes and his quaint expressions. He never lacked for recreation, though work might be his play. He had no time for frivolity or for the minor vices of adolescence. It was not so much that he felt himself superior, or a prude, but to him, there was so much he had to do, there was no time to waste in wasting time! His fun was wholesome fun — of being with people, of doing with people. Yet, let no one think his life was dull; it was fuller, much fuller than most.

J. E. Pomeroy, the eldest son, called Tom his buddy and confided to him his dearest ambition — to be mayor of Pasadena when it would incorporate. He is now a successful water well contractor (McMasters & Pomeroy Water Well Drilling), and he and Tom can reminisce, since their businesses often bring them together. Oddly enough, Pomeroy is director of the Pasadena State Bank, while Tom's son, Howard, has an interest in its competitor, the First National Bank of Pasadena. And another curious twist — McMasters, not Pomeroy, was indeed once mayor of Pasadena.

When Tom returned to Houston late in the summer of 1910, he stayed with a Mrs. Clayton, whose boarding house was on Caroline near the intersection with Jefferson. His work on the Carter Building, later the Second National Bank Building, took him up sixteen floors. In those days there were no construction elevators scaling the skeleton walls with their web of steel. He climbed these sixteen flights not only in the morning and at night but down and up at lunchtime too. He helped build foundation forms for what is now the West Building, and this at least kept him on the ground, but there were other considerations. Good weather in the middle of the rainy season once kept Tom working two days and two nights without sleep. The four dollars a day he received was considered good pay.

Tom's fling at house plans was not an idle whim. He had kept on sketching and while at Mrs. Clayton's decided to enroll at the Y.M.C.A. for a class in architectural drawing. He actually attended only three formal sessions but happened to show his teacher the detailed floor plan he had been working on at night. So impressed was the teacher with the layout, he persuaded Tom to allow the school to have it published in a Houston newspaper.

Later Tom sold this house plan to the Houston Land Corporation, who were developing Montrose Place, named after a royal borough in Scotland. He not only sold the plan but sold himself: he was hired to build the house! It was the first to be built in Montrose Place on the other side of the SAP tracks. The address is

4102 Mount Vernon, which is the corner of Mount Vernon and West Main. It is a handsome, interesting-looking house and no one would dream it was built forty-five years ago.

Actually Tom's first contractual construction was for a Mrs. Myers on Leeland Avenue. For $300 he added three rooms to the house, which now stands as Tom completed it. Before this, he had obtained for Castle & Podd the remodeling of the Jantzen home at 3101 Leeland Avenue. Tom did the carpentry and soon after this he became a boarder with the Jantzens. Tom found employment on the interurban overpass being constructed for the Houston Belt & Terminal Railway Company and this was not far from the Jantzen home. His next job was for the Magnolia Compress Company in Harrisburg. His work on the Rice Institute power plant brought him somewhat closer to home. Daily he would walk the five miles from the Jantzens to the Rice Institute campus.

Building the Montrose house gave Tom a real sense of accomplishment. It had two stories, with three bedrooms and a bath upstairs; entry, living and dining rooms and huge kitchen downstairs. There were two fireplaces, one in the living room and one in the front south bedroom. The cabinet work was outstanding. Bookshelves, counter-height, divided the living and dining areas. The kitchen had a well designed arrangement of cabinets and shelves. The ceilings in the living and dining rooms had trimmed beams, and the whole flavor of the house was unusual with an accent of something foreign, Norway, perhaps. The roof line and eave and window trim confirmed this. It cost $3,200 to build. Tom was pleased with the $200 he got out of it — his labor and profit.

Tom decided to go to Tvedestrand. He had saved enough money for the trip even though he had periodically sent part of his wages to Tora. Her last letter had been wistful, and she had written of her growing friendship with Ingeborg. They shared their letters from Tom and the girl would sit in the front room with Tora, watching her agile fingers, and they would talk. Tom could picture these occasions, and his blood ran faster at the thought of his lovely Ingeborg and his mother — together. His mind was made up. If Ingeborg would have him, he would bring her back to Texas as his wife.

It was early May, and the boat out of Galveston bound for New York carried a group of gay passengers. Among their number, besides Tom, were one of the Podd brothers and his wife — off on a honeymoon. Both had passage also on the White Star Liner from New York to Liverpool. Yielding to Podd's insistent invitation, Tom was inveigled into a card game. Since Tom had observed a good deal of gambling in Panama, he could recognize the professional player. He acted the innocent and was allowed to win fifteen dollars. And he quit! No amount of coaxing could induce him to return to the game. Podd saw the joke, and his amusement added to the pique of the card sharks who continued to harass Tom for the remainder of the voyage.

The steamer nosed its way into the harbor at Arendal. Tom was the first to disembark. Ingeborg awaited him on the wharf. Tom was suddenly shy, and the phrases he thought in English sounded awkward in Norwegian. They laughed together as they realized Tom's predicament. The strangeness was lost in their laughter, and they were a boy and a girl in the May sunshine. Tom was home again. They went by horse and buggy down the coast to Tvedestrand. It was a wonderful reunion, and Tora smiled to see that, for the first time, Tom's attention was divided. He seemed to listen for other footsteps. But she understood.

Tom and Ingeborg were married on the first day of August, 1912. A wedding is essentially a bride's memory.

Ingeborg loved her wedding dress, designed and carefully stitched by Mrs. Knutsen, mother of her friend also named Ingeborg. The bodice was of chantilly lace, with long sleeves and high neck. The lace extended, tunic fashion, halfway down the silk chiffon skirt. The net veil fell loosely into a short train. It was gathered at the forehead by two nosegays on a short embroidered headband. Her bouquet was large and made of garden flowers, tiny corsages being pinned to white silk ribbons which cascaded from the center of the bouquet. The bride's attendants carried similar bouquets.

The steeple of the Lutheran Church is visible from any part of Tvedestrand. It was nearly five o'clock and Ingeborg's heart beat faster as her carriage approached the church. Her father helped her descend to the street, and she took his arm as they mounted the steps. The organ was playing softly as they entered the church and waited in the room to the right of the door. The wedding party had gathered but Ingeborg was scarcely conscious of the excited whispers of the girls, quieted by a stern glance from her father. He stood very straight and did not smile as he looked down at her, but his eyes were kind, and

65

in a moment Ingeborg divined from that look the love he bore her — unspoken but nevertheless real. She treasured his strength now. The bouquet trembled perceptibly and he leaned over to make her hold more secure. Then the music became louder, and the strains of the wedding march summoned them to the doorway. Ingeborg walked slowly as if in a dream. Then, suddenly, there was Tom, standing by the altar. Now she was herself again, and as she faced the minister with Tom at her side, she was completely composed, and there was no hesitation in her clearly spoken answers.

Carriages took the wedding party and the invited guests back to the house of Miller Master Larsen. All the furniture from the first floor had been carried to the upper floors except the long dining table and chairs. Here dinner was to be served. Friends and relatives filled the rooms and thronged the garden where the photographer was posing the bride and groom for their formal picture. Then the attendants grouped together with Tom and Ingeborg seated in front of them. Behind them, the Norwegian flag could be seen, draped from the carriage house.

Ingeborg's father read from the Bible, and the guests joined in singing hymns. There was much conversation and exchange of experiences between relatives who had not seen each other for some time.

The dinner was a gay affair — seven courses: among them, a bouillon on whose surface floated tiny Norwegian dumplings; fish; chicken; a roast of beef surrounded by potatoes and vegetables; dessert and of course wedding cake and coffee. So numerous were the guests that the dinner was repeated several times, in order that all might be seated at the table.

The house was a profusion of flowers, sent by friends. The large number of wedding gifts too were displayed, and all day telegrams were received. The telegram forms were ornate, with beautiful colors and much use of gold. They were written in the picturesque script of Miss Julie Gutormsen, who was manager of the telegraph office in Tvedestrand, and the daughter of Tora's landlord. These telegrams were a measure of the popularity of the bride and groom, and these amenities were considered very fashionable indeed. Each was read and applauded as it arrived. Tom and Ingeborg received over a hundred, from places as far away as Kristiania. Most of the messages were formal and

Tom, age 15, taken at Marseilles

Bride and Groom—August 1, 1912

Tora and Tom, Tvedestrand, 1912

Hortense, Tora, Howard, Ingeborg and Lorraine
Tvedestrand, 1923

Slim Alexander and Tom's first truck, 1919

dignified. "Good luck for the day and also the future." Occasionally a lighter note smiled in — one read "Hip, Hip Hurra" and another "Hurra for Ingeborg."

Tom and Ingeborg did not meet again until the next morning. They would go to Oslo for a few days before taking a boat back to America. Ingeborg's mother bid her farewell at home, but her father walked with her down the street to the wharf; her luggage had gone ahead by cart. She hardly noticed his taciturn manner. Early that morning her mother had helped her into her handsome new suit, with the Russian cut to the coat. She smoothed her hand across her skirt — it was luxuriously soft, with deep pile. The touch brought involuntary tears to her eyes, and she glanced away from her father, lest he see her cry. She still felt about her shoulders the pressure of her mother's embrace. No words had been spoken, but standing in the shadowy hall, she had bent her head to her mother's cheek, and the arms that held her close had trembled.

Tom was surrounded by friends who had come to see them off. The post boat would take them out to meet the steamer. All was gaiety. As her father turned to leave her, Ingeborg could detect a sudden quiver of his prominent and almost-defiant chin. He walked away to the end of the pier. They boarded the boat, and as Ingeborg looked back, and as the boat moved away, she saw her father walking back and forth, his cane tapping on the planks. He did not look up. This is how she remembers him, and it was the last time she was to see him.

Tom and Ingeborg sat at the captain's table on the trip across the Atlantic. The vessel was a combination freight-passenger boat and touched at Newport News before heading for Veracruz and Tampico prior to its docking in Galveston. It would have been possible, timewise, for Tom and Ingeborg to have gone up to Mexico City, but the revolution which then convulsed Mexico made it unwise to do so.

The newly-married status of the young couple must have been pleasantly evident, and Ingeborg was cautiously and wistfully discovering a sense of freedom from the narrow religious atmosphere of her old home. One of their fellow passengers, a well educated man of means, made this prediction: "Someday she'll be the belle of Texas." What nicer compliment could there be than that a husband of some forty-four years should, in reminiscing, say in agreement, "and so she has come to be!"

The boat docked at Galveston. At first glance it was not too unlike other harbors Ingeborg had seen. Craft of varying description moved at cross paths intent on missions of their own; cargo was being loaded and unloaded to the loud cries of longshoremen and other workers on the wharves. The burlap bales of cotton caught her attention. There were so many, piled like toy blocks in long-eaved warehouses. The shrimp boats with their center-deck cabins peaked like a captain's hat, the nets pulled high in back, looking for all the world like the ruffled tailfeathers of a sea gull — these were new to her.

Tom and Ingeborg took the interurban into Houston. It was not yet a year old, and the green leather seats were shiny, and the mahogany interior of the car was rubbed to a high gloss. Looking eagerly out the windows, Ingeborg experienced a rude awakening. For miles at first there were swampy inlets, and then the seemingly endless stretch of saltgrass prairie. The swaying cars passed untidy Negro shacks with mattresses hunched on leaning porches, clothes spread to dry on broken fences. Scrawny, half-dressed children stared at them as they rumbled by. "Where, where in the world have you brought me?" she asked.

The Jantzens gave Tom and Ingeborg a warm reception. They had draped a portiére at one end of their living room so that the couple might have a sitting room in addition to their bedroom. All Tom's friends gathered there on the still-warm September evenings, and Ingeborg was touched by their friendly and affectionate welcome — she who was accustomed to more reserve and formality. Shyly, she gave Mrs. Jantzen the knitted things Tora had made for her son's friends.

House hunting became the order of the day. Ingeborg was distressed by what she saw. The orderly households and spotless kitchens of Norway were a far cry from the untidy and crudely finished apartments at which she looked. Tom tried to soften her judgment, but as a man, could not wholly understand. "For you, we will have a little Norway," he told her. "You'll see."

For ten dollars a month they rented a little three-room box house around the corner from the Jantzens, next to the German landlady, a Mrs. Mueller, and Tom was as good as his word. He transformed that little house into a veritable doll's house with a paint brush as his magic wand. It was a frame house, one room wide. He grained and stained the floors and papered some of the walls and ceilings. The exterior was repaired and trellises built to flank the veranda with its four columns and low balustrade. On these, Ingeborg planted the climbing roses she loved so much. As a wedding present the Jantzens gave them draperies from their shop for the windows of the little house. Ingeborg had brought woven things from home — made on the family loom. The lovely doilies, the throws, the tapestry, the hand-woven rugs from Norway, all added charm and sophistication to the modest rooms. Tom built most of the furniture in the lean-to shop at the rear of the house. Not a nail or a screw were used, only dowels. Some of these pieces are still in existence in the Rector's Sacristy of the Church of the Redeemer, and upstairs in the church's Educational Building where a branch of the Houston Public Library is located. The old-world cradle Tom made for Howard, who was born April 16, 1913, unfortunately was not preserved. The house at 1506 Palmer Street was a show place — of a man's skill in creating beauty from so little, and as a token of his love for his wife and family.

Montrose Place had proved a popular location, and Tom had contracted for a lot from the Houston Land Corporation. He built a house on it for sale. Kipling dead-ends at Audubon, and the house looked down Kipling. On Sunday, Tom and Ingeborg would ride the streetcar out to the house together with Howard and the baby carriage, and wait for prospective buyers. The house was sold for $3,400 to Dave A. Weis, manager of the Prince Theater. It bore Tom's own particular brand of design and individuality.

The houses in Montrose brought Tom a fair amount of recognition as a builder. One of such early clients, and a lifelong friend, was Mr. Hugh Waddell, founder of Waddell's House Furnishings. For a son, Reed Waddell, Tom built a home similar to the house he'd had for sale on Audubon. When the daughter married, Tom drew plans and built a house for her. At the father's request, Tom remodeled the family home on Caroline for still another son, H. K. Waddell. It was this job that first caused Tom to become a literary subject. It came about this way.

Across the street from the Waddell home on Caroline lived Judd Mortimer Lewis, who was to be designated the first Poet Laureate of Texas by the State Legislature in 1932. When Tom first met Lewis the latter had, for many years, written a column of poetry and prose for the *Houston Post*. His generous frame and his interest in finding homes for orphan babies were well known, and he was much beloved in Houston. On two occasions Tom did work for Lewis. When, in 1917, Lewis bought a car too long for his garage, he called Tom to remodel the garage. Later he decided to pave the driveway. The weather man must have frowned upon such extravagance because Lewis wrote in his column of March 27, 1919:

It rained for forty days and nights. The world was all
    a-sozzle.
It slobbered down out of the skies like water from a nozzle.
It dripped down off the eaves, it did, and overflowed the
    gutter,
And all the earth felt to the feet like gobs of homemade
    butter;
The city streets were overflowed, the country roads were
    oozes,
And almost everybody's toes went "sqush, sqush" in
    their shoeses;
My driveway sort of half dissolved, I could not navigate it;
I used to get up out of bed at midnight to berate it; at last
The rain still falling down, as sometimes drops of booze'll
Go chasing one another down a southern colonel's goozle,
I called a man who builds driveways, rock hard and all
    cementy
And figured on a new driveway and it cost me a-plenty;
    and all
The while he worked the rain came down in one big
    torrent —
It's really a fact the rain to me grew quite abhorrent.
But on the day my drive was done so I could go a-calling
The rain which rained all the time straightway let up its
    falling.
But if I had not built that drive it would let up never.
It would have rained and rained and rained and rained
    and rained
Forever!

In early 1914 Tom had drawn the plans and built a house for Paul Jones at 3012 Leeland Avenue. It also has the down-

swept roof, the distinctive porches and the Nordic look. The Jones'
still live there. An amazing feature is the outside paint — it is the
original coat. Although showing signs of mildew and weathering, it is
still presentable. Tom recalls the middle-aged Englishman who mixed
his own paint from white lead, oil and pigment:

"Tom," said Jantzen when he first beheld the completed house, "that paint job's no good. I'll wager it will peel
off in a year's time."

If Tom had been a betting man, he would have won
that wager forty-two fold, at that.

There were ups and there were downs. Tom under-
charged. Each job challenged him, and if it was possible to improve
some feature he would do so, ignoring his own estimates. He never
thought to consider the imposition on his time and what it might
cost him in dollars and cents. Andrew Ness, a friend of Tom's and
for whom Tom had a real affection, came to him with a contract to
build a house on West Gray. The two went in together. Unfortunately, the owner could not pay Tom and Andrew on schedule.

Not since the early days had Tom been quite so broke:

Tom opened the door to a peddler. The man was
thin and stooped and his nearsighted eyes peered at Tom.

"I have pins and sundries — and real sharp knives."
The whining voice was weary and the hand not steady as he
held up a bread knife.

Tom hesitated. "How much?" he asked.

"Only forty cents."

Tom reached in his pocket. Two quarters, a dime,
three nickels and five pennies. He took the knife and gave the
man forty cents. The remaining coins made a cheerful sound
as he closed the door. Tom's heart was light although the forty
cents remaining was the sum total of his cash resources at the
moment.

There was nothing to do but go to work for someone
else. Tom took a job for Castle & Podd on the Dubard Building on

the corner of Elysian and Lyons in the Fifth Ward. It was a combination hotel and storage building, and Tom was general superintendent. From the very first, Tom sensed a reluctance on the part of Podd to discuss financial details of the job. Tom wondered why, and this time his anxiety was real. If this proved another failure, how would he support his wife and child? His apprehension was well founded. Castle & Podd went bankrupt, and the men were laid off. But good fortune often masquerades as bad, and when the representative of the bonding company came to Tom to ask him if he would complete the building for what they had in it, Tom recognized his opportunity. He borrowed $600 from his fishing friend, Richard Krupp, a brother-in-law of Mrs. Katie Jantzen. This enabled him to contract to finish the building. On it he made a profit of two thousand dollars.

This Tom called "another beginning."

Contractor

Unless the Lord builds the house,

those who build it labor in vain

When Tom and Ingeborg were married, the Lutheran minister in Tvedestrand, Pastor Kringen, gave them a copy of the Bible. On the flyleaf he inscribed the date and place and wrote a reference to the Biblical text: Psalm 127, Verse 1. It is this dedication which introduces this chapter.

It was known in Tvedestrand that Tom had followed the carpenters' trade when he first came to America. The townsfolk were also aware that when he returned home in 1912, he was a man in business for himself—a contractor. This may have guided the minister in selecting the text, but he could only have divined from some intuitional source how really apt was his reference.

Tom Tellepsen was destined to be a builder for the Lord as well as for mankind, and what has been built for man has been done with the reverent and humble knowledge that it must first be good in God's sight.

The wonderful, formative years of Tom's childhood and young manhood instilled in him the love of work, independence, perseverance, determination to succeed. To these, he added the flavor of enterprise he found in Texas — the imagination, the initiative and the courage to try new methods. The years from 1914 until he incorporated as Tellepsen Construction Company in 1929 were to establish Mr. Tom as a contractor not only of merit and imagination as a builder, but as a business man of conscience and integrity.

In October of 1914, Tom and Andrew Ness formed a partnership. It was to bump over a rocky path until the late spring of 1917. Their first major job was to remodel the old Harris County courthouse located in downtown Houston. They also continued in residential construction.

Standing aloof of the old Houston-Galveston highway, poised on the bluff above Sim's Bayou, adjacent to Milby Park, the palatial home of a former president of the Katy Railroad, C. E. Schaff, has become a Houston landmark. Ness & Tellefsen built this beautiful residence in 1915-16. A palm-bordered drive once lead to the porticoed entrance. The house is a southern mansion with a Nordic air — the same charming mixture of influences as one can detect, even now, in Ingeborg's soft accents.

The house stands today against its background of trees as if regally posed for a portrait. Off to the right a note of incongruity creeps in — no doubt completely ignored by the proud old home. The stacks and flare of the Goodyear Synthetic Rubber Corporation and the Sinco Plant (Sinclair Pipe Line Company) can be seen just over the hedge of distant trees.

When Tom and Andrew built this house, it was one of the most imposing and expensive in Houston — and a real accomplishment for the builders.

Yet there were moments of anxiety too:

It was late when Tom waved dismissal to the last workman and climbed wearily into his new Ford. "Mr. Schaff should be pleased with what we've done today," he thought. Ness had already left the job to see about materials which were to be delivered next day.

In the dusk, Tom recognized the middle-aged man walking along the road. He hailed him. "Where are you going, Mac?"

"Into town, Mr. Tellepsen."

"Want a lift?"

"Oh boy, do I. I'll be glad when they get streetcars out here."

As they talked of the rapid development of the South Houston area, Tom noted the rising fog. He slowed as he approached the railroad crossing on Leeland Avenue, just west

74

of Dowling. Nothing in sight. He started across. Out of the grayness there appeared a solid surface in front of him. A flat-car had come from nowhere.

Wham! The impact of the collision turned the car over and it slithered into the ditch. The accident attracted immediate attention. People came running from every direction.

Willing hands helped Tom and his passenger out of the car. "Mac" was driven to the hospital but later dismissed with minor injuries. Tom was completely shaken, but the problem of extricating his car from the ditch distracted him from any thought of hurt. Suddenly he heard a familiar voice, sharpened by anxiety. It was Ingeborg, summoned by one of the neighbors. He hastened to assure her he was all right.

The railroad was clearly liable for the accident. There was no signal at the crossing, and no watchman had been there to flag the car's approach. "Mac" collected thousands of dollars for his injuries; Tom not one — for self or car. And why? It was typical of Tom — he didn't even file a claim.

Andrew and Tom together built the Eastwood Elementary School, now named after a former principal, Dora B. Lantrip, who held that position during the time Tom's children were in school. The school was located in a neighborhood which was fast becoming one of the most desirable residential areas in Houston. The oaks and pines which shaded Park Drive reminded Tom of Norway. "This is the place. I must live here," he said. The site he chose was a lot on Park Drive next to a corner bounded by Maplewood Street. Later they bought the corner lot and the lot to the west of the house as well.

It was about this time that Tom dabbled briefly and gingerly in oil speculation. He had continued to invest what he could in land, *per se,* but this time he bought a share in a well being drilled in the Humble field. Prospects were good and became more so as the drilling proceeded. There was even a party to celebrate. His friend, Olaf Bergesen, grieved because he had no part of this enterprise! He badgered Tom into selling him one half of his share. It was a dry hole, and thus Tom had halved a loss instead of a gain!

In the meantime, Tom had become a United States citizen. He applied for citizenship on December 17, 1915, just eleven days before his intention papers would have expired. His good friends, George and Philip Tharp, were his witnesses. He signed himself "Thom Tellefsen," a general contractor. He took the Oath of Allegiance on April 10, 1916. He was now the father of two children: Murial (Hortense) had been born in September of 1915.

The Oath of Allegiance gave Tom a chance to indicate any change in his name. He did not avail himself of the opportunity. The transition of the letter f to the letter p in Tellepsen was a gradual process. His signature on the Oath shows how much alike Tom wrote the two letters. Tom decided the p must have seemed more logical, and sounded better to the American ear. He was about to give up on it. Let it be a p.

For some time now Tom had felt that his family needed a larger and more substantial house. For over a year he had talked of this, remembering the hurricane that mutilated Houston only a few weeks before Hortense was born. The storm had come up late in the evening. Tom was bone-weary from the day's labor and slept in spite of the shattering of windows pushed inward by the angry wind, the shuddering of the frail house. Next morning, Tom had found in their yard an uprooted chinaberry tree which had been carried by the wind for several blocks.

Now that he owned property in Eastwood, he would build a new house. Tom did much of the work himself. This was late 1916 and by early the next year, the house was ready for occupancy.

Soon thereafter it became apparent to Tom that his partnership with Andrew Ness could not continue. To make the break complete, he decided to leave contracting for the time being.

* * *

This is the story that a jack built.

Tom was always alert for opportunity. Early in 1917 he had been approached by a man who had designed and built a lifting jack. It had a threefold use: it could lift up to twenty tons; it could serve as a clamp; it could pull wire. The man demonstrated on a telephone pole which he jacked up fully three inches before Tom stopped him. On the basis of this demonstration, Tom took a franchise for the Gulf Coast counties of Texas, for which he paid two thousand

76

dollars. The jacks would retail for seventeen dollars and would cost him seven dollars.

Tom sent out two salesmen. They sold not a single jack. He considered the situation. Two thousand dollars was no small investment in 1917. And besides, he was thoroughly convinced that the jack *was* superior.

So-o-o-o . . . well, why not? He'd go out himself and prove it:

Tom had a strange feeling that he was on the wrong road. He'd set out for Bay City, but must have missed the turn. Sure enough — the next marker read "Sealy 5 mi." He was on the Katy Highway. At Sealy, he inquired for a short cut and was directed down a narrow road across the prairie. About fifteen miles out, the trail came to a half-demolished bridge over a dry creek-bed. Rather than turn back, Tom dipped his model T into the gully and bogged down, bending the radius rod and the front axle. It looked as if the car were kneeling; both front wheels were flat on the ground!

The situation appeared hopeless. But not for Tom. He was all alone. Through the late afternoon he could see a single farmhouse in the distance. Then he thought of the jack he carried as a sample.

"That's it," he said to himself. "I'll use my jack to raise the car and then to straighten the rod and axle."

He jacked the wheels free of the ground. Tugging a broken piece of concrete from the old bridge, he poked it under the car so that he might release the jack. He removed the rod and axle and spread them out on the stringers left on the bridge. He adjusted the jack to its clamping position and forced the bent metal into shape. Replacing the straightened rod and axle was but a matter of minutes.

"Now," said Tom aloud, "how to get back out of the ditch without further damage?" He walked around the car. Why hadn't he thought to bring along a piece of chain or rope. Never again would he be caught without something. He shrugged his shoulders and set out for the distant farmhouse.

"Sure, sure," the farmer was dubious as he headed for the shed, "but I still don't see how you'll get out. If you'll just wait a bit, I'll hitch up the team . . . ."

"Thanks," said Tom, "the rope is all I need," and hastened back to his car.

He put the rope around the rear axle and threaded it into the jack, now in the wire-pulling position. The car inched backwards.

Tom returned the rope to an astonished farmer. "I better have the car checked," he thought as he re-entered Sealy. The garage mechanic was unbelieving.

"Say that again," he said, and Tom warmed to his story, which grew even more amazing in the telling!

"Let's see that jack," the mechanic asked.

And before you could say Jack Robinson or Jack Tellepsen, that is, Tom had sold his first jack. And as his story spread, he had orders for twenty more before he left Sealy! Thereafter, this experience became his principal salestalk, and a mighty convincing one it was, too.

Tom decided to combine business and pleasure. Corpus Christi was in his territory, and Ingeborg and the children would love the bayshore and a brief vacation. He installed them in a rented cottage set on piling. It was a great adventure for the children. Hortense in particular loved to climb and swing on the timbers underneath the house. One day she ventured out too far, and her screams brought Ingeborg running from the upper room. Howard was out on the ledge behind Hortense:

"Titter, stop crying, titter. Sit still. I'll get you."

Titter stopped crying and submitted to rescue by her big brother.

Tom had noted the number of piling left standing in the bay after the superstructures had been wrecked by tide or hurricane. He went to see the water commissioner at Corpus and pointed out that his jack could be used to remove these piling which were, in fact, a threat to navigation. The commissioner was not too receptive, but agreed to let Tom experiment. Tom had already done this on the piles in the inlet by the cottage. In front of the Nueces Hotel, in water over his head, Tom succeeded in locating the chain and in using his jack to pull a designated pile. It took him one hour and was not only strenuous work, but dangerous. Result: the sale of one jack to the city of Corpus Christi!

He was more successful in nearby towns:

Coming through Refugio one forenoon, Tom noticed a group of people gathered on the square. It was a holiday. He stopped his car, took out his jack and addressed himself to the crowd. His spiel was well rehearsed by now. The men listened with interest. He explained the three functions of the jack.

"Why," he said, "this jack will even pull stumps."

The overalls with the red hair moved forward. "All right, fella, prove it! There's a stump just down the road. Let's see you pull *it* up!"

Without hesitation, Tom went to the stump, the crowd following. He secured the chain beneath a gnarled, protruding root and encircled the stump. It seemed dry. If Tom was doubtful, he did not show it. Threading the chain, he tightened the jack. The chain crew taut. Tom thrust his weight downward on the handle. Again. Again. The chain strained. The stump creaked. The men guffawed, and Tom felt a prickling sensation at the nape of his neck, not caused by perspiration alone. Suddenly, the stump gave way and pulled free of the ground. A cry of congratulation went up, and Tom sank back, his arms tired but his spirit refreshed. The men crowded around, and he sold sixteen jacks on the spot!

On his way back to Corpus from Hebbronville one night, Tom hit a sandy stretch of road. His wheels spun and he came to a stop. Scarcely had he dimmed his headlights than a farmer appeared with his team and offered, for ten dollars, to pull him the sandy mile which lay ahead.

"What a way to make a living," thought Tom, realizing this must be a common occurrence, "cultivating misfortune instead of cotton." But he paid the ten dollars. Later on that same night Tom made a wrong turn into a ditch which looked, for all the world and in the moonlight, to be the road. Although he did manage to pull himself out by use of his jack, he decided to bunk in the car. The road forked in front of him and, with the ebbing luck he'd had all evening, he wouldn't chance a decision as to which road to follow. Daylight discovered him on the outskirts of Falfurrias.

But, however eventful his jack-selling experiences had been, Tom knew he would return to Houston and to contracting.

Houston 1917. Mayor J. J. Pastoriza presided over City Council meetings. Main Street was called Main Boulevard and placards in the automobile salesrooms read "A car is now a necessity." Ed "Strangler" Lewis, appearing in Houston, was soon to make his bid for the champion's jeweled belt. War was declared in April, and the Houston papers headlined progress of the troops. Eggless, milkless, butterless cakes were all the rage. The first Liberty Loan drive solicited a $36,000,000 pledge from Texas, of which Houston's portion was some five million dollars. By June 15 Houston had exceeded its quota and set a precedent in civic participation. But Houston was to make news in not so favorable a way. On the night of August 23, a race riot spread terror throughout the city. Negro troops from Illinois, billeted at Camp Logan, became rebellious at the arrest of two of their number after an argument with city police. One hundred and fifty men left camp and marched on the city. For some ten sinister hours, panic stalked the streets of Houston. Thirteen people were killed, nineteen wounded. One of the last acts of Governor Ferguson before his impeachment was the declaration of martial law under Brigadier General John Hulen. Tom well remembers the incident. He and his family had been back in Houston scarcely a month.

Tom experienced some difficulty in getting back into the swing of things, but with characteristic doggedness, he set out to find jobs. At first they were small, but they grew in number. One such was for the city of Houston which was experimenting with a plan to treat sewage for fertilizer. Tom built the plant, and on this job used his own cement mixer, one of the first gasoline-powered mixers in Houston. To do this he employed his Model T as a hoisting device to lift the buckets of cement. This job was hectic for more than one reason. Tom would arrive at the job only to find some of his material confiscated because of need elsewhere on a war production project.

Tom now began to operate in two different locations concurrently. The first out-of-Houston job was a creosoting plant in Somerville, built in the summer of 1918. Thus he started commuting between jobs. Two handsome residences were built in Beaumont for W. A. Preddy and Perry Weis. At the same time, a foundry for oil field tools was being constructed for the Mack Manufacturing Company. To the demands upon his ability to organize and delegate responsibility, upon his time in traveling between jobs was added a further complication — the old bugaboo again of client failing to meet his obligation. That Tom could survive this combination of circumstances proved him to be well established as a business man.

The concrete buildings of the foundry were bid at sixty-five thousand dollars. Tom was paid on schedule for the first two estimated completion periods — five thousand dollars each. When it was time to pay the third installment, the company informed Tom there was no money available. He could foreclose or take a mechanic's lien against the plant and complete it. He did not act without considered opinion. He consulted bankers, architects, and other builders and then did just the opposite of what they advised. He went on to finish the buildings. Call it intuition, call it faith — Mr. Tom has many times made such a decision in the face of adverse conditions. For a long time, over two years in fact, a token payment dribbled in — amounting to not more than five thousand dollars. It was discouraging, and Tom began to doubt his own impulses and his judgment. Finally, he instructed his lawyer to foreclose. That very day he had a call from Mack Manufacturing Company. The Niels Esperson estate had bought the entire plant, and a check was in the mail reimbursing Tom in full and including ten per cent interest for the period of the delinquency. Tom's lawyer was paid one thousand dollars. The plant today is known as Reed Roller Bit Company.

Almost every job has a story authored by physical circumstance or the whims of human nature. This is perhaps why the construction business is so fascinating — and so hectic. Tom was low bidder on an addition to the Lubbock School out on Harrisburg Boulevard, but when he began to lay out the job, he found the architects had made a critical miscalculation. According to their plans, the school would extend halfway into the street! Rather than have the plans redrawn, bids resubmitted, valuable time wasted, as would be the procedure today, Tom suggested an alternate plan. He would widen the building and provide the same amount of floor space. To counterbalance the greater cost of this construction, he would put down piers to support the beams, instead of pouring a solid concrete foundation. The architects, who protested this was the only mistake they ever made, nevertheless accepted Tom's proposal with alacrity, as did the school board.

But Tom's efforts were not always so well accepted. Here human nature intervened. Tom was called to bid on construction of a service station to be leased to the Eagle Oil Company at South Main, McIlhenny and Bremond. It was to be built of concrete and to have graceful arches to support the roof over the service area. Since remodeled and made larger, it was a type well favored in the early twenties. Tom worked conscientiously to meet every requirement. The architect had formerly been employed by the city of Houston and he knew Tom and the caliber of his work BUT:

"Tellepsen," the man stood with feet placed apart and hands upon his hips. "Tear up that slab. I didn't check the sub-grade, and I distinctly told you that would have to be done. I surveyed the front area all right but didn't have time to do the side. You had no reason to assume it was done unless I told you. Tear it up."

And another time:

"Tellepsen, I've measured this arch and you've made an error. You are a thirty-second of an inch off the radius!"

No, it wasn't always smooth sledding. And Tom would fume. He did tear up the concrete, and it cost him a thousand dollars, but the arch remained.

Tom had his union problems, too, and in retrospect, these had a humorous aspect. Tom, a union contractor, was awarded the contract to build the Beaumont Iron Works. The president of the B. I. W. was also president of the Open Shop Association in Beaumont! It meant quite a bit of conversation to persuade him to allow use of union labor in the construction of his plant. This job remains in Mr. Tom's memory, too, because it was necessary to pour 120 yards of concrete in eight hours. This he did by use of a one-sack concrete mixer. Can it be done? He did it. And not long ago he had occasion to check the concrete and found it still in good condition.

The almost reverse of the above predicament, as it refers to unions, occurred when Tom was building the carpenters' union hall in Houston. Scarcely had he begun, than a jurisdictional dispute arose between the carpenters and the sheet metal workers in Houston. Who should install hollow metal windows? The other trades sided in with the sheet metal workers. The carpenters withdrew. Tom could not use any of the other trades on the carpenters' hall as long as he used union carpenters. The hall stood idle five months during a rainy season, but finally Tom, and the weather, brought the carpenters around to agreeing that he use nonunion labor to complete the building! The carpenters did whatever jobs they could do, but whimsically enough, refused to let Tom set the windows because "only a carpenter should do it," and although Tom had once been a member of the carpenters' union, he had of course resigned when he became an independent contractor.

This situation on the carpenters' union hall caused Tom to go nonunion for a short time. The Rice Institute Chemistry Building was caught in the squeeze and Tom had nonunion Mexican brick layers on this job. But we are ahead of our story.

Prior to this, and now that jobs were multiple, it was necessary for Tom to work at home at night to keep up his books and do his estimating. One night late in 1919, Mrs. Magdalene Clicquennoi, Katjie Tharp's mother, poked her head around the door of the study. "Mr. Tellepsen," she said, "you ought to find an office and get someone to help you with your paper work." The upshot was that Mrs. Clicquennoi did both! She had for some time been manager of a building supply company in New York. She was very efficient, had a ready wit and was indomitable. Tom chuckled at the nonchalant way she handled certain labor situations; the men might not have been so docile with him! On one occasion, Tom being out of town, a crew of iron workers could not do their specific jobs because necessary material was not available at the site. According to labor regulations, they were entitled to two hours' pay because they had reported for work.

"All right," Mrs. Clicquennoi said cheerily, "just go back and work at anything for two hours. I'll have the money for you then."

They did. She did. No one complained.

Mrs. Clicquennoi stayed with Tom until 1928 as secretary and bookkeeper, and she proved a valuable asset to a growing business and was a dear friend of the family:

"Mama Clicquennoi," Ingeborg's voice was soft over the telephone so as not to awaken the baby, Lorraine. "Howard and Hortense are coming on the streetcar. Would you meet them please and take them to the movies? Before Tom left for Beaumont, he said he had checked with you, and it was all right."

"Of course, Ingeborg. Let's see — they'll get off at Fannin and Congress. I'll try to get there before they do. Goodbye."

But before she could leave the one-room office in the Prince Theater Building, there were other phone calls. She half ran to the corner and saw the streetcar approach. It whizzed by without stopping. She looked about. No children were anywhere in sight. She waited for the next car. Still none.

"I must have missed them. They're probably at the office," she thought hopefully and hurried back. No one there. She called Ingeborg who was immediately alarmed. Mrs. Clicquennoi hastened back to the corner of Fannin and Congress, this time in undisguised dismay. Then she returned to the office to summon help. The police were called; the neighborhood alerted.

Howard with Hortense by the hand walked wearily down Maplewood Street and up the back steps to the door. It was a long way from town. They had gotten off the streetcar at the wrong corner and gone on to the office. Finding no one there, Howard wisely decided to go home. He simply followed the streetcar tracks the way they had come.

To the solicitous relief of his mother, Howard was righteously annoyed. "I knew where I was all the time," he said.

Hortense looked up at him with pride and confidence. She also knew they were never lost.

In the fall of 1921, Tom found a right man who was also looking for a right job. It was a happy coincidence. E. A. Kruse had come to Houston in 1920 as Project Engineer for Burrel Engineering & Construction Company who were building the American Maid Flour Mill on the ship channel. Kruse had had experience in the designing and estimating of flour mills, elevator construction, etc. While looking for cement finishers for the American Maid plant, he had the opportunity to inspect various concrete structures in Houston, and he was most impressed by Tom's buildings. Facing transfer east and wishing to stay in Texas, Kruse decided to look around. A friend suggested Tom Tellepsen. Kruse went down to Tom's office in the Prince Theater Building and applied for a job.

It was a logical time for Tom to take on a man to help him in his estimating. At the moment he had three sets of plans on the boards, and each one averaged more than half a million dollars. Anyone familiar with construction will realize the implication of this statement. Thirty-three years old; a resident of Houston for only twelve years and a full-fledged contractor for but four of these; and yet Tom felt himself in a position to bid three jobs totaling a million and a half dollars!

Kruse knew excavating, concrete and reinforcing steel but admitted his ignorance as to finishing techniques, etc. "I may not do it (estimating) according to Hoyle," said Tom, "but I will show you how *I* do it," and the pact was sealed.

Kruse pitched in and took off the First Baptist Church plant, and a church is one of the most complicated types of buildings to estimate. Tom did the pricing. They were low on the opening but the building committee of the church hesitated. Tom Tellepsen? What had *he* done?

The committee revised the plans and resubmitted them. Four times Tom was low, but on the fifth, the American Construction Company got the job. Ironically, when it came time to start construction, the project could not be financed. Bids were asked for the Sunday school building alone.

Tom and Kruse reshuffled their estimate, and Tom took in their bid. He was wearing his Masonic pin. In 1921 Tom had joined the Temple Masonic Lodge. Frank Jones, then potentate of Arabia Temple, was a member of the building committee of the Baptist church and he commented on Tom's pin. Tom was given the contract. Later Tom went on to lay the foundation for the auditorium of the church and finally to build the entire plant.

When the church was dedicated, Tom was invited to the ceremony to formally present the keys to the building committee. For a while that evening, he wished he had kept them! When the subject of pledges arose, Tom and Ingeborg discreetly withdrew, only to find the doors locked. As members of the congregation came forward to make their pledges and were acknowledged by those present, few paid any attention to the two standing forlorn and embarrassed by the door. Finally, Oscar Holcombe, then mayor and a member of the building committee, recognized their dilemma and let them out!

On July 3, 1954, Howard Tellepsen, as president of the Houston Chamber of Commerce, spoke from the stage of the Miller Memorial Theater in Hermann Park during a program honoring the one-millionth Houstonian. Howard's thoughts must have traveled back to 1922 when his father built this theater and he himself, at the age of nine, was water boy. This was his first construction job. John Nelson, superintendent, taught him to drive the Ford and he would go on errands.

However, for transportation home and back — some six miles — he relied on his bicycle:

"Tom," said Ingeborg, "you must go look for Howard. It's almost dark outside. It's been raining off and on all day, and it's so damp. He had a starting head cold this morning, and I'm worried."

"Nonsense," Tom never worried about Howard, "he's been delayed. John said he had something for him to do on the way home tonight. But, if you'll feel better, I'll go and see."

Tom drove slowly along the route Howard was likely to take and found him bogged down in mud near the 4600 block of Leeland. The muck was too deep to permit him to pedal, and the boy walked along, prodding the bike ahead of him and raising mud-laden boots with obvious, weary effort. He saw his father's car and cried out, his relief dissolving into tears. Tom returned home with Howard, bicycle and mud — all loaded in the car!

The Houston Ship Channel prior to 1915 had been a crusade to far-sighted Texans who saw in its development the establishment of Houston as a major United States city. President Woodrow Wilson officially opened the port in November of 1914 and in August of 1915 the first large ocean-going vessel, the *SS Saltilla* docked at the 1,300-foot wide turning basin.

In 1922 Tom Tellepsen built the second wharf of any consequence on the channel. It was called the Manchester Wharf. At first it was under the administration of the city of Houston and a navigation department in the city government. Later the wharf became, during the time of its construction, the property of the newly formed Harris County-Houston Ship Channel Navigation District. Completion of the installation was to be under the City's jurisdiction, although operation of the wharf was strictly the domain of the Navigation District.

Tom was particularly diligent in its building, and he tangled here again with human nature. The Port Director, who was head of the city's navigation department, visited the job in progress and without consulting Tom, interviewed newspaper reporters. The gist of his remarks ballooned in headlines "Houston is Losing Thousands Because the Manchester Wharf Construction is Behind Schedule." Tom knew nothing of the teapot tempest until he read about it in the newspapers that night. He paced the floor until dawn — in indignation and anxiety. Next morning he went to see the city engineer and showed him progress charts and reports. He demanded and got retraction.

Kruse went out on the Manchester job and he, too, came to verbal blows, this time with a member of the Navigation District staff. The facilities of the Manchester Wharf were being widely publicized and promoted. Ships were encouraged to dock before the project was completed: case in point, the water lines had not yet reached the dock. Drinking water was not available and ships moored at the wharf had no fire protection.

With the approval of city officials, Kruse bought a number of old cisterns and mounted them on a hill behind the wharf. He arranged to fill these by pumping from wells of the adjacent American Maid flour mill. Thus the ships at Manchester could be serviced and be safe. When Kruse presented his bills to the city, he was told that this was an operating cost, and he must go to the Board of Directors of the Harris County-Houston Ship Channel Navigation District. After several repeated visits back and forth, the board finally refused payment on the ground that regulations required a previously dated work order. Kruse had none.

"There are two boats docked at Manchester right now," typically Kruse did not raise his voice, "and one of them was taking on water when I left. They'll be surprised when I cut off their supply. There'll be lots of publicity, all right — all bad."

The official was startled. "Surely you wouldn't do that?"

"If your regulations won't permit you to pay our bills, then it's our water system. I assure you when I leave here, I'm headed for Manchester to tear out the tanks and salvage what I can."

Regulations suddenly became flexible. The bills were paid.

Tellepsen Construction Company remodeled the Manchester Wharf in 1949 and uncovered a nail bar and sharpshooter left there during its original construction. Because contractors can be sentimental, these mementos now decorate a wall in the office building. That contractors are practical as well, is evidenced by the placard that accompanies the display. It is a terse reminder to workmen to look after their tools!

This remodeling job is of interest in another respect. We have previously noted that Tom's ingenuity and awareness were often the margin between profit and loss. Here again, application of a different approach was to rewrite in black what very well might have been in red. The some 500 feet of concrete retaining wall originally poured by Tom in 1922 had to be demolished in order to replace the piling and a part of the footing which teredos had eaten away. The wall itself had chunked out in places. Previous tactics called for chipping out the concrete. The wall was two feet across the top and slanted to a base of twelve feet. Its height from footing to wharf was eighteen feet.

Tom surveyed the situation and considered. The old method was time-consuming and expensive. There must be an easier, quicker way.

Excavating the fill behind the wall, he had holes drilled at intervals horizontal to the footing. Similar holes were drilled vertically from the top surface. Into these holes, rock jacks were inserted and as they spread under hydraulic pressure, the concrete cracked in jagged, heavy segments of rock. Holes had been drilled on the top surface for lewis pins fastened to slings so a derrick could lift out the grotesque pieces, some weighing as much as twenty tons. The derrick rode on a barge moored in the channel beside the wharf.

And what's more — Tom found a market for his unexpected by-product. The Champion Paper & Fibre Company down the channel bought the broken concrete for riprap and Tom retrieved almost the cost of the wrecking operation.

Back in 1922, Tom undertook a second wharf — for the Houston Compress Company — the 1,700 foot Long Reach Wharf. Tom knew that Anderson, Clayton & Company hoped to load cotton off Long Reach at the season's end, and this meant that his workmen must race against the nimble fingers of the cotton pickers and his pile driver must compete in time with the creaking wagons bearing the sacks of bolls to the cotton gin.

This was the first time concrete piling had been used in Houston. The inspectors would not allow jetting or heavy hammers for fear of injury to the piles. It took an entire day to drive the first fifty-foot pile. Impatient and apprehensive that their goal might not be reached, Anderson Clayton insisted that Tom employ a second pile driver. There was one hitch. Tom had only one "follower," a kind of metal cap used to cover the concrete pile to prevent its shattering under the impact of the driver. The follower was manufactured in New Orleans. Tom ordered a second follower and Anderson Clayton contacted their representative in New Orleans, Holger Jeppeson, to expedite its preparation. The cap was made and expressed to Houston but by the time it had arrived, Tom's crew, with the one driver, had already driven the over two thousand piling necessary to complete the wharf. The second follower was never used.

And there had been other complications. Original plans allowed Tom an area near the job site for a warehouse to store his materials and tools and sufficient space in which to cast and stack his piling. Before the job was under way, this area was dredged away by mistake. In return Tom was given a similar site six miles down the channel at Clinton. This meant barging all his materials to the job. How many times at night did the phone ring, "The barge is sinking, Mr. Tom," and off in his model T Tom would dash, shirttail out, eyes half open, to help a tug and crew from Harrisburg pump out the water which had leaked into the barge. One night a Mexican helper fell overboard, and Tom still remembers the tragedy of accidental death, an ever-present anxiety for all who build.

The wharf was completed and ready for use in less than ninety days. Two weeks ahead of schedule, ocean-going ships took Texas cotton on board. Anderson, Clayton & Company rewarded Tom with a fifteen thousand dollar bonus!

In all the mosaic of Tom's construction experiences, perhaps the example of the Rice Institute Chemistry Building is the most typical of his ingenuity and his ally, coincidence.

William Ward Watkins, Professor of Architecture at Rice Institute, designed the Chemistry Building and specified a face brick to match the other existing buildings. He knew a man, he told Tom, who had a kiln in Conroe and who had access to the proper clay. Tom was given an outright contract for $650,000 which allowed fifteen dollars per thousand for the brick. This allowance Watkins considered ample. One million brick were needed. Tom placed the order casually because Watkins had been so confident. Time came for delivery. The stone was laid out in readiness to complement the brick. No brick. He called Conroe but was evaded. He called Watkins, on vacation. "That's your lookout," was the reply. Tom in desperation made the muddy road to Conroe and found — a few drying pans, a mud mixer, no kiln, a small pit. Heartsick, he pursued his inquiry. A $600 mortgage held by the local bank stood against the doubtful assets. The owner pleaded. He would borrow more money and would fill the order. Tom took heart. But the man did nothing. By this time, the administration at Rice was apprehensively aware of the situation. They took over the Conroe plant and asked Tom to run it for them (for no other return than the production of the brick he needed to complete the building). Tom agreed and built a kiln of raw brick. He had sent a sample of the clay to Houston to be analyzed, but his new kiln was half full of formed brick when the analysis arrived: the clay, when fired, turned black; it was no good.

The clay would have to be obtained elsewhere:

"All right, Tellepsen, what can we do?"

Tom thought a moment. Providing the brick had been no obligation of his. This was surely passing the buck, and the brick, he thought grimly. Only a professor well insulated by academic detachment might do so. "Who supplied the original clay?" he asked.

"Well, as best I can recall his name was Williams and I think he mined on Brady Island, near Harrisburg, but he is dead now."

"Who had the formula?"

"Williams," was the reply.

"Well, I'll try to get a sample. I have barges now on Long Reach, and we'll go to Brady Island." Tom's voice was anything but enthusiastic. It was a forlorn hope.

"Good, good," said Watkins, "you'll make out — you always have."

Tom felt weary. On the way home he stopped by the job in progress at McKinney and Dowling — the Standard Sanitary plant. Tom had had his share of trouble here, too. The job had almost been shut down yesterday because the architect insisted that one, not two, sacks of cement be processed in the mixer. But the inspector, W. B. (Bruce) Leach, had found the batching good and persuaded the architect not to interfere. As he drove up, Tom saw Leach leaving.

"Hello," Leach called to him, "everything is running smoothly today, Mr. Tellepsen."

The cordial voice invited confidence. "Thanks, Leach, if I could only say that about the job at Rice Institute."

"Now what's your trouble. It never rains but it pours, I guess."

Tom blurted out the entire situation.

"Williams — Ted Williams," Leach's voice was incredulous and his sudden shout of laughter startled Tom. "Why, he's not dead. He lives next door to me. I know all about the clay; I've heard him tell the story many times."

Coincidence? I'll let you judge.

They located the clay on the banks of the bayou, and it was sacked and sent to Conroe. Tom formed it, fired it, and it was perfect.

But there were anxious moments. The kiln fire had to be kept going. Should it die out, they would lose all brick being fired and ruin the kiln besides. Often Kruse would be awakened in the middle of the night with a frantic call for fuel oil. To get these supplies to Conroe by rail was quite an operation. It involved first loading the fuel from the oil company onto the Port Terminal Railroad which would carry it to the Southern Pacific switch and it would then be transferred and go on to Conroe!

To meet sudden emergencies, Tom would drive over the pitted, muddy roads where cattle roamed at will. Once, with Kruse, Tom almost plowed into a herd, and as Kruse put it, he "sailed over the shoulder," righted the car and went on. The car Tom had been driving expired noisily, and he literally wore out a new one. They made the million brick all right, but at a cost of ninety-five dollars per thousand instead of fifteen, but the miracle was they were made at all.

Yet Tom's problems did not end here. His crew had carefully rubbed down the brick, cleaning and oiling the surface. It was found not acceptable. He was required to repeat the process and in doing so, eliminated practically all of the profit he had in the job.

Although Tom had, by now, added a second room to his office in the Prince Theater Building, quarters were cramped for his increased staff. He bought the entire 3900 block between Bell and Polk Avenues across the Houston Belt & Terminal Railway tracks. Bringing in a street which became Clay Avenue, he built not only offices but warehouse and yard facilities.

Tom kept on building. In 1924 it was the two wings of the Art Museum. This would more than double the capacity of this beautiful building. Roofs were a troublesome quantity that year. The steel frame for the roof of the Art Museum came prefabricated, but all wrong, so that Tom had to tear it down and rebuild it completely. At the Golfcrest Country Club, Tom found that, if built to specifications, the roof would have fallen in! He added supplemental supports to insure sound construction.

Besides problems of overhead in 1924, there were also problems on foot, namely, horses. Tom had a lift station job and the laying of sidewalks in the new River Oaks subdivision. Horses were used to haul sand, gravel, etc. from the railroad to the job site. They hauled for the Art Museum job also. A makeshift corral was located across the street from the Art Museum and where the Warwick Hotel now stands.

This was the first time Tom had used quadruped employees and he was uneasy about them. When a brisk norther pounced on Houston, Tom called Kruse to get the horses to enclosed shelter. Only a short distance down Main Street from the Art Museum, Kruse located an empty cement shed on the Rice Institute campus. The chemistry building was nearly completed and Tom had not yet moved all of his construction shacks. To help him move the horses, Kruse sought out the elderly Italian who was handyman-watchman at the Museum job. When the man was made to understand what he was to do, his dark eyes rolled in panic and his already broken English shattered completely. It seemed that he was afraid of horses. By this time it was almost dark and the increasing cold made some action imperative. Patiently, Kruse showed him how to lead the horses, promising to precede him slowly in his car. Finally the man agreed, saying "me not scared." Off they went down Main Street — the car weaving slowly as Kruse leaned out to shout encouragement to the string of four horses led gingerly by one excited Italian. To make matters worse, the horses balked at entering the shed: they were not accustomed to floors and ceiling!

Tom built the Palmer Memorial Church on South Main Street for Mrs. E. L. Neville in memory of her brother, Edward Albert Palmer. Mrs. Neville was a wonderful person to build for, so appreciative and considerate. The church is a replica of one in Italy. On this job Tom gave a summer vacation job to Robert Quin, son of the Rt. Rev. Clinton Simon Quin, Episcopal bishop for the Diocese of Texas. Tom remembers Bob, a student at Rice, as a fine, conscientious young man who worked along with the Negro laborers in excavation, that being the only type of work available at the time. Later that summer, Bob went to Europe with his family. He became ill with typhoid fever and died on shipboard.

Tom found in the construction of the Palmer Memorial Church the special kind of gratification he associates with the building of any church, and he has constructed over a dozen for different creeds and different races.

The building to house the Gray and Temple Masonic Lodges was one of 1924's outstanding buildings. Tom's pleasure in its building was clouded by the accidental death of one of the workmen. In Mr. Tom's experiences these occasions are rare, as he and his company have long stressed safety measures, and in fact are pioneering in safety in the construction field. He recalls each such death with deep personal sorrow.

A record was established in the construction of the William Penn Hotel in 1927. An average of three floors each week was poured until completion. Proud as he justifiably could be, Tom nevertheless remembers this job with regret. He had taken a second mortgage in lieu of final payment and was finally forced to discount the note for half its face value.

In 1927, a new kind of endeavor was added to the repertoire of Tom Tellepsen, General Contractor. He went into underground work comprising the laying of sanitary sewers, storm sewers, waterlines, etc. He financed all his own equipment and trained a special crew. Up until the time Tom left this field in 1946, Tellepsen Construction Company put down perhaps more water and sewer lines than anyone in the business.

But tragedy was in attendance here also.

The telephone rang insistently. Tom picked up the receiver.

"Yes — who — when did it happen?" The excited voice jangled in Tom's ear and carried across the room as Ingeborg stopped in the doorway.

Tom put down the receiver and reached for his hat.

"There's been an accident on the sewer job. Davidson got his sleeve caught in a cog on the ditching machine. It pulled the arm around with it and the arm is badly crushed. They've taken him to the hospital. Is Perce's car in front of the house?"

Ingeborg rushed to look out across the street. Dr. P. A. Sloane was Tom's good friend, and Tom relied on him for all industrial accidents as well as in matters of his family's health.

"Look, he's just leaving." Ingeborg ran out and waved.

Dr. Sloane waited for Tom, who was gesticulating and shouting. In a moment the car was under way and the two men were headed for St. Joseph's Hospital.

They found Davidson in the emergency ward. He was in shock and the resident doctors were very pessimistic. They went into conference with Sloane.

Presently, Tom felt Perce's hand on his shoulder.

"Tom," he said, "they recommend amputating immediately."

Tom's heart ached with pity. "Isn't there anything we can do? If there's a chance, any chance at all, save his arm. He's a fine man. Don't spare the expense — I'll take care of that, but if you can - - - don't let him lose his arm."

Tom instinctively rubbed the forefinger of his right hand. His thoughts went back over the years to a small boy in his mother's arms being told that his finger would always be stiff. When, later, he stood by the quiet form in the shaded hospital room, he prayed, and in his unassuming way, he urged Davidson to believe, as he did, that with God's help, his arm would again be strong and well.

Two years — years of pain and doubt, but today the arm, its strength restored, enables E. E. Davidson to perform a valuable job as General Shop Foreman for Tellepsen Construction Company.

In his life as contractor, Tom Tellepsen has been plaintiff in only one suit. It was declared a mistrial, and Tom let it rest there. But that's not the whole story by any means. In 1927, Tom was putting in a storm sewer trunk line — which meant tearing up the entire stretch of Shepherd from the bayou south to Westheimer. Soil conditions proved bad — the dry sand was as fine as flour. It was necessary to shore the sides of the street with sheet piling, and the cost of the concrete was excessive and had not been included in Tom's estimate. The contract he had signed with the city of Houston had a contingency clause referring to extra cost for shoring against quicksand. Methods were the same except that in the present situation, the protection was against a dry sand and not a wet sand. The head of the city's sewer department refused the plea of added cost. Even the chief inspector on the job for the city recognized the unfairness of this attitude, and persuaded Tom to seek redress. Most of the City Council agreed with Tom, but it became evident that to secure action, a suit was necessary. Judge Allen B. Hannay in declaring a mistrial indicated that when certain errors of a legal nature were corrected, Tom would have a strong case. Tom was delayed in re-filing and in the meantime received from the City a check for $10,000, the amount of his additional costs!

The people of the Brazosport area were amazed to see a bridge being built over dry land! This project was so unusual, in fact, that it became grist for Ripley's mill and achieved world-wide publicity as a "Believe It or Not."

The shoaling conditions caused by Brazos River currents and periodic floods in the hinterland had long hampered the development of the natural harbor at the mouth of the river near Velasco and Freeport. In 1925 a navigation district had been organized in Brazoria County and bonds were voted for the purpose of diverting the stream and making the lower seven and one-half miles a land-locked arm of the Gulf. Tom Tellepsen was awarded the contract in 1928 to build the bridge that would cross the diversion channel to carry Highway 36 to Brazoria, Sweeney, etc. The bridge was built over dry land before the course of the river was changed.

Success of a construction job often leans heavily on the ingenuity of the contractor. Tom's inventive mind and his willingness to approach problems in an unorthodox manner, if need be, have always stood him in good stead. The Freeport bridge is a good example of this. He got permission to try a new method of preparing and pouring the center, pivotal pier. A square concrete caisson, without top or bottom, was sunk into the new river bed by slanting the bottom edges and excavating the dirt from the inside of the box. As the dirt inside was removed, the pressure outside and the weight of the box itself caused the structure to subside. Piles were driven along the outer sides to guide it down and to prevent it from sinking too rapidly. When the caisson had been lowered twenty feet, wood sheeting around the walls extended up another eighteen feet. At thirty feet below the surface of the ground, piles were driven on the bottom inside the box to support a four-foot concrete footing.

On this the central, round pier was formed and poured and the caisson backfilled to the surface.

The bridge is a turning bridge, to permit large vessels to pass up the river. The cost of machinery to turn the bridge was found to be prohibitive and instead a hand-operated device was installed. The specifications required that the bridge could be opened by one man. The one man chosen to demonstrate the bridge before it was accepted was Tom Tellepsen.

Tom's strength derived from the rest and inspiration of his recent trip to Norway to see his mother. Birger Jorkjend had written that she was in poor health and almost morbid in her desire to see Tom. He landed in Bergen and went overland by train, through impressive scenery he had thus far only read about. Coming out of a semicircle of tunnel, Tom, in a front coach, could see behind and below him the observation car just entering the tunnel. Chasms to the side of the track held a glint of water while on the other side, trees fringed moss-covered ground that rose upward into stretches of exposed rock, topped by white-collared mountain peaks.

The nine days he spent with his mother were an elixir. For long hours they talked, and when she rested, Tom would walk the familiar streets, and every footstep was a prayer. Tora lived for seventeen years to the age of eighty-four. She who had given him life, received it back from him in the love and faith which he had learned from her.

When Tom returned, he found Kruse very glad to see him. The Farmers' Market was being built and there had been union difficulties.

In fact, the day after Tom sailed, a delegation of union officials visited Kruse with the ultimatum that unless the Freeport bridge job hired union hoisting engineers, instead of the nonunion men then employed, the carpenters who were building foundation forms at the Farmers' Market would go out on strike.

Kruse knew he faced a tough situation. He asked for a day's time. That evening, he called his one hundred carpenters together on company time, and climbing up on the platform of a flatbed truck, he quietly explained the situation. The men in question on the Freeport bridge job were manning gasoline equipment which hoisting engineers were not trained to handle.

Kruse's glance kept returning to the intent face of one big fellow in a blue shirt, standing near the truck. "Because of those two men who are doing a special job in Freeport, you'll be asked to strike."

The voice of the big man interrupted him. "Who says so? Mister, if what you say is true, there'll be no strike."

And there was none.

After Tom had been back a while, it was decided that he should incorporate as Tellepsen Construction Company. Kruse had proved his worth and, in contributing to the growing success of "Tom Tellepsen, General Contractor" had earned a twenty-five per cent interest in the business. Incorporation would put the relationship on a legal basis. Tom became president. Kruse, as second in command, was vice president and a member of the Board of Directors.

"Toil and Trouble"

"Double, double toil and trouble
Fire burn and cauldron bubble"

MACBETH
ACT IV: SCENE I

The witches in Macbeth must have been brewing a special potion meant for Tom Tellepsen and the youthful Tellepsen Construction Company.

The early years of the Company's existence were to be difficult years. It was depression — 1929. President Hoover urged loyal citizens to support our free enterprise system by investing and expanding in order to bring back the spiral of prosperity. Tom thought the matter over very seriously. He decided to build four warehouses on his property in the vicinity of Leeland, Clay and Cullen Blvd. Warehouse facilities were needed in Houston, and it seemed like a good investment. Besides, by building, Tom could keep the Tellepsen Construction Company staff and crews employed. Tom put into the project not only all of his personal capital, but in addition borrowed $250,000 from The Rice Institute.

The first warehouse was built on the corner of Clay and Cullen. The second was located on Ingeborg Street south of Leeland Avenue. These two were completed by Tellepsen Construction Company with union labor, but while the third was under construction at Jefferson and Sidney, a situation arose which forced Tom into open shop. The A.G.C. (Associated General Contractors) had agreed to reject a demand for an increase in carpenter's pay from nine to ten dollars a day. One by one, the other members of the A.G.C. yielded

98

The Montrose House, built in the fall of 1911 and
the spring of 1912

Chemistry Building, The Rice Institute

Offices of the Tellepsen Construction Company

The East End State Bank

Melrose Building

The Shamrock

Medical Towers

— all except Tom, who held to the agreement. Also, the union had boycotted Tom's superintendent, MacCracken. During the several years Tellepsen Construction Company did operate open shop, several sizable contracts were lost because of it.

But this was not the major crisis as far as Tom was concerned. His warehouses, which had proved profitable during the first few years, were suddenly emptied of their principal contents — cotton. This was due to the application of the Bankhead Inland Storage Act. The latter was a political maneuver of the Democratic régime ostensibly to build up public storage facilities inland, but in reality it was a gesture to favor certain larger companies who had supported the Democrats in the 1932 campaign. Tom protested but to no avail. He had first-hand information that his buildings were not only adequate but superior to many being used.

Tom found himself in real financial straits. Since his decision to build the warehouses, he had been handicapped by a lack of liquid assets. Construction in the Houston area was practically at a standstill. Without income from the warehouses, default on his loan seemed unavoidable. He was able, however, after appealing to the Rice Institute administrators, to keep up the payments on a reduced scale. The land that he had bought in 1928 out on Telephone Road, and which is the present location of Tellepsen Construction Company, lacked $15,000 of being clear. Ironically at this time of crisis he was offered just that amount for the entire plot although it was worth many times that figure. Through Tom's contacts at the City National Bank, the latter took over the balance of his loan with the First National Bank.

Thus Tom worked his way out of these precarious and anxious years, but in looking back, he knows it was a miracle that he did not lose everything. It was to take time and perseverance to re-establish the kind of financial framework Tom felt necessary, personally and for the company. It was to take time and considerable courage to erase the bitterness over the cause of his predicament. The injustice of his treatment by the Government had far-reaching effects on his personal life and on the early welfare of Tellepsen Construction Company. If it had not been for this warehouse fiasco, the situation at High Island and again at Corpus Christi might not have seemed so perilous. If it had not been for the sense of desperation derived from this same stalemate, the Mexican episode might not have ever happened. But, be it as it might have been, Tom consoled himself that every business enterprise has its hazards, its complications, its head and heartaches. He had found that contracting not only is no exception but seems to lead the field. Consequently, almost every job is a "story" in itself, a story of overcoming obstacles and ironing out situations. In recalling each, there is either a grimace or a grin — depending on the outcome.

For Mr. Tom there were both. He met the complications of Nature with determination and ingenuity; he met man-made complications with a persistence and simple honesty. Over all, he sensed and acknowledged the guidance of a power superior to Nature and to Man. He was ever aware that God had a stake in Tom Tellepsen. His ways might be obscure, but Tom did not question the ultimate good. Herein lies the essence of true religious faith. However impatient Tom might become with a situation; however he might storm and rant and pace the floor — and he did all these — still his bitterness, his anxiety quieted when he turned to his God. He trusted in His wisdom and accepted the problems confronting him as yet one more test of his determination and conscientious effort. Events substantiate this belief and this confidence.

For example, consider the episode of High Island, and its epilogue. In the middle thirties Tom took over a rock quarry near Huntsville when the owner defaulted on a note Tom had co-signed. The rock was of low grade and the machinery makeshift and rusty. But it became one step of a treadmill that took Tom from Houston to Huntsville to Galveston — to High Island.

High Island is a sleepy little town on the Intracoastal Canal between Beaumont and Galveston. Drilling derricks break the monotony of the flat stretches of coastal land. Tom secured a PWA contract to build a railroad bridge for the Santa Fe Railway Company over the Intracoastal. This meant crossing the Canal with a temporary bridge, demolishing the one presently in use and building the new one. It seemed advisable for Kruse to take up residence in High Island.

Verily, complications of situation and human nature soon indicated that the imp of misadventure was riding the pile driver! In the first place, Tom immediately realized that the length of piling specified for the bridge was wholly inadequate. It required piling twice that long! It would take weeks to obtain these longer piling, not to mention the extra time required to drive each pile. This would also apply to the temporary bridge which had first to be built so that railroad service would be continuous. Two inescapable delays, and they had scarcely started!

100

The bridge was a turning bridge such as Tom had built in Freeport, but this time it was to carry machinery to operate the bridge automatically. A cofferdam was constructed and piles driven for the square footing of the center pier. The top of the footing would be ten feet below the water line — mean low tide. Forms were put down and the concrete poured. Inspectors came from Galveston to obtain cylinder samples of the concrete. These must age for as long as twenty-eight days before testing, but because time was running out, Kruse made his own analysis and proceeded to prepare the reinforcing steel and to pour the circular pier which would support the center of the bridge.

One morning the phone rang and Tom answered:

"Tom," Kruse's usually unruffled voice had an edge of anxiety, "you'd better come over."

"What's the matter, Kruse?" Tom was weary. This commuting was getting him down. Howard would be graduated in a few days from the Georgia Institute of Technology and he planned to drive to Atlanta to join Ingeborg and the girls. It seemed to him that all he did was drive, drive, drive. "You got the steel all right? I had the invoice this morning."

"We're ready to erect it. But Tom, Colonel Marks called. They've condemned the concrete in the lower portion of the pier."

There was silence. Kruse's voice toughened. "I'm sure there's a mistake. I know the concrete's good, Tom. I am sure of it. But here's a mess to get straightened out, and there is so little time. If we don't go on, we'll be penalized on completion. We're in the dead middle of this."

"I'll see Marks this afternoon. And drive on over. And Kruse, what about coring? If I can't get satisfaction from the Colonel, I'll appeal. You see about the coring."

———————

Colonel E. H. Marks, District Engineer of the Galveston District, Corps of Engineers, swung around to face Tom. "I'm sorry, Tellepsen. You'll have to tear it all out." Then pointing to a broken cylinder of concrete resting on the window sill, "There's your concrete."

101

Tom took a careful, appraising look. "That's not our concrete, Colonel."

"O.K. You have a legal right to contest our findings." The Colonel was brusk. "Make your preparations for coring and I'll make arrangements with an inspector from Pittsburgh Testing Laboratories to be on hand when you're ready to core. You're aware your time is almost up. That time penalty clause can't be avoided. Again I say I'm sorry. We have found your work satisfactory in everything else."

Tom and Kruse went out to the bridge together. It was late afternoon and the tide was ebbing. The muddy water swirled about the controversial pier. "That's a hundred thousand dollars, Kruse."

"Tom," Kruse refused to even consider the possibility of rejection, "we'll find the pier is O.K. Say, remember the coring machine we have in the warehouse, the one we had to take over for nonpayment of storage? Can't we use it? I've called all over and a machine to get a six-inch core is hard to find."

Tom's confidence was kindled by Kruse's purpose. "We can certainly try it. We have to have four different cores."

Over a month of valuable time passed before four cores of acceptable size and shape could be provided from the areas of the pier designated for coring. Pittsburgh Testing Laboratories had tested the first cylinders which were judged unsatisfactory. Although they did agree to supervise the second coring operations, they requested that the actual test on these be made by another laboratory. It was agreed to take the cores out to the Rice Institute and use their presses. If the cores stood up to standard, the Government would pay the expenses involved in the second test and absolve Tellepsen Construction Company.

From the grapevine, Tom learned the engineers in the Galveston office of the U.S. Corps of Engineers were betting on the outcome. He told Kruse he knew how it felt to have a race horse entered in a derby with bets down. Kruse laughed. "I'd like to have some of that," he said. "It's a cinch to win." The engineers must have felt the same way as they were all in favor of Tom except the one man directly responsible for the job:

102

The testing of the cores was well attended. Besides Richard B. Gillette, Jr., who had served with the Army Engineers and the Galveston District since 1903, Tom counted four more government men from Galveston. The first core went under the press. It was a tense moment.

Gillette turned to Tom. "If it goes over 2200 pounds, you're safe," he said.

The gauge swung upward - - - 1000 pounds - - - - 2000 pounds. It seemed to Tom as if the atmosphere weighed more! How many hours can a moment be? The silence certainly must shatter before the rough cylinder would break. 3000 pounds — and Gillette was pounding Tom upon the back and congratulating him! Neither this core, nor any one of the other three, broke under 4000 pounds.

The explanation of the contradictory cores finally came out. The inspectors who took the first cores had scraped the footing after it was poured, and their samples were the inferior upper wash, friable and of course lacking in strength.

Thus, this hurdle was successfully passed. But there was a time deadline. Tom knew he had a logical claim to latitude, but again he must face rules and regulations and then —

Surely, Justice's scales were all askew. Two days before Tom and Kruse would have submitted the bridge for acceptance, a tidal wave hit the coast. The tracks, the fill to the apron of the bridge, all were washed away by the high water. Another delay — the agonizing wait for receding tides, the struggle with muck and treacherous sand.

When Tom talked to Colonel Marks about the $10,000 penalty against Tellepsen Construction Company for failing to complete the job in the time specified, the latter agreed there were extenuating circumstances but explained he had no recourse but to follow terms of the contract. Tom did not have the heart to appeal.

This was 1934. In 1937 Tom bid on the Parcel Post Building in Houston. It is rare indeed for bids to be identical, but R. E. McKee, Contractor, of El Paso and Tellepsen Construction Company presented the same figure — two hundred and seventy-six thousand dollars. Rumor had it that McKee, because of greater political activity, would receive the contract. Tom's friends in Houston rallied to his support: calls, telegrams, personal contacts in Washington. As a result, Tom was summoned to the Nation's Capital. The successful bidder would be decided by lot.

This was the first time Tom had been in Washington on business. His Houston acquaintances were glad to welcome him and offer advice and encouragement. There was Wyatt C. Hedrick, then consulting architect to the Treasury Department: Hedrick had supervised the plans for the Post Office building. Jesse Jones was an old friend and many of Jones' staff knew Tom, or knew of him.

Everyone wished him luck:

The letting committee sat about the long table. There was a great deal of overlapping conversation, and Tom could sense they were eager to have the drawing begin and be over with.

Tom could see two plain slips of paper in front of the chairman. The latter indicated that Tom and McKee's representative should each take one.

Alphonse-and-Gaston-fashion, they held back. Finally Tom squared his shoulders and picked up one slip. Tom drew the winning lot.

Some minutes and documents later, Tom emerged into the Washington sunshine. He was strangely at peace, although he thought guiltily, "I should be very excited." "But it was to be this way," he mused.

A hearty greeting brought him back to reality. It was Colonel C. N. Avery, who had an interest in a limestone quarry near Austin, Texas. Tom, with the contract for the Parcel Post Building in his pocket, was now a potential customer. "Congratulations, Tellepsen," he said. "I've just heard the good news. That's the way it should have gone in the first place. A local man, you've a fine reputation for excellent and conscientious work, and you'll do a good job."

"Thanks, Colonel Avery," said Tom. "You know I'll try."

"Say," Avery took Tom by the arm, "I'm having a stag party at the hotel for Admiral Peoples — he's head of Public Buildings, you know — fine guy. How about coming? You've got a reason to celebrate."

"Oh, I don't know if I can," Tom hesitated, "I thought I'd better see about getting back to Houston."

104

"Later, later." Avery's enthusiasm was hard to turn aside. "You'll meet some interesting people. The Attorney General and his assistant will be there — and assorted congressmen. You owe it to yourself. Who knows what might come of it?"

Who knew, indeed, that that evening Tom, finding himself talking to Homer Cummings, the Attorney General, and Bryan McMahon, his assistant, should, in the course of conversation, impulsively pour forth the story of High Island.

Impressed with Tom's quiet sincerity, his intent and direct statements, Homer Cummings listened closely and came to an astonishing conclusion.

"You have been unjustly treated," he said. "I'll not only get back your $10,000 but I'll see that you get twice that much in settlement. You had a legitimate claim to time extension and since the Department was in error in holding you up for that second coring test, they were liable for the delay. They owe you not only the $10,000 you paid them as penalty, but $10,000 more for having kept you from putting up your steel when you were ready. In all probability you could have completed the bridge before the tidal wave. Mr. Tellepsen, you have a case!"

Tom's eyes crinkled at the corners. "This has certainly been a day," he thought to himself and involuntarily chided his own lack of faith. "I must remember not to be too impatient in my prayers," he said out loud, and Cummings, grasping his unspoken thoughts, laughed and shook his hand in agreement.

But Tom was not one to wait on wheels, even of Justice. Next day he went directly to the office of the Corps of Engineers U.S. Army, and repeated his story, quoting Cummings and McMahon. His reception was cordial but evasive. Tom left Washington, not knowing.

Ten days later he received a check reimbursing him for the penalty payment. He did not press for the other $10,000.

* * * * * * *

The witches stirred the brackish waters of Corpus Christi Bay for a hair-raising story, or rather, as Kruse put it, a "hair-graying" story — his hair!

In 1937 a former employee of Tellepsen Construction Company, now in business for himself, asked Tom to co-sign a performance bond with him. The man had worked with Kruse on the Manchester Wharf and had gone on to achieve a fair amount of recognition in his field. Tom was glad to accommodate him. The particular subcontracting job for which the bond was required called for laying 36" cast iron siphon pipe for a sewer line under the turning basin at Corpus Christi and also three smaller utility lines at the mouth of the ship channel on the bay side of the bridge. Tom had given the plans and estimate a cursory inspection, and when nothing was heard from the subcontractor or primary contractor, he had assumed all was going smoothly. He was completely unprepared, therefore, for a call from the latter, MacKenzie Construction Company, to the effect that the pipe contract had run into difficulty and would Tom please come to Corpus immediately and take over? Ordinarily, the default would have been made known to the bonding company, who would then hire someone to complete the contract. Tom would have been ultimately responsible, so MacKenzie wisely figured that if Tom would go ahead on his own and work out the situation, it would save time and money for everyone concerned. MacKenzie never even notified the bonding company.

Apprehensive, Tom made the trip to Corpus Christi:

He found chaos. The pipe had not been lowered to proper grade; the pipe joints had come loose in places. It was a case of improper procedure from the very start. And almost all the money was gone. A further irony became apparent when Tom started looking for a dredge. The pipe would have to be taken up from the bottom of the turning basin, its bed redredged, and the new and/or salvaged pipe relocated. A large dredge used in deepening the ship channel was still moored in the basin but had been demobilized. A smaller dredge was brought over from a nearby coastal town, and the effort was made to revamp it for the job; but this proved not feasible. The owner of the larger dredge offered to do the work for $15,000, which was about six times the price originally quoted the subcontractor while the dredge was working in the basin.

It was about this time that Kruse moved down to a cabin on the beach and took over on-the-spot supervision. The fate and future of Tellepsen Construction Company depended on the early completion of the job at minimum cost!

Dredging proceeded without incident. Then came the task of lowering the 36″ jointed pipe into place. It was hauled by pontoons to location and lowered by winch. The first attempt to lower the pipe failed because water in the pipe used to weight it shifted under wave action, and one end submerged faster than the other, breaking cable progressively. Workmen were tossed overboard like buttons snapping from a fat man's shirt! On the second attempt, concrete weights were used, and the pipe was lowered evenly. But the third joint from the end broke loose, and it required a diver to repair it. Connection was made with the junction chambers already installed on either side of the turning basin. Tom and Kruse heaved a sigh of relief.

But the time of tribulation was not passed. As if problems with natural causes weren't enough, hairsplitting by the city inspector and the PWA inspector over acceptance of the joint at the junction chamber may account for some of those gray hairs on Kruse's head. It was an absurd situation because it was a known fact that the city of Corpus Christi intended to abandon the sewer line after it was accepted. The pipe was down, had been tested and was water-tight. A small amount of seepage was discovered where the pipe entered the junction chamber. The inspectors required repair. For a week attempts were made to stop the seepage. It was insignificant and actually of no importance, but the inspectors held out.

Kruse threw up his hands in exasperation. It was Thanksgiving Day and his birthday to boot. "You know as well as I do you have no intention of putting this line into operation, and yet you've kept us here a week on a petty thing. I'm through. And so is Tellepsen Construction Company. You can do as you please about it!"

The matter was dropped.

In the meantime, between the first and second attempts to lay the 36″ sewer line, the three smaller utility lines near the bridge had been successfully placed. But even this was accompanied by untoward experiences. When the pipe was ready and the weather was favorable, the Harbor Master was notified so that the port might be closed for a few hours. It was then discovered that they must also have permission of the United

107

States District Engineer in Galveston. The latter cited a regulation that notice must be given two weeks in advance.

"What about the weather?" Kruse asked.

"Take a chance," was the reply.

The pipe floated in wait on the side of the bay where it had been fabricated. The watchman was instructed that when the two-week period was up, or shy of it by a few days — if the wind lay, he was to call Kruse, day or night, so that the pipe could be towed into the channel near location and kept in readiness for lowering when the port was officially closed.

At 2 a.m. on the Saturday morning preceding the Sunday deadline, Kruse heard a hammering and a ferocious knocking.

"Bay's calm as a lily pond," came the watchman's voice.

Sleepily, Kruse pulled on his clothes and groped for the coffee pot. The harbor was closed only four hours; from eight to twelve noon on Sunday, "so the seamen could go to church" grinned Kruse.

At one time it looked as if the job would show a loss of close to one hundred thousand dollars. As it was, it did represent a substantial loss, but not as much as was feared. Tom and Kruse considered themselves lucky to be done with it.

As partial repayment, Tellepsen Construction Company took over a few pieces of equipment owned by the subcontractor, who had suffered a nervous breakdown. Tom let the situation rest. He was not one to hold a grudge or a burdensome debt over an unfortunate human being.

But the blindfolded lady with the scales does have vision! A short time after the three lines near the bridge had been accepted, a ship dropped emergency anchor to prevent sideswiping the bridge and the anchor severed the utility lines. The city of Corpus Christi put out the repair job for bids and Tellepsen was low. Kruse was understandably weary of the situation, and when another company offered to buy the contract for $4,000, he wanted to sell. But Tom's intuition prevailed. They went on to do the work. By getting permission to substitute beach shell for the more expensive oyster shell as backfill, they managed to make a profit and lessen their previous deficit. They found this type of fill was more satisfactory, anyhow.

108

There is an additional touch of whimsical justice *a la* Mr. Tom. Some fifteen years later, the bonding company wrote Tom a letter of appreciation for his having stepped in and done the work. Although they had never even been notified of this troublesome situation when it occurred, they had in the meantime learned what had happened. In recognition, they deposited $15,000 in Mr. Tom's East End State Bank and have never drawn upon it!

* * *

Toil and trouble! Tom built the Buick showrooms at Milam and Clay. Tom had been called in to bid because The Rice Institute owned the property, and they recommended him. Competition was keen, and looking over the other bidders, Tom sharpened his pencil to a fine point, shaving his profit to $1,200 and this on a job totaling one hundred and forty thousand dollars. Tom got the contract and, to indicate the accuracy of his bidding, made almost to the penny of what he had figured. But if you would like to assign a monetary value to anxiety, it would certainly have shown a loss.

The architect had specified a patent plaster which was a new material. The coloring was already in the gypsum plaster. Tom had had no experience with it — nor had the architect. Personally supervising the application and following the manufacturer's instructions, Tom was aware that the finish was not perfect; the color was not uniform. Tom checked and rechecked the procedure recommended by the factory; there could be no mistake. The architect's reaction was the same as Tom's — only violent! He fumed. He stormed. He blustered. It was obvious to Tom that in his present state, the man could not be talked to!

Tom entered the Buick showrooms with a lagging step. No solution to the predicament had come to light after many sleepless hours. The architect was waiting, but today, his demeanor had changed. He did not look at Tom directly.

"Tellepsen," he said, "I guess I lost my head yesterday. I've no reason to accuse you of not following the instructions that came with the material. It is not what I expected, and you'll have to admit you feel the same way."

109

"Yes," agreed Tom. But this wasn't the point. "What can be done about it?" After all, the threats of rejection were still ringing in his ears.

"I'll take care of it. I've wired the factory."

And then as Tom was about to turn away. "Tellepsen — ah — I want to ask a favor."

Tom was surprised. Their relationship at this point hardly invited favors.

"When you get back to your office, you will find a letter from me. Please tear it up." The voice was apologetic now.

There was a letter, and Tom did tear it up, unopened. Days later, as these things sometimes happen, a friend of Tom's stopped him on the street. "How is it with you and . . . . ?" he asked.

Tom briefed the situation and the friend smiled. "I happened to be in his office when he wrote that letter. He said he'd break you on this job; that after this, you'd never get another contract."

* * * * * * *

Fire burn . . . . The episode in Mexico is on the debit side of the ledger. There was no laughter over Mexico. It is a combination of *Dragnet* and *Foreign Intrigue*.

This is a story that began in 1935. An acquaintance by the name of Calvin, a mining engineer, had recently returned from Mexico and described to Tom and Kruse the desperate need of the City of Puebla for an adequate water supply. It was a critical situation: water was to be had only a few hours of each day. In his estimation, based on what he had seen and heard, a sufficient water table existed, but there was a lack of engineering know-how. He had contacts in Mexico City, he said, and why didn't Tom and J. A. Sauls (Tellepsen engineer) and himself go to Mexico City and see if they could get the job?

There was little construction work in Houston or thereabouts. Tom was growing restless. He decided to have a try at it. Leaving Howard and Kruse in Houston to handle things, Tom set out with Sauls and Calvin. They added the services of a Frenchman by the name of M. Nippell, who resided in Mexico City and was an architect and engineer. He would serve as interpreter. Nippell

110

knew a Mr. Simmons, a native-born Texan who had been educated in England and now lived in Mexico and had married a Mexican woman. He claimed to have contacts too.

The first step was accomplished in short order. They obtained a verbal agreement with the Governor of Puebla. According to the agreement, they would proceed with geological exploration and draw up engineering plans. J. A. Sauls had formerly been water engineer for the city of Houston and knew his business. His job would be principally in Puebla on location. Tom would stay in Mexico City to work out legal and financial details. Tom and Sauls found their inability to speak Spanish a decided handicap, and Tom immediately took issue with the accepted habit of the outstretched palm. To straightforward Tom, it was an unsavory custom. "Moochers," he called them. It might be high class mooching, like some fees of the legal profession, or low class, petty mooching like commissions to the go-betweens, but one and all, they irked him.

Leaving Sauls in Mexico, Tom made several hurried trips back to the States. At this time the highway to Mexico City was under construction, and on one occasion a landslide blocked the road and Tom was forced to spend a day and two nights in an adobe hut on a diet of *frijoles*. Back in Houston, Tom's friend, Dr. P. A. Sloane, noted symptoms of malaria and warned Tom he was still susceptible. This was the first reoccurrence since his Panama days. Ingeborg and the girls accompanied Tom on one trip into Mexico, and it was a glamorous experience for them. The blond beauty and sophisticated manners of Hortense and Lorraine, fresh from the campus of the University of Texas, were heralded by the suave and handsome gallants of the Capital. On the other hand, the picturesque city, the courteous attentions of the young men, the quaint customs, the beautiful music made their visit very exciting!

But Tom had other things to think about than music and gallantry:

It was late afternoon. Tom was impatient to be back in Mexico City. You couldn't make time on these winding mountain roads. It was all of 150 miles between Puebla and Mexico City, and to Tom it seemed to take forever.

Sauls was asleep beside him. He had been very elated when Tom picked him up. Prospects were excellent for a first well. With banking arrangements completed, they were now ready to draft the final contract before going into actual construction.

Nippell was in the back of the car, talking constantly, as was his wont. Tom half wished he'd go to sleep too, but he had to admit that the chattering at least kept him awake at the wheel.

Suddenly, as Tom dipped down a steep incline, he saw a car approaching in the middle of the narrow road. It was driven by a native woman and was overflowing with children. Instinctively, Tom slowed from his pace of thirty miles an hour and waited for her to take her side of the road to permit him to pass.

On she came, without giving a foot. The bright eyes of the children were upon him as Tom swerved frantically to the right to avoid collision. He heard Nippell shout as the car headed down into the ditch. A rock caught the front right tire, and the steering wheel spun under Tom's hands as he was thrown upward against the top of the car. Tom struggled to regain control of the writhing car; it seemed to have a will of its own. A tree rose up in front of them. Tom's feet were braced on the brakes; he fought with the steering wheel. There was no response. The car skidded into the tree.

When Tom regained consciousness he felt as if he had been hit in the face with a block of ice. He did not know how long he had been sitting thus — slumped over the wheel. Suddenly it felt as if his face was on fire. Dazed, he lifted a hand to his mouth. The contact gave a further sensation of pain, and his hand came away covered with blood. His tongue hurt, and dully he realized he was half-choking on blood and the loosened teeth which filled his mouth. He coughed again, and again.

He turned slowly. Sauls was sprawled beside him. He was unconscious. Then Tom became aware of the groaning from the back seat. Nippell was glassy-eyed and seemed to be out of his head. His gibberish was in French, and he would alternately shout wildly and then cover his face and be convulsed with piteous moans. He made no effort to get out of the car, nor seemed to be aware when Tom dragged himself to a sitting position on the running board. Shock passed through Tom in sickening waves. He was nauseated. He could see Sauls' foot; it was hanging loosely at the ankle. Tom knew it must be broken. All was so quiet except for the weird crying of Nippell. Tom shuddered.

Suddenly he heard brakes. Cries of surprise and alarm came down to him from the road above. Fortunately Tom's car had been recognized by friends making the same trip from Puebla to Mexico City. They lifted Sauls out of the car and gently laid him on the grass. Their assurances filtered dully through the maze of Tom's mind. He still sat by the car. "Ambulance," "next town," "car all smashed," "whole front caved in," "Tellepsen half out," "Nippell not injured" — it was as if he were in a dream.

An ambulance did come from the next town — an hour later.

The law in Mexico as to accidents is very peculiar, and a little bit barbarous. You commit a crime if you have an accident. You are liable for a fine. Instead of a hospital, the three men were put in jail! It was a small room, with a dirt floor, already occupied by literally hundreds of flies. They were kept here for several hours with no first aid of any kind. Tom stopped his bleeding as best he could, tying a handkerchief across his lacerated lips. He had not tried to talk. The friends stayed on in the small town, and in what seemed to Tom a lifetime of waiting, an ambulance came from Mexico City. The accident occurred at approximately 5:30 p.m., and it was 3:30 the next morning before they had medical attention.

Sauls was admitted first, then Nippell who by this time had reached a point of hysteria. Tom was last. Sitting in the next room, wearing his bloody mask, Tom heard himself discussed.

"It looks as if he's bitten off at least a half inch of his tongue," the doctor was saying. "He'll never talk again."

But Tom knew differently. He didn't wince when the wounds on his face were stitched, nor did he avoid the doctor's eyes. Tom had faith and he prayed.

He was taken into the same room with Sauls, and though it seemed strange to have to gesture or nod your head to make yourself understood, he was patient.

The worst was yet to come. One day Sauls called Tom's attention to his foot. "Look," he said, "I can move it." Tom applauded silently. The next day gangrene set in. It advanced very rapidly, and the first amputation at the knee had to be

113

followed by a second one at the groin. Sauls was weakened by shock and the initial loss of blood. The physician told Tom that Sauls' heart had almost stopped beating when he was on the operating table. His recovery was slowed by apathy, and Tom had to turn away from the haunting, hurt look in the man's eyes. When a dear friend came from Houston, Sauls took heart and slowly gained strength.

Three months later they were discharged from the hospital, Sauls bravely maneuvering on crutches, and Tom learning to speak all over again, like a child - - - but *speaking!*

It had been a harrowing experience to say the least, but now they faced the future with confidence. All was ready for the Governor's signature. Tom had been notified that the water well contract had favorably passed the congress of the State of Puebla. Now, they were sure, they would build the waterworks! But:

The general smiled ingratiatingly as Nippell translated. He stood at attention, his resplendent uniform without crease or fold. "He must never sit down," thought Tom.

The smile disappeared from Tom's thoughts as he realized the full implication of Nippell's words.

"He says the Governor wants $75,000 as his part in securing the contract. He wants it in advance and in American money — and then he'll sign."

There are no words to describe how Tom must have felt at that moment. The physical pain he had endured was dwarfed by the agony of mind at the useless months — a year almost. His anger rose as the whole fabric of deceit, of graft, of dishonesty spread out before him. As quickly it subsided. "What use," he thought. "This is a foreign land; these are foreign ways. I've learned a bitter lesson. Let's be done with it."

"Tell him," he said, turning to Nippell and indicating the Governor's messenger, "that I must first go to the United States to raise the money. I'll fly out tonight if there's a plane." He had

114

no intention of returning. Now he had to have an excuse to get out of the country.

The general looked doubtful, but he shrugged his shoulders. Nippell kept up a soothing conversation in his plausible way.

The plane landed in Brownsville — Tom's first flight, by the way. He took a train to Houston, and as his car blurred across McKinney to the rhythm of the swinging warning lights, Tom looked out the window to see his automobile first at the crossing — the girls leaning out the back and Ingeborg waving. Their white, anxious faces touched him and he took heart. This had all been a nightmare.

No one said, "I told you so," but Tom knew they must have thought it. George Brown had warned him; Brown & Root had built a highway and encountered much as this. And others. Tom found out later that his was the third company to be taken in on the waterworks — and milked! He lost about $15,000 and aged as many years.

But this is not yet the end.

In December of 1936, after Tom, Sauls and Nippell had been back in the States scarcely four months, Tom received a $10,000 offer for the transfer of the Puebla waterworks contract and all engineering plans, etc. The offer was made by Nippell's friend, Simmons, as agent for a German whose name Tom later learned was Brandstetter. The meeting was to be held in Laredo.

From here on the story reads like the script of a Grade B thriller. It is a fantastic sequence of plot and counterplot:

Tom and Nippell arrived in Laredo on Friday, December 4. The meeting was scheduled for the morning of the fifth. About 11 a.m. on Saturday, Simmons called long distance from Monterrey asking that Tom and Nippell come to Monterrey as he did not expect Brandstetter until Sunday night. Tom's coming to Monterrey would expedite the closing of the deal.

Tom was apprehensive. He had been advised not to re-enter Mexico; his abrupt departure from Puebla had left certain moochers unsatisfied. However, Nippell had gone into Nuevo Laredo the day before and had been unable to discover any charges against Tom or the company. After calling Kruse,

115

who said "Be careful," Tom decided to risk it. Nippell and Tom drove to Monterrey and met Simmons at the Imperial Hotel.

There seemed no cause for anxiety. Simmons was affable and confident. Together with a Greek friend of Simmons, they went to a wrestling match Saturday night. They drove to Saltillo for Sunday dinner — the match and dinner both at Tom's expense. South of the border, time is not of the essence, but by ten o'clock Sunday night, Tom was beginning to fidget. A call came through for Simmons. It was Brandstetter's secretary with a message from Brandstetter who was in Tampico. He would not be in Monterrey until Wednesday as he had business in Mexico City Monday morning. Tom was exasperated. He'd come 500 miles already for two appointments with an individual whom he had neither met nor talked to.

"Wire Brandstetter," he said grimly, "that we'll meet him in Mexico City tomorrow."

It was midnight and the 500 miles of mountain roads between Monterrey and Mexico City made hazardous driving. Spelling each other, Tom and Nippell made the trip in fifteen hours. They cleared customs and got their Mexico City driver's licenses. Simmons took them to the Hotel Bolonia Roma, a small second-class establishment. Tom was anxious not to publicize his presence in Mexico City. Brandstetter had not arrived. He was not on the 7:30 p.m. train from Tampico. Simmons talked to Brandstetter's girl friend and induced her to try and locate Brandstetter. Her call to Tampico was completed and Brandstetter assured her he would fly to Mexico City on Tuesday. With this, Tom had to be content. It had been two days since he and Nippell had been to bed and even apprehension did not keep Tom from sleeping soundly.

Tom whittled away the Tuesday morning hours wandering about Mexico City, as Nippell had taken the car to visit relatives. Simmons met both the 11 a.m. and 1 p.m. flights from Tampico. Still no Brandstetter. This was the last straw. Tom had received a mysterious phone call that morning. A voice spoke rapid Spanish but Tom could make out the words *ingeniero* and "Tellepsen." He told Nippell and Simmons that he believed he was being watched.

"We're leaving, Simmons," Tom informed him. "If Brandstetter is still interested in our proposition, he'll have to

116

come to us or at least furnish earnest money to back his intentions. This run-around may have a reasonable explanation, but I'm not going to waste any more of my time here."

Tom and Nippell checked out of the hotel and loaded their luggage into the car. Nippell started the motor and at that moment two plain clothes men approached with orders from the Labor Office requiring Tom to stay in Mexico City to answer certain charges. He was placed under constant police surveillance — even at night a guard was stationed in the lobby of the hotel. Tom and Nippell moved back into the same rooms they had just vacated.

Tom sought out the American vice consul, a Mr. Wilson, who advised that any charges against Tom would have to prove violation of the Mexican Constitution if Tom was to be restrained from leaving the country. A law firm in Mexico City, Swift & Priego, had formerly handled legal matters for Tom, and Tom presented his predicament to them. They were reassuring — there must be some mistake. They agreed to find out for Tom just what the charges were. However, at Simmons' home, Tom inadvertently overheard a telephone conversation which lead him to believe that Brandstetter was in Monterrey with Simmons' Greek friend, and also that Velasco Russ figured in the deal.

Velasco Russ had already played the villain in Tom's early dealings in Puebla. He had professed a willingness to be of assistance to Tom. On one occasion when Tom was attempting to get financial backing from one of the banks in Mexico City, Russ had written a letter of introduction to a banking firm. However, this bank refused Tom's loan. From the very day Tom and Sauls had begun their unfortunate negotiations in Mexico, casual acquaintances such as Russ had continually harassed them. Russ had been a general in the Mexican Army, but was now in official disfavor. He had been cordial and effusive, and Tom had at first been impressed with his bearing. But he had reappeared on the scene time and again: at Tom's expense. Tom had felt that Russ had been behind the Governor's exorbitant demands in the first place. Now he was sure.

It was Wednesday, December 9. Tom was advised that his case had been set for Friday. He was also shown a legal document, notice of charges, which he was supposed to have signed on November 26 in Mexico. It was a forgery. Tom was in

117

the United States at that time. It was clear to Tom by now that he had been enticed into Mexico under false pretenses. He doubted that there was a German named Brandstetter who had any interest whatsoever in buying his Puebla contract and plans. Simmons protested his innocence, saying that he, the Greek and a Mr. Church had been approached to make arrangements and were to get a commission on the transfer of the contract and technical papers. They were to receive eighteen thousand dollars. Tom had agreed to accept ten thousand dollars. Nippell was inclined to feel that Simmons was telling the truth and had himself been duped by Velasco Russ. The Friday hearings would answer a lot of questions.

But there was the gap of Thursday to live through. Tom couldn't sit idly. He made the rounds — going first to the lawyers' office. Here Priego suggested bond, but Tom decided it was too risky. On the way to Simmons' office, Tom and Nippell ran into Mrs. Velasco Russ, who called Nippell aside. She had just had a telegram from her husband instructing her to call off the police as he, Russ, was bringing Brandstetter into Mexico City on Friday. Brandstetter was prepared to do business. This contradictory state of affairs made Tom more optimistic, tho his skepticism remained. He and Nippell joined Simmons, and they worked out details of the negotiation to be entered into on the morrow.

That night Nippell called on Russ's attorney, who had filed the yet unrecited charges. He was told that there were two more characters in the plot. Two gentlemen of Puebla had actually started the proceedings. They had some sort of financial agreement with Velasco Russ.

The situation with all its various ramifications was a nightmare to Tom. He, who usually fell asleep the moment his head touched the pillow, lay awake in uneasy thought until three-thirty in the morning.

Swift & Priego met Tom at their office with the table of charges: back wages due Russ at two thousand pesos per month for twelve months and three months' extra salary for dismissal without notice. In all it totaled thirty thousand pesos. Also there was an additional claim of fifty thousand pesos to be explained later. Priego had approached the judges for alternatives. Tom could give bond for eighty thousand pesos to guarantee his appearance at the time of trial, or it was intimated that a no-bill could be obtained for a fee of five thousand pesos to each judge. Priego got the bribe down to fifteen hundred pesos.

By this time Tom knew Russ had reached Mexico City. He had sent word to one of the policemen guarding Tom that he wanted to talk to Nippell. Nippell went to see him. Russ bluntly demanded that Tom name an amount he was willing to pay for his freedom or Russ would expedite all charges. He further insinuated that Tom's life was in danger if he didn't prove reasonable. The well worn bait was again dragged forth. Simmons had received a telegram from Brandstetter in Monterrey saying that if Tom would meet him on Tuesday, they could do business.

Tom refused to swallow the bait this time and accused Simmons of complicity in Russ's scheme. Tom had in the meantime decided that paying off the judges would be the cheapest and quickest way out, but upon arrival at the hotel, another notice of suit for five thousand pesos was served, and it became evident that these trumped-up charges would increase in variety and frequency, their very number and the time required for hearing each, etc., might prolong Tom's stay in Mexico City for months, to say nothing of the cost of no-billing each one! Russ, in appealing to Nippell, claimed that Simmons had double-crossed him by trying to arrange a secret meeting between Brandstetter and Tom.

"The pot and the kettle," thought Tom desperately, "and to be trite about it, I'm between the Devil and deep blue sea — of graft."

But the charges recited to Nippell by Russ made Tom's hair curl. Russ showed Nippell copies of the legal documents to substantiate his statements:

1) Russ had tried to have Tom's car intercepted on the way to Mexico City, supposedly after Simmons' double-cross, but Tom had made better time than was expected, and the road block missed him. However, the Governor's car had gone through the block at Victoria and, not being recognized, it was fired upon by the police. Tom was held responsible.

2) An accident had occurred not far from Valles, and the car which caused it had sped away but not before it was identified as Tom's car.

3) At Tamazunchale, a car bearing Tom's license number had hit and killed a Mexican citizen and failed to stop.

119

4) The Attorney General of Mexico had given notice to investigate Tellepsen Construction Company with regard to Puebla operations.

5) Some eight or ten additional charges were in the mill.

Russ admitted that Tom would be successful in disclaiming some of the charges, but he emphasized their nuisance value. It was apparent, too, he resented the intercession of the staff of the American Embassy in Tom's behalf. They had called him in for questioning.

To Tom the most serious aspect of the frame-up was that Russ had succeeded in involving claims which concerned the Mexican Government. If he did manage to get out of the country, it was possible that he would be extradited to face these charges, however false.

Russ seemed surprised when Nippell told him that Tom had previously instructed Simmons to offer Russ a settlement equal to the no-billing pay-off. This ignorance lent some credence to the double, double-cross. Thus mollified, Russ suggested that a compromise be reached. Tom would give a power of attorney to Swift & Priego to handle the Puebla negotiations, and Tom would pay Russ $2,000 as compensation for his part in the transaction. In return, Russ would secure withdrawal of all suits against Tom Tellepsen, giving him a notarized "letter of release" in which he renounced any claims against Tom should the latter ever re-enter Mexico. Russ agreed to arrange for the sale of the Puebla contract and documents. He even went so far as to produce Brandstetter's son-in-law, whom Nippell remembered from Puebla as a representative of a pipe and valve manufacturer. Brandstetter was reputed to be this manufacturer.

Sunday, December 13 — the day of decision. Tom weighed all possible procedures and decided to meet Russ's conditions. Even Wilson advised him to do so as the next step would undoubtedly involve criminal proceedings against Tom. Tom offered Russ his personal check. It was refused. He called Kruse to wire the two thousand dollars. It was now necessary to avoid Simmons and associates for fear they, too, might exert similar pressures. Tom secretly hoped Simmons would catch up with Russ — what a meeting that would be!

It took Monday and part of Tuesday for all the snarls to be untangled. Swift & Priego held the stakes as well

120

as the power of attorney. Swift had an ironic tale to tell after making the rounds of courts and police station with Velasco Russ. One colleague collected a thousand pesos for his share in the plot; another thousand pesos was diverted to an undisclosed official channel. Russ complained to Swift that of the seven thousand three hundred and forty pesos swindled from Tom, he would have about five hundred left when he had settled with all individuals involved.

Tom and Nippell left Mexico City at 2 p.m. Tuesday, December 15, and drove to the border without incident. They arrived in Houston on Wednesday at noon.

* * * * * * *

And cauldron bubble! In the Varner Building (Fannin and Capitol) Tom's reputation for superior workmanship and close figuring introduced an unusual condition into the contract. The building was to be built for a guaranteed cost, but the owner was to share in any savings which Tom might effect. This was depression, 1938. The fall rains were heavy this year, and an unprecedented weight of water in the ground pushed in one of the basement walls. Even the footings moved inward. From an engineering standpoint, the architect agreed that this was not Tom's fault, but rather an error in specification on depth of the footings. The entire wall had to be wrecked. In determining who would bear the cost, the architect was sole arbitrator. In view of the clause granting the owner a share in savings, the architect ruled that for all intents, the owner and builder were partners and therefore must share in this expense. As it turned out, however, Tom managed to come within the guaranteed cost anyway. This job at one time looked as if it might have High Island complications. A cylinder test of concrete from the transit mixer was condemned but before Tom could core, the architect withdrew the condemnation.

* * * * * * *

The witches allowed Tom a respite and a chuckle. On the corner of Burkett and Simmons Streets stands a Negro church. There is something distinctive about it. The peak of the roof is rather narrow and steep. The stained glass windows are simple but attractive. The grounds are neat; there are sidewalks, curb and gutter.

The lawn is landscaped with shrubbery and trees. Even a foot scraper is mounted discreetly near the entrance. A bulletin board in the front of the church announces the services and sermon and the name — Rev. T. Vincent Harris. The immediate impression is that this church was built with greater care and attention than most Negro churches. Mr. Tom had his finger in the planning of the St. Luke's Episcopal Church; in fact before it was over, he was in it up to his elbows.

In 1937, Tom was member of the city-wide building committee for the Episcopal Churches of Houston. James Anderson was chairman. The committee had a request to build a Negro Episcopal church. The other members of the committee turned to Tom, "How do you recommend we proceed?" Tom suggested having a Negro architect draw a plan and that bids be taken from Negro contractors. This was done. The plan was very acceptable, and bids came in ranging from $2,000 to $10,000. It was immediately discovered that the $2,000 bid did not include a roof for the building. The second low bid was for $4,000. Tom had in the meantime made his own estimate and knew that the church could be built for $4,000. The builder, however, could not qualify for surety bond and offered instead a personal bond backed by a local lumber company. Again the committee deferred to Tom, who could not see his way to advise accepting such a bond and suggested instead that the builder let the committee supervise purchase of all materials and that he contract the labor only, receiving payment from the committee as he progressed. It would be necessary for him to act as foreman and he would not receive his profit until the job was done. This he refused to do, saying, "I'm a contractor and do not do the work myself."

Confused, the committee again turned to Tom. He shrugged his shoulders. "If you want," he said, "I'll hire a Negro foreman and let him get his own crew. I'll supervise the purchase of materials and the actual construction."

And so it worked out.

Tom derived much satisfaction from the obvious pleasure the congregation took in their church. The foreman, hat in hand, thanked Tom for "all I have learned about construction from you." Tom recalls with a chuckle the night of the dedication of the church. It was very crowded; no standing room was available. Dark faces appeared at all the windows. The Rt. Rev. Clinton Quin gave the principal sermon. Tom and Ingeborg and Mrs. Quin sat on the front row. Beside them a Tellepsen employee by the name of White kept up an intermittent applause, shouting "Amen" every time the Bishop said something which appealed to him in particular.

* * * * * * *

The witches' activities have allowed Tom but few real vacations. However in the late spring of 1939, Tom and Ingeborg visited Norway. It came about this way.

Several years before they had made the acquaintance of a Captain Andersen, whose Norwegian vessel docked in Houston. Captain Andersen and the Tellepsens became good friends. He visited in their home and in turn, Tom and Ingeborg dined and spent pleasant hours aboard the *Tabor*. It was Captain Andersen's idea that Tom and Ingeborg go back to Norway with him. His owners' quarters were luxurious, with living room, bedroom, anteroom and private bath. It was an enticing offer and Tom said, "Some day." The some day came in 1939. Captain Andersen wired from New Orleans that the reservations he had had for his return trip had been cancelled — the quarters were vacant — and come on! Tom and Ingeborg made up their minds in a hurry! The whole family went to Galveston to see them off. It was a wonderful trip. The boat touched at Newport News, where Tom and Ingeborg visited with the Taylors, friends from Houston.

They spent three weeks with Tora and with Ingeborg's family and were loath to leave, but the threat of war was in the air, and every headline gave encouragement to their anxiety. Erik, Ingeborg's nephew, offered to drive them over the mountains to Bergen. It was a breathtaking and beautiful journey. The ferry trip over Hardanger Fjord on the way to Bergen was unforgetable.

Tom and Ingeborg took passage on the *Queen Mary* out of Southampton and it was a pleasant crossing. War was indeed close on their heels. The next trip the *Queen Mary* was to make to the United States would find her decks made into improvised sleeping accommodations for tourists and refugees seeking the safety of our shores.

* * * * * * *

Back home Tom found the witches had not been idle. Particularly at the floodgates job just outside Freeport, they had been up to their usual mischief. Gates were being built on both sides of

123

the diversion channel, or New Brazos River, where it intersected the Intracoastal Canal. The soil condition was the first hurdle to excavation. The muck had a slimy way of slipping out of the grasp of any machinery. A by-pass had been dredged above the site of the floodgates to permit uninterrupted canal traffic. A pontoon bridge carried men and supplies out to the job site. A hurricane hit the coast that summer and lifted the bridge out of the water, leaving it up on dry land. By cornering the dredge underneath it, Tom finally got it back in the water. Most of the dirt work had to be redone. The war came along about this time and raised prices and increased labor problems. It was an unprofitable job.

Mr. Ernie Cockrell Sr. turned to Tom. "This floodgate you're going to show us — it's something new, isn't it?"

"Yes," said Tom, with his eye on a bumpy section of Highway 288 between Angleton and Freeport. "It is designed to hold back the flood waters of the Brazos, keep out debris and that kind of thing. Sometimes the current is so bad, tugs can't go through and have to tie up on either side. It is a treacherous river. War will probably interrupt flood control projects, but some day it may be better."

"How long do you think it will take you?"

"I believe another twelve to fifteen months, Ernie. I'm having trouble already getting materials. Labor has to commute to a great extent. There's really a tremendous housing shortage here; what with the Dow Chemical Company moving in."

"Look, there's your bridge, Tom." Mrs. Tellepsen was pointing ahead to the right as they approached the intersection with Highway 36 going to Brazoria and Sweeney.

Tom told the Cockrells the intriguing story of the "bridge over dry land." Turning just short of the bridge, Tom stopped the car and they walked out on the bridge, examining the bronze plate and looking down at the river.

"There should be tarpon in here," said Tom, and just then Mrs. Cockrell called out and pointed at a silver body rolling in the clear green water.

"Oh, this is so exciting," she said.

"Should have brought our tackle, Tom," grinned Ernie.

Back in the car they crossed the cattle guard and were immediately surrounded by curious, white-faced cattle, mostly Brahmas or scrubs with a Brahman ancestry. They laughed at their clumsy movements and inched along until they were clear of the herd. As they approached the temporary canal, Tom could see a crew working although it was Sunday. Anxiety nudged him. "Something is wrong," he said.

And something was wrong. A tug coming through had hit the pontoon barge bridge and sunk it — preventing any boats or tows from going either way. Tom had not been notified. The foreman and crew were working frantically to raise the barge.

"I'm afraid we'll have to get some divers, Mr. Tellepsen," Jack Kale said. "If we can get just one chamber afloat . . ."

Ernie Cockrell surveyed operations with a dour expression. Tom took him in a rowboat across to the now "island" where the control house for the gates would be located. One look at the muck, the mud-laden machines —

"You can have it, Tom," he said. "I wouldn't want any of that grief. There are headaches in my business, but nothing like this! I'll stick to the pleasant, quiet little gamble of drilling for oil!"

In the Big Time

When the war spotlight fell upon Houston and the Gulf Coast in the fall of 1939 and early 1940, Tom Tellepsen and his construction company were standing in the wings, awaiting their cue. Their role in wartime construction was to give the small but tested organization the boost it needed to enter the big time.

Tom was ready. He was now past fifty, with thirty years seniority in a profession he had learned literally from the ground up. He was soon to step down from the presidency of the company in favor of his son, Howard, and to become Chairman of the Board of Directors. It would still be the vision, the drive, the tenacity of Tom Tellepsen which would characterize the company. He had given it a reputation for integrity; he had financed it soundly; he had staffed and equipped it wisely; and he was to encourage its expansion into new fields. From here on, the story of Tellepsen Construction Company is less a personal story. Yet in one sense, every achievement of the company is a monument to the abiding faith and adventuring spirit of Tom Tellepsen. And think not that Tom is not minutely aware of every job under construction! His trained eye and divining sense are everywhere apparent. In the words of old Slim Alexander, his oldest employee in point of service, "Mr. Tom drives by slow, but he knows what's goin' on, yes, sah!"

In 1940 there was little construction work in Houston. Thus the building of an air base at Ellington Field was a coveted contract and competition was keen. Tellepsen Construction Company was successful bidder on the first section which included, besides the wrecking of 1917 buildings (Tom had installed a water tank here at that time), the construction of barracks, mess halls, chapels, warehouses and miscellaneous buildings. Since this was the only job of any consequence in the Houston area, labor was plentiful. The men formed literally block-long queues at the Clay Avenue office and mile-long lines of automobiles at the field. It was even necessary at times to have police supervision at the field to keep order among the job seekers.

Tom set up a subsidiary mill on the job site so that lumber might be handled more efficiently and economically. At first in the early fall when the ground was dry, materials were transported by Tellepsen trucks. With the coming of the rainy season, the field became a morass, and all materials had to be sledded into place. This meant the use of tractors and was a very expensive procedure. Tom faced a tough proposition, and he and his staff worked day and night to meet the challenge.

The cost of materials began to rise due to wartime demand and Tom experienced difficulty in having lumber accepted because of excessive moisture content. The government inspectors at Ellington Field rejected load after load of precious timbers. Yet the driver would merely go on to the next project and the material would be used. In fact a driver was heard to say to a certain inspector, "You gonna inspect it? Never mind, I'll just take it over to Camp Wallace. That'll save time!"

Tellepsen Construction Company had a deadline — March, 1941 — and Colonel E. D. Dunstan of the Construction Quartermaster Corps in San Antonio made no bones about what would happen if the deadline was not met.

It was not difficult to see that the company would lose on the job, but they completed the work by March and gave a good account of themselves in excellent workmanship as well. In the meantime, jurisdiction over camp construction had been transferred to the U.S. Corps of Engineers in Galveston. The Engineers had a more realistic point of view, and, in approving of Tellepsen Construction Company they made possible a second contract to do the streets, lay utility lines and construct more buildings. On this contract, Tellepsen was able to balance out its loss on the first.

Other government contracts followed. Tellepsen Construction Company built hangars at the Bryan, Texas air field; three chapels and other buildings at Camp Hulen at Palacios, Texas; and warehouses for the navy training camp at Clinton, Oklahoma.

Tom is especially proud of the Ellington Manor housing project at Meadowbrook. Here two hundred houses were built for

127

Ellington Field officers and their families. The contract included streets, sidewalks, utilities, a playground for the children and even landscaping. Against a background of pines and oaks, it was a most attractive layout. The project amounted to a million and a half dollars, and Tom managed to save the government ten per cent of the estimated cost, or one hundred and fifty thousand dollars. Here Tom learned a sad political lesson that he has never quite forgotten: it isn't always the best man who gets the government nod, but more often the one with the most active political connections. Tom had been called to Washington and asked for a cost estimate on Ellington Manor. The work would be on a fee basis. He later learned that a similar project had been let in Dallas for a like estimate, only there the builder, instead of saving the government ten per cent, exceeded his estimate by ten per cent. But who then was approached to construct other housing projects in Texas? The Dallas man!

Camps were being scheduled for all over the Gulf Coast, and the estimating staff at Tellepsen Construction Company worked day and night. Cots were moved in to permit a quick nap in the otherwise uninterrupted procession of figures. Howard had been graduated from Georgia Tech, receiving a reserve commission of second lieutenant, and he expected to be called into active service. But Howard was the one who spearheaded the whole estimating brigade at Tellepsen Construction Company and Tom didn't see how he could do without him. Tom assumed all responsibility in deciding what should be done. He talked first to Army personnel in San Antonio and even went to Washington. Here he was advised that Howard should forego his commission, stay in Texas and continue building for the more vital war needs of the United States. Tom persuaded Howard that in this way he could more directly and effectively serve his country. In reality, he would contribute more in doing what he knew best which was construction and this was what Uncle Sam needed so desperately, and in a larger sense, construction ultimately won the war. Regretfully, Howard finally agreed. He redoubled his efforts, and it seemed to Tom he never rested. Tom recalls one instance when Howard, coming from the site of a new job at Camp Wallace, was due in San Antonio on another bid at nine the next morning. It was late at night, and he scarcely had enough time to shower, dress and be off. He was alone at home and decided to chance a brief nap before leaving. He, like his father, was a fast driver, and he'd figured the time carefully. So exhausted was he, that, in spite of the alarm clock, he slept through,

128

and when he awoke it was nine o'clock or the time he should have been in San Antonio.

Matagorda Peninsula and Matagorda Island are part of the Gulf Coast hem line of Texas. Only a small cartilage of land connects the peninsula to the mainland just below Sargent. The narrow strip of land then runs many miles with the Gulf on one side and Matagorda Bay on the other, finally pointing a skinny finger towards Matagorda Island which continues down the coast. The end of the peninsula and the opposite end of the island are the site of the Matagorda Air Base which Tellepsen Construction Company built in 1942. This was the largest over-all job for the company up to this time.

It was to be an interesting job but a provocative one. Not only was the field to be a self-contained unit with barracks, mess halls, hospitals, etc., but a small counterpart had first to be provided to house the workmen on both peninsula and island, with segregated areas for the Negro laborers. Men and materials were boated to the job sites. Headquarters — office building and yard — were at the head of Port Lavaca Bay, some twenty miles from the peninsula-island. Barges, towed by tugs, transported materials from the storage yard at Port Lavaca, which was supplied by a railroad spur, to storage yards on the island and peninsula. Cranes were required for much of the loading and unloading.

Four motor boats were purchased to take supervisory personnel, inspectors, etc., to the job. Two shrimp boats were under lease to do nothing but convey the workers back and forth. Labor turnover ranged to 700 per cent in the eight months during which the air base was built. Top employment was around 1,100 men. Personnel was recruited from all over the state of Texas; constant advertising was necessary to fill the vacancies. It was an exasperating situation; a large number were shiftless, working only until they had enough money to quit. Pay for the ten-hour working day was good. Yet it was the custom of some to sign on for the weekend, taking advantage of overtime, and to lay off the following Monday. And there were other considerations which complicated the labor situation. Living on the island was a rugged experience. Mosquitoes came in droves, and although the men slept under mosquito nets, working and moving about on calm days was very unpleasant. On such occasions, they breathed mosquitoes like smoke. Then, too, there were problems of food and drink. Dysentery was prevalent, from what source it was never clearly determined. Great care in purification was taken, but

129

the crowded conditions made it difficult to be perfectly sterile. Two doctors and nurses were in constant attendance at both peninsula and island. Serious cases were flown out by plane to nearby hospitals on the mainland. None of the men were critically ill, but it was an epidemic that weakened and distressed. Morale was low. The psychological factor of fear, too, worked among the men. Shortly after the job was under way, a Mexican tramp steamer was sunk off the island by a German submarine. This was not the only incident of its kind, but such events did not appear in the newspapers. The crew came ashore at Matagorda in life boats, and the half-sunken hull was visible to the workmen. Half the camp quit at this time. Later on, gear from a Swedish vessel was washed up on the shore. No boat was seen, but rumor spread.

It would be hard to imagine a more hectic situation, and building under such conditions taxed the drive and ingenuity of the supervisory staff. Their experiences, too, were often in the category of danger and adventure. The Garwood cabin cruiser *TC2,* traveling at high speed, hit a submerged boiler in Port Lavaca Bay. They were out of traffic lanes temporarily to avoid target practice of training planes from Victoria. The occupants of the motorboat half-swam, half-waded ashore. They recall, "The rats swam alongside."

And the time deadline was inexorable. Tom was constantly being reminded of this fact by visiting Army representatives who, in reviewing labor difficulties, were doubtful if the camp would be ready on time.

Tom set himself a demanding schedule. He visited the job twice a week; this meant leaving home at 3 a.m. and arriving at the dock in time to catch the 6 a.m. boat taking the superintendent and his staff to the island. He would stay at the job until the boat returned in the evening and would not arrive back in Houston until ten or eleven o'clock that night. It was summer time, and it is characteristic of Mr. Tom that, in spite of the worries and anxieties, he remembers the early morning drives with pleasure. Many times the sun would be rising as the moon was descending — often both over water, as the coastal road he took crossed many causeways and the water washed on both sides, sometimes sending soft spray into his face. The physical beauty of the landscape, the feeling of closeness to God that such quiet moments always brought, served as an inspiration to face the difficulties and the problems he knew he must overcome.

Altar of the Church of the Redeemer

The Church of the Redeemer

Lorraine, Mrs. Tom, Hortense

The Tellepsen Family, 1918

The Tellepsen Family with Katjie Tharp
and Mrs. Clicquennoi, 1918

The Tellepsen Family, 1956

House and Yard—4518 Park Drive

It seemed that he was always met by a delegation, bearing their complaints. On the occasion when Superintendent Fred Glaser was ill and had to be taken by plane to the hospital in Victoria, Tom was told, "The whole camp is about to die."

But no one did die, and the air base was built, and built well, and completed ahead of schedule. Tom was told that this was something of a record. It was the only base built within the time allotted!

It was fortunate for Tellepsen Construction Company that this was so. The Army eagerly moved into the camp shortly after completion. A hurricane hit the Texas coast soon thereafter. The camp was evacuated except for one officer who suffered a mental breakdown after the experience. The buildings withstood the several feet of water that covered the installation, but there was considerable damage to the roofs. Tom was given a verbal order to make the necessary repairs. Tellepsen facilities at Port Lavaca had taken a severe beating in the hurricane. The tidal waters had, in fact, demolished the warehouse building. The cement sacks stored therein became chunks of rock. However, Tellepsen was able to muster a repair crew, and the Army was soon able to reoccupy the base.

The check from the government for $1,200,000 for storm damage was taken by Mr. Tom to the City National Bank of Houston, of which he was then a director. Reminiscent of the occasion of his 1909 deposit of three one thousand dollar bills, this deposit created quite a furor: it was the largest single deposit in the City National up to that time.

Tellepsen Construction Company bid on war projects other than camps and air bases. Several of these were government-sponsored petroleum and chemical plants. At first, Tellepsen built conventional structures, such as office buildings, but through these contacts, they became aware that there was opening up a new and exciting field of opportunity in plant construction and installation. This would require designing and engineering, especially for the youthful chemical industry. Recognizing the similarity that existed between petroleum and chemical plants, a division of Tellepsen Construction Company was formed in 1943 to devote itself entirely to this field. It later adopted the name Tellepsen Petro-Chem Constructors. Thus the Tellepsen Construction Company, known previously only as *general contractors,* expanded their title and became *contractors and engineers* offering "complete design, engineering and

131

construction of petroleum, chemical and gasoline plants and allied types of installations." It was a long step forward.

The initial job of this nature was an acid regenerating plant in Beaumont, Texas, for the Southern Acid & Sulphur Company. Today, thirteen years later, Tellepsen Construction Company is considered one of the leading contractors capable of building in the petro-chemical field. National magazines and trade journals such as the *Petroleum Refiner* advertise this fact.

For some eleven years Tellepsen Construction Company maintained a branch office in Freeport, Texas, site of the Texas Division of the Dow Chemical Company. Maintenance as well as new structures were bid on by Tellepsen. The branch office was discontinued in 1953, but work is still being done for Dow from a field office in Freeport. The cordial relations between Tellepsen Construction Company and Dow Chemical Company attest to the mutual respect and benefit derived from this association.

A recent development in the petro-chem field is original research and pilot plant operation involving treatment of natural gas. Tellepsen Construction Company is also interested in a generally similar project at Llano Grande in West Texas. Tom Tellepsen and Tellepsen Construction Company are pioneering.

Pioneering, too, in other countries in the Western Hemisphere. In 1952 a subsidiary company, Tellepsen de Mexico, built the first Frasch method sulphur plant in Mexico:

The bow of the boat thudded against the rope buffer on the wharf. Tom pushed his vizored cap back from his forehead. It was hot and the humidity was oppressive. The Tehuantepec Isthmus was some 15° closer to the Equator than Houston.

"Welcome to San Cristobal, the future sulphur capital of Mexico, Mr. Tom." Lyle de Witt extended his hand in greeting and to assist Tom to the dock.

Tom grinned and soon forgot his discomfort in a tour of the plant. Everything seemed to be running smoothly. Materials were sometimes delayed as they had to be barged from Coatzacoalcos. De Witt and his staff made the trip daily by boat. Common labor had been easy to find, and most of the men lived with their families in a nearby village.

"Got a surprise for you, Mr. Tom. We've been invited to lunch in the village. Then you can say you've eaten real Indian food in an authentic adobe hut."

Tom was amused by the bright-eyed, round-faced children who seemed to peer from every corner. The primitive, straw-roofed hut had a dirt floor, but the surface was hard and seemed dustless. The guests were provided with camp stools, hastily recruited from the job. The food was served by dark-skinned women who never raised their downcast eyes, and from what Tom could tell, never changed expression. The basic tortilla baked over the coals was more tender than Tom remembered its American version. The dish — something "con pollo," which Tom recognized as chicken, was tasty, although rather highly seasoned for Norwegian taste.

It was all very interesting. With his innate delight at places and people, Tom relished the contrasts the scene before him brought to mind. It was as if he were in a different world, in a different century.

But Tom Tellepsen was not to find this job any more profitable, dollar-wise, than his previous experiences in Mexico. This time, the fault lay not with the Mexican authorities, but with a promotional scheme that had originated in the United States.

Tom had no way of knowing that his company's interest in the petro-chemical field would ever require that he volunteer as ballast. But so it did. It all came about in this way.

In 1951 an affiliate company had been organized in Venezuela, to be known as Trans-Caribbean S.A. Mr. J. G. Coultrup, who originally headed the petro-chem division of Tellepsen Construction Company, took charge of the new venture. The first client was Shell Oil Company and the first job was to construct a five and a half mile dike along the banks of Lake Maracaibo, where withdrawal of oil and caving in of sand formations caused subsidence of the ground and threatened swamping of the oil field area.

Shades of Corpus Christi! The second job required the laying of pipe in water. In this instance the pipe measured up to 30″ in diameter, and the water of Lake Maracaibo was up to 60′ deep. Actually, the job was bid by Tellepsen Construction Company, who also had a license to operate in Venezuela. The job was then sublet to Trans-Caribbean and consisted of fabricating and laying

133

61,500 feet of pipe line for a gas-gathering system to serve a gas conservation plant in the Bolivar coastal field for Creole Petroleum
Corporation, a subsidiary of Standard Oil of New Jersey.

Tom had followed developments with more than usual interest:

The plane dipped slightly, and Tom executed a
half skip to avoid stumbling. The plane carried a cargo of elbows.

"Elbows," Tom grinned to himself, looking over at
the eight-foot sections of pipe, curved slightly. Their open ends
measured 30" in diameter. "These are elbows for the armor of
a giant."

This was an emergency run. The Trans-Caribbean
crew needed these fittings and in a hurry. Those that had been
furnished by the owner, as was customary, were defective, and an
S.O.S. had gone out to the Houston office to secure the correct
fittings. These had been supplied near Milwaukee, trucked to
Chicago because the local airstrip could not accommodate the
plane that Tellepsen had chartered from Slick Airways, Inc. It
was a constellation, with a greater wingspread and perhaps some
ten feet longer than a regular transport.

The elbows nestled together in a neat geometric pattern and were web-strapped to the plane. There was a space in
back where you could walk, a chair or two and a water cooler,
but going from the quarters in the tail to the cockpit meant
literally stepping from one rounded surface of pipe to the next.
This required agility, balance and constant alertness to the
rhythm of flying.

The plane had stopped over in Houston to clear
customs and to fuel and take on the necessary supply of high
octane gas that weighed almost as much as the cargo. The pilot
informed Tom that the plane could carry up to three hundred
additional pounds.

He inquired, "Anyone want to go along?"

"There's your chance," Kruse said. Since early morning they had been standing by for the arrival of the plane, and
it would be noon before take-off. Tom had been wanting to
visit the job for some time. Regular flights took up to twenty
hours with layovers in New Orleans and Caracas. Now he could
go direct in less than seven hours. It was too good an opportunity

to miss. Tom couldn't resist; he went, and thus began, as he puts it, his "promenade over pipe."

Ironically, when the final estimate of weight was certified, so close was the figure to the maximum that it was thought convenient to omit the listing of the sandwiches carried on the flight!

Tom had no worries about the caliber of the plane's complement of officers. This consisted of Slick's chief pilot and three other top pilots — none of whom had been in Venezuela and who wanted to go along for the ride.

Tom reached a seat beside the co-pilot. It was already dusk and he knew that no planes landed at the Maracaibo airport after dark. Looking down on the indistinct blotch that was the beginning of Lake Maracaibo, Tom wondered if Coultrup had been able to keep the custom officials overtime in order to clear him so that he might go on to the Trans-Caribbean camp and marine terminal, which was located on the shores of the lake to the south of the city. A Creole truck would be waiting to transport the precious cargo, and Tom was anxious to be on hand for the morning's operations.

The plane circled and Tom settled himself for the landing. As he swung down from the side opening, he saw Coultrup and a group of men standing by the sheds to greet him. "All is well," he thought, with the pleasant excitement of a successful flight, and in anticipation of the morrow.

Tom found sleeping accommodations in one of the four-man cottages. Besides office and shops, the camp boasted a mess hall, a house for the superintendent, and a number of these cottages for the crew. "The bathrooms are not exactly A-one," thought Tom the next morning. "Let's see — towel racks..." Mentally he made note of certain improvements to make the quarters more livable.

He was soon aboard one of the tugs towing the pontoons on which rested the mile-long sections of prepared pipe. These were made up of 40' pieces of pipe that had been welded together, cleaned, wrapped, "doped," reinforced with wire mesh before being encased in four inches of concrete. The weight of the section was considerable, and towing was difficult. Once at location, the end of the line previously laid was raised and the new section joined to it in a manner similar to the original fabrication.

The wash of the water against the side of the tug reminded Tom of the beginning of the job, when equipment worth more than half a million dollars was put on a barge to be taken to Venezuela. The transportation fee was a whopping thirty-two thousand dollars. The converted oil barge measured up to 220 feet but proved not to be seaworthy. Scarcely had it reached open water than the force of the wave action split off the bow up to the bulkhead, a distance of approximately twenty feet. The tug was able to reach Morgan City, Louisiana, and to limp into New Orleans. With the delay for repairs, it had taken three weeks for the equipment to reach Venezuela. Yesterday he had flown over in some six and a half hours. Tom frowned.

"Ah, well," he said aloud, "it's all in doing something new." The sound of his voice was dwarfed by the noise of cable bringing up the pipe. The captain looked up inquiringly, but Tom shook his head and smiled.

There were to be other occasions of an exasperating nature. A clerk's oversight was to cost Trans-Caribbean $40 a day — in interest on $300,000 which represented a ten per cent hold-back on final payment pending acceptance after completion. The job was finished and approved. But the check was not forthcoming. Finally, a wire to the New York office of Creole Petroleum Corporation brought action, and a duplicate check was immediately remitted. The original had been carefully and neatly pigeonholed while a clerk was on his vacation!

Tellepsen Construction Company was one member of a syndicate of seven concerns bidding on the Falcon Dam project, the second largest earth-fill dam in the world. The others were: C. F. Lytle (Sioux City); Foley Bros. (St. Paul); Edward Peterson Company (Omaha); Massman Construction Company (Kansas City); San Ore Construction Company (McPherson, Kansas); Amis Construction Company (Oklahoma City), and their engineers used the Tellepsen Construction Company Houston office as headquarters in preparing their estimate. Falcon Dam Constructors, as well as Constructora Intercontinental S.A., their Mexican counterpart, were low bidders.

The dam was a cooperative project of the United States and Mexico and had been negotiated through the International Boundary and Water Commission. It was not entirely completed by

136

the date of the dedication, which had been set well in advance at the convenience of President Dwight D. Eisenhower and President Adolfo Ruiz Cortines.

Officers of the syndicate companies were on the official guest list for the dedication. The Tellepsen party had driven to McAllen the night before the dedication, and the next morning they flew to the construction camp where they had accommodations for the day at the guest house. Besides Tom and Ingeborg, there were Howard and his wife, June, and children; Karen, Howard, Jr., and Tom. Also in the group were E. E. Gose, Jr., and his family, Mr. and Mrs. Jim Keith and Mr. and Mrs. W. A. Abrams.

The children were especially excited at the prospect of seeing the President:

Tom fingered the folded paper Karen had given him. He remembered with a sudden twinge how dismayed she'd been when he tried to discourage her. "I don't think I'll have a chance to talk to the President." "Please, please, granddaddy, *you* can!" Hope restored the glow to her pixie face. Who could refuse such confidence?

And he had tried. Dale Miller of San Ore Construction Company gave him encouragement. As invited guests of the President, they were seated army-style, in a huge tent at the camp set up for the troops accompanying the President. There were hundreds of people being served a sumptuous meal, complete to champagne. Tom could see President Eisenhower and President Cortines and other dignitaries and officials exchanging informal toasts. "There seems to be no lack of understanding — language or otherwise," thought Tom.

At Miller's insistence, they made their way to the front table. Governor Allan Shivers was seated at the end, and on impulse Tom stopped and spoke to him, explaining his mission.

"Someday you'll have a grandchild, too," he reminded the Governor, who smiled back in agreement.

"And I'd want to do for mine as you do yours, Tellepsen," he said, "but I'm afraid this isn't the time. It would disrupt proceedings even if they let me ask him, and if he gave one autograph, there'd be requests for a hundred more - - - you understand. But I promise you I'll get little Karen the autograph somehow, sometime soon. You tell her that." And Tom had to be satisfied, not knowing that the Governor would, in the course of time, send him two pages of Mrs. Shivers' stationery on which President Eisenhower had penned his name.

After lunch Tom and Miller hurried out on the bridge and took seats in front of the dais where the presidents were to speak. They were only ten or fifteen feet from the lectern. This was the boundary between the United States and Mexico — halfway across the dam. The American and Mexican flags stood side by side, their colors intermingling. Here also were poised the two monuments, still veiled.

The bands began to play. As Tom looked out over the lake already filling behind the dam, he could see sailboats and motorboats making irregular patterns across the slight rippling the wind was making in the water.

Loud clapping interspersed the martial music and the presidents made their way to the center of the platform. First, President Eisenhower addressed them. Then President Cortines spoke in Spanish, and Tom could grasp only scattered words and phrases, but he was fascinated by watching the American President's mobile face. He smiled and nodded or contorted heavy brows in concentration, following the musical syllables which he seemed to understand.

The building of the dam closed out as a financial loss to the syndicate of some two million dollars. There were several reasons for this. Difficulty in getting materials was one: for example, priority in reinforcing steel was not adequate to supply the job. Then, too, there were constant engineering changes in the plans, and these caused delay and expensive alterations. In all, it was a year past the originally scheduled date of completion before the project was finished. Then the ironic "last straw" was an unfavorable drop in exchange: seven pesos to one dollar dropped to twelve to one, which represented an outright loss of over two hundred thousand dollars. The syndicate has filed a claim for losses due to delay and circumstances which they considered the liability of the governments as represented by the International Boundary and Water Commission.

Restitution will no doubt be long drawn out, if not meager. But there was little postponement in the obvious benefit of the dam. Soon after the dedication in 1953, floods of the upper Rio

138

Grande filled the reservoir to capacity, a feat it would ordinarily take years to accomplish. Experts claim the savings in flood damage to the lower Valley alone have already repaid the cost of the dam. Add to this the value of water conservation and waterpower potential, and the importance of the project can hardly be overemphasized.

When speaking of dams, and the Texarkana Dam Constructors (Tellepsen Construction Company and two of its Falcon associates) were low bidders on a project to dam the Sulphur River in northeast Texas, Mr. Tom is apt to stress the word unduly, but on purpose. The contract called for outfall structure with machine house and gates, concrete spillway and dirt dam amounting to four million cubic yards of fill.

Tom's associates insisted that a Tellepsen man, Lindsey Hall, be superintendent. However, they outvoted Hall's recommended estimate, which was $250,000 more than the figure finally bid. Contention arose early in the project, and the associates reversed their opinion of Hall, demanding that he be replaced. Tom refused, and instead bought them out on the basis of the bid and including their proportionate share of anticipated profit. Only there wasn't any profit. Tellepsen went on to finish the contract in a manner which reflected credit upon the company. The loss approximated $250,000, due principally to difficulties over engineering details and changes. Had Hall's estimate prevailed, there would not have been a loss, and the bid would have been low anyway. This kind of hindsight irony is quite typical of the construction business, as we have seen.

Perhaps here is a good place to insert a bit of parenthetical comment on the nature of this business. It may by now be obvious to the reader, but nevertheless bears repetition.

All business ventures are a gamble in the sense that the end result is unpredictable, but we can conclude from what we have learned of Tom's adventures, that the odds in construction are long odds. Kruse had cause to chuckle in recalling the day Tom happened upon a group of workmen shooting craps. Tom was audibly distressed — not so much at the breaking of company rules but at the venturing of their hard earned wages on chance! "And you, a contractor," Kruse could not resist the ribbing. Tom grinned in acknowledgment that chance, indeed, had contrived to lose a hand for many a contractor — even him!

Of course all jobs can't lose money, or the contractor couldn't stay in business. Some jobs make money, some lose, some break even. Tom considers himself very fortunate that not until

1933, when he was forty-five years old, did a job actually lose money. In this instance, work had to be done by hand when Tom had figured to use machinery in laying a water line under the railroad tracks of the Houston Belt & Terminal Railway on Texas Avenue. The error lay in inaccurate drawings by the City of its water and sewer system. Tom had no recourse.

Prior to this there had been certain, shall we say "exaggerated," expenses due to the quirks of the trade. For example, back in the twenties Kruse and Tom had bid and were low by $20,000 on the construction of the Crockett Street bridge. They were elated since, having completed the second ice plant for Bill Irvin, they needed to locate their equipment and surplus lumber. Tom had no yard or storage facilities at the time. Tom talked to the mayor about moving to the job site and was told to go ahead. However, the job after an interval of weeks was not officially let. Tom became aware that material was being stolen and he posted a watchman. The delay was expensive. He had given a certified check with his bid and thus his funds were impounded. He went to the mayor again and the latter alibied that right-of-way and pro rata costs were not as yet cleared by the Katy railroad whose tracks would run under the proposed bridge. Tom knew C. E. Schaff, president of the Katy, and appealed to him, only to learn that the railroad had long since fulfilled what was expected of it. The mayor was still evasive but permitted Tom to substitute a bidder's bond and thus retrieve his check. Nothing was done until one year later when new bids were required. Tom put in a bid identical to his previous one and this time was $20,000 over the low bidder. Actually the bridge cost well over $20,000 in extras. This experience cost Tom some $6,000 in expenses incurred to bid and lose this one particular job. Yet, by comparison, this was a mere drop in the dragline bucket!

In 1951 Tellepsen Construction Company lost a million dollars gross! Yet the year showed only a small net loss. Reasons for losses are various: sometimes it is due to errors in estimating; sometimes in construction procedures or personnel; sometimes bad luck. Yet Tom has never failed to finish a job awarded to him, and only once did he ask to be released from his contract. He was refused. In figuring a school building after World War II, the estimator inadvertently omitted the totals of three pages of foundation costs. The PWA official in Dallas agreed to resubmit, but the Pasadena school board held Tom to his bid. Tom built the school and took the loss.

On the other hand, there are jobs such as the one early in 1954 when Tellepsen Construction Company was asked to bid on a marine job at Lake Charles, Louisiana. It involved laying 8"pipe under the Intracoastal Canal. The Tellepsen bid ran around $20,000. Nothing came of it until eight months later when Tellepsen Construction Company was approached to submit a new bid. Somehow Tom was not too impressed with the prospects, yet a hunch nudged him on.

"If caissons can't be used, we'll have to get divers," he told Abrams, who had prepared a tentative estimate.

"And that's not only dangerous but expensive," was the latter's comment. Tom agreed.

"What's your figure?" he asked.

"$34,000."

"O.K. turn in a bid at $45,000."

Tellepsen Construction Company was notified they were low bidders. Did they want the job? Tom made one of his quick trips and sized up the situation. He accepted the job. It took divers, yes, and three weeks. Tom cleared $29,000.

Yet there were other debits, not only *on* paper, but *in* paper. In recent years the timber of East Texas has brought a comparative boom to the area in the manufacture of paper products. Tellepsen Construction Company was awarded the prime contract to build a $30,000,000 wood pulp and paper plant at Evadale, which plant is owned jointly by Time, Inc. and the Houston Oil Company of Texas. Initial work was delayed from May to September because of labor difficulties. Completion goal was December, 1954, so that the merchandise might be advertised as available in January of 1955. Although plagued with continuing labor demands and disputes, the engineers, contractor and owners exerted every effort to meet the deadline. To Tellepsen, this meant overtime and overmanning, which proved very expensive. The roll reached fifteen hundred men, and a weekly payroll figure of $155,000, the highest in Tellepsen history for any one job. The job had been awarded on a fixed fee basis. Tom shrugs his shoulders and points to the sad but significant fact that by December 1954, $20,000 worth of small tools had disappeared. The East Texas Pulp and Paper plant is a credit to East Texas and will give employment to hundreds of workers. Nearby towns have already felt a favorable impetus in business due to housing projects, etc.

Perhaps the greatest world-wide recognition given Tom and Tellepsen Construction Company was in connection with the building of the fabulous Shamrock now the Shamrock Hilton. This hotel is famous in its own right as well as famous for its colorful ex-owner, Glenn McCarthy. It was well publicized in Tom's native land, and he received many letters from all over the world because of it.

The opening was scheduled for March 17 (St. Patrick's Day) 1949:

It was March 15. Heavy seasonal rains had made an unplanned lake out of the hotel grounds. Landscaping under such conditions was difficult. As Tom sloshed through the mud, he reflected on the luck of the Irish. "Maybe it has something to do with this being Texas and not Ireland," he thought grimly.

Tellepsen Construction Company draglines were engaged in planting jumbo-size palm trees around the pool. It was a rather unorthodox request, but Tom had agreed, knowing the anxiety of the nursery men and the hotel staff that all should be in readiness before the lavish celebration.

Besides, as Tom looked back over the past two years, his association with architect, owner, superintendents, inspectors, subcontractors, etc., had been very harmonious — extraordinarily so, in fact. Mr. A. G. McNeese, Jr., attorney and representative for McCarthy, had cooperated in every respect with Tellepsen Construction Company and made the relationship a very pleasant one. H. F. (Red) Ulrich, vice president of Tellepsen Construction Company, had spearheaded the construction and done an outstanding job. The name of Tellepsen Construction Company on the cornerstone as general contractor had meant and would mean excellent publicity for the company. It was a beautiful modern hotel, unique in Houston and the Gulf Coast. If all the witches could brew was a little wet weather, they did not succeed in dampening Tom's spirits!

"And Ingeborg and the girls in their new evening dresses," thought Tom complacently, "can just step out of the car into the garage and slip into the hotel without endangering a single spangle."

It was a "gala affair." Tom was as much a star as Pat O'Brien or Dorothy Lamour or Leo Carillo.

Tom had less formidable competition for star status five days later when he celebrated his sixty-first birthday at The Shamrock. The music of Russ Morgan and his orchestra was being broadcast over a national network. Tom was startled to hear, as part of the program, the announcement of his birthday party - - - "Tom Tellepsen, builder of The Shamrock" and the band blared forth a rousing "Happy Birthday to you." The waiter brought to his long table a festooned birthday cake, whose candles flickered in the elegant gloom of the Emerald Room. Later, dancing with Mrs. M. D. Carlisle, one of the guests, Tom remarked, "It's like old times," referring to the early 1930's when Tom was known as the best foxtrotter in that congenial group of friends who met weekly for an evening of dancing, cards and good fellowship.

The Tellepsen sign with its trademark has in recent years been a familiar sight on Houston downtown streets. Battlestein's Inc., Sakowitz Bros., Melrose Building, Houston Bank & Trust Company, City National Bank Garage, etc., are among the most prominent buildings constructed by Tellepsen. The twenty-two story Melrose Building was noteworthy in that it was financed as well as built by Tellepsen Construction Company. On this occasion they dealt with banks in New York. The loan they negotiated amounted to five million dollars. This is quite a contrast to the $600 Tom borrowed in 1914 from his fishing pal, Richard Krupp, and which permitted him to complete the Dubard Building and get a new start as a contractor.

Tom speaks with considerable pride of other construction jobs, notably:

The Houston Coca-Cola plant he considers "one of the most, if not the most, outstanding in the world."

The modern plant of the world-famous Schlumberger Well Surveying Corporation, pioneers in oil well logging, consists of office building and shops, including facilities for manufacture of their highly technical instruments. There is also an equipment-testing laboratory, where pressures up to 25,000 pounds per inch approximate bottom-hole conditions.

A new addition to the renowned Texas Medical Center is the ultramodern Medical Towers — seventeen stories of doctors' offices. Tellepsen Construction Company was already represented at the Center by their "at cost" construction of the Childrens' and St. Luke's Hospitals. During the 1956 campaign for polio funds, the uncompleted Medical Towers bore a 179' x 12' x 8' sign proclaiming "Boost the 1956 March of Dimes." How typical of the Tellepsens!

Another beautiful and modernistic building (1956) is the Mayfair Apartments at 1600 Holcombe Boulevard. The striking facade is similar to that of the Melrose Building and Medical Towers. The window-wall front is fabricated of aluminum windows and frames (to the floor) and porcelain enamel panels.

In 1949 Tellepsen Construction Company moved from its several-times remodeled office and warehouse at the Clay Avenue location. Tom calls the present installation at 1710 Telephone Road "ideal, well located and suitable for the construction business." The office and warehouse employ approximately 125 men and women. The warehouse boasts over sixteen thousand square feet and houses small tools, supplies, etc. The machine shop's modern facilities fabricate light structural steel as well as repair almost all company equipment, automobiles, and trucks. The planing mill prefabricates forms, etc. A pipe fabricating plant on Holmes Road took over men and equipment when Tellepsco Industrial Piping Company, a Freeport affiliate, was dissolved in 1953. Thus Tellepsen Construction Company facilities are extensive.

"Mr. Tom's" Bank

One might think it a far cry from an icehouse to a bank. Still, the underworld has certain slang expressions referring to the monetary value of "ice." Yet it was through building an icehouse that Mr. Tom became interested in banking.

W. H. "Bill" Irvin asked for bids on a five-story ice plant and warehouse to be built on Hemphill Street just off Washington Avenue. Tom was low bidder. The relationship of ice and highballs is more obvious, and it was when the owner, architects and Tom met to discuss their plans, that Tom was induced to take his first drink of hard liquor. He was thirty-two years old.

"Tellepsen," Irvin waved aside Tom's refusal, "You've got to be sociable, be a regular fellow. It goes with the job. Now sit down and have a drink with us."

Reluctantly Tom took the glass. The liquid burned his throat, and he choked. Instantly he retched and grabbed for his handkerchief. His sputtering and coughing mingled with the audible amusement of the older men.

"Now or never," Irvin thrust the glass towards Tom.

Tom steeled himself. This time he managed to keep it down. Irvin regarded him. "I'm going to like you, Tellepsen," he said.

And what was more, Bill Irvin learned to respect Tom and to admire his painstaking work. This was 1920 and Tom himself

145

supervised the building of the plant. One day when they were in the last stage of construction, Irvin asked Tom if the hoisting tower might not be removed as he was ready to put the delivery platform into operation, and the tower was in the way. Tom agreed and instructed his men.

Next day, Tom was met by an irate Irvin. "Well, Tom, there's your tower, still standing! You said you'd have it down by today."

Tom's shoulders squared as they always did when he was under fire. "Bill," he said, "that tower will be down in two hours."

"Ha," was all that Irvin would say.

Tom called over the Negro watchman and himself wielding a wrecking bar, he soon had the man carrying and stacking the dismantled timbers as he feverishly jerked them loose. Tom was strong and his will was stronger. That hundred-foot tower was wrecked in an hour and a half. Irvin had been unbelieving, but was boisterous in his approval.

"Tom, you old son of a gun," he said, "I didn't think you could do it. For my money, you're the one to do any work I need done — and that's what you'll do it for I reckon — my money," and Irvin chortled at his own joke.

But Irvin meant it and in February of 1921, Tom was summoned to build a second ice plant near the bridge on Jensen Drive (then Hill Street) over Buffalo Bayou. According to Irvin, Tom could do no wrong, and he *could* do the impossible. "Say, Tom, I want to change the name of this plant to the *Zero Ice Factory, Inc. (1921)*." Tom surveyed the neat lettering on the wall - - - *W. H. Irvin Ice Company.*

"The plasterers are on strike, Bill," he said.

"Well, do it yourself," replied Irvin impatiently. "It won't be the first time. And I want it done right away!"

The roof extended over the platform and Tom climbed up — suspending a plank to raise him to the height of the lettering. He chiseled the unwanted letters and carefully set the fresh cement. With a pattern cut from cardboard he laboriously traced the long name. It was a precise job and done in probably less time than it would have taken a plasterer. This is just another example of Mr. Tom's self-practiced preaching, "You can do anything you put your mind to."

146

The letters are still exceptionally clear cut. In fact the plant is in excellent condition. It is a significant commentary that most of Tom's early buildings are well preserved today — the Montrose houses, the Dubard Building, Miller Memorial, to mention only a few. It must be that the sound construction and loving care that went into them has been recognized by their owners — who, in turn, were inspired to maintain the standards set by the builder.

But to return to the circuitous route by which Mr. Tom became involved in banking, Bill Irvin held a block of stock in the Gulf States Bank and served as honorary vice president. Along in 1923 he was approached by the Board of Directors of the Citizens State Bank to be their president. He sought out his good friend, Tom Tellepsen.

"Tom," he said, "I can't serve two masters. I can't stay in both banks. I want you to buy my stock in the Gulf States Bank — for what I paid for it, mind you, and you take my place as honorary vice president.

Tom protested. "I can't, Bill. I don't know anything about banking, or being a director — far less being a vice president."

"There's nothing to it, Tom. You're a good business man, and you've had a lot of dealings with banks as a client. It'll help you along. You've got to take my place."

Bill Irvin was as stubborn as Tom, and very persuasive, and besides, banking was glamorous to Tom. He had never forgotten the respect given to three one thousand dollar bills. "Banker," he thought. "It has dignity and stability — and I will be in a position to help others." Never was this ambition far from his mind.

"All right, Bill," he said gravely, "but you'll have to teach me the ropes."

The Gulf States Bank was located in what is now the West Building. As Mr. Tom pushed open the doors of the bank, he thought back to the days when the building was first constructed, and he was a carpenter fitting lumber for the foundation forms. "Well," he thought, as he joined the other directors in the conference room for his first directors' meeting, "this is a foundation of another sort." At the head of the table sat D. S. Cage who was president of the bank. Cage was one of those farsighted men responsible for the Harris County-Houston Ship Channel Navigation District. For seventeen years he was to serve as member first of the Harbor Board, later the Board of Directors of the Navigation District. Tom had known him when he built the Long Reach Wharf, and he had, in fact, at that time transferred some of his banking business to the Gulf States Bank.

Eli Marks was executive vice president of the bank at this time. To give financial advice and assistance, it is necessary that a banker know his client's character and his client's business. Tom discussed his construction problems with Marks and the two became fast friends. Together with Dr. P. A. Sloane they were to form a congenial triumvirate. The men — one a banker, one a doctor, one a contractor — were different also in racial background — Jewish, Irish, Norwegian — and yet they had humanity in common. Each in his own way had dedicated his life, directly or indirectly, to helping other people.

One December 24 Tom was in the bank on business, and looking across the crowded banking floor, he saw Dr. Sloane, who was also a customer of the bank. Tom hailed him. "Perce," he said, "let's get Eli and have lunch together."

Marks protested. "Boys, I'd like to, but this is the day before Christmas — one of the bank's busiest days. Look at that mob. I don't suppose I'll get away from my desk all day."

"Oh come on, Eli," Tom was insistent. "See here — I'm a stockholder and a director. I officially request you to have lunch with us!"

Sloane grabbed Marks' hat and coat and, still objecting, he was propelled through the lobby and out the door. Thus a tradition was born. For many years until Dr. Sloane died in 1936, the three lunched together on Christmas Eve day.

Bill Irvin kept track of Tom, and when the Citizens State Bank scheduled a new building in Houston Heights, nothing would do but Tom should build it, even though he was not the low bidder. "Look here, Tom." Irvin's voice had that do-not-argue tone that Tom had come to recognize. "Go ahead and build it for this lower amount. You know you can do it." And Tom did. And made not a cent. His original estimate was painfully correct. "Well," said Irvin, "I won't argue with you again. You know your business all right. But thanks, Tom."

In the middle twenties the Guarantee Trust Company proposed a merger with the Gulf States Bank, which had grown to some $700-800,000 in deposits. The former had been organized by J. A. Elkins, then Harris County judge, and Willard Keeland, and had approximately $300,000 in deposits. The new bank would be known as the City Bank & Trust Company. Location would remain

148

in the West Building. The Board of Directors of the Gulf States agreed to the merger. Mr. Cage was in poor health and stepped down from the presidency in favor of Judge Elkins. Marks remained as executive vice president. The board was reorganized, and the position of honorary vice president was abolished, but Tom remained as a director and served continuously on the board until 1946.

It became immediately apparent that the accommodations in the West Building would not continue to be adequate for the thriving bank. The board of directors discussed the alternatives of enlarging their present quarters or leasing a larger building. Elkins and Tom looked over the first floor of the old Masonic Building at Main and McKinney. The occupant was Shepherd's ladies' ready-to-wear. Tom, with his happy faculty of visualizing what could be done, mentally removed partitions, added beams on a new foundation and transformed the appearance of the building. "Elkins," he said enthusiastically, "it can be done, and it will make a fine bank. It's a good location."

Arrangement was made to transfer the lease held by Shepherd's and to negotiate a ninety-nine year lease which would include an extension clause for another ninety-nine years. Remodeling began. The result was a handsome banking floor, with attention to detail of convenience and good looks. Tom was impishly content with Jesse Jones' comment, "Well, I didn't know anything like this could have been made of this building — if I had, I'd have done it myself!"

These facilities were adequate to meet a continual growth in banking activities for over a decade. The depression brought an uneasy period to Houston banking circles. At one time rumor was abroad that the City Bank & Trust Company was in difficulty, but it proved to be but a rumor. Tom persuaded his friends and business associates to deposit, rather than to withdraw.

In 1934, the Board of Directors felt it expedient to become a national bank, and the name was changed to the City National Bank of Houston. Wartime nourished the need for wider financing on the part of local industry and the bank increased its capitalization. Deposits rose from $17,000,000 in 1940 to some $117,000,000 in 1946. During this period, the bank took over the upper two floors previously occupied by offices of the Masonic lodge. The banking floor was remodeled several times to give more lobby space.

During the years, Mr. Tom had added to his ownership of stock in the bank, either by purchase of additional shares or by stock dividends declared by the bank. By 1946 he was one of the principal stockholders. He liked the atmosphere of the bank. Here he felt at home. He attended board meetings regularly and took his role of director very seriously.

Eli Marks had resigned in the early 1930's to go into the oil business, and Willard Keeland had taken his place as executive vice president. He and Tom were very close in those days, and he called Tom one of their best directors. There was something in Tom's quiet faith and assurance that invited confidence. "Never give up," said Tom, "to the idea that it won't work out. You've got to go forward. The momentum of your faith will carry you through." "Tom," said Keeland, "I don't know what I'd do without you — you're the salt of the earth."

The rift between Mr. Tom and the City National Bank that culminated in his selling his stock in 1946 and forming the East End State Bank is largely a matter of misunderstanding — a misunderstanding that has been neutralized in the intervening years. Witness the fact that Tellepsen Construction Company in 1954 was awarded the contract to enlarge the City National Bank Garage.

There was a definite need for a bank in the East End area. As has happened before, and will undoubtedly happen again, Mr. Tom's interest, drive and ambition coincided with the need. The idea took root in Mr. Tom's mind and imagination. He talked to Howard, and at the latter's suggestion, H. C. Donahoe, who was employed by Tellepsen Construction Company at this time, was sent out to contact key people in the East End area and to solicit their interest and support. In March of 1946 Mr. Donahoe went to Austin to consult Lawrence Johnson, Banking Commissioner for the state of Texas. Johnson informed him that there had already been an application for a bank in that area but that the application was over six months old and, since it had not been processed, it might be disregarded. Mr. Donahoe convinced the Commissioner of the very active intentions of the applicants he represented and came back to Houston with instructions on establishing a state bank. It was necessary to show need for a bank — a petition bearing thousands of signatures was prepared. A second requirement concerned the financial ability of the founding group; a roster of prospective stockholders was more than adequate. On May 27, a charter was granted the East End State Bank.

Notice to Stockholders was mailed May 30 and on the evening of June 7, some thirty people gathered in Tellef Hall of the Church of the Redeemer for the first stockholders' meeting. Donahoe called the meeting to order and Tom was elected chairman with S. S. McClendon, Jr. as secretary. Business necessary to the establishment of a new organization was conducted and the directors elected. It was voted to increase the board from seven to eleven. Besides Tom, E. A. Johson, Louis Dietz, R. D. Strauss, S. S. Mc-Lendon, Jr., E. A. Kruse, J. C. Suttles, E. A. Moody and C. M. Knipe were elected. R. E. Pierce and F. L. Senter later completed the board.

Tom opened the meeting with a brief talk in which he quoted United States currency, "In God We Trust." Tom's talent for judging character held him in good stead in the selection of Louis Dietz, formerly vice president of the bank at Sour Lake, Texas. Mr. Tom acted as president of the East End State Bank from 1946 to 1952, when he resigned in favor of his executive vice president, Dietz, to become chairman of the board. Dietz has proved to be outstanding in his field, well qualified and well liked. He has been ably assisted by Ralph Pierce and Ed Luton. E. A. Kruse and E. A. Johnson have been invaluable to the Board of Directors and the loan committee.

It was decided to locate the bank on Leeland Avenue and a right-hand side of the street driving towards town location was deemed most desirable. Such a site was finally obtained by Donahoe under rather amazing circumstances. Having canvassed the 4200 block without success, he was summoned for a return interview by the property owners at 4215: "We've decided to sell for the $10,000 you offered us," he was told, "right away." Hastily Donahoe scribbled an escrow agreement on a scrap of paper and reaching in his pocket, drew forth a ten dollar bill which became earnest money for the location of a bank that now has over a million dollars in capital, surplus and undivided profits! That scrap of paper rests in the vault of the bank today.

Construction of the bank building by Tellepsen Construction Company was begun immediately after purchase of the site but was interrupted by a three-month long general strike. The minutes of that initial meeting had anticipated an August first opening, but it was the eighteenth of September before the bank opened its temporary doors across the street on Leeland Avenue in the bread shop of the Fehr Baking Company. The staff of life indeed! "The Bread Box," as the employees of the bank came to call their for-the-time-being bank, was situated on the corner of Leeland and *Ingeborg*

151

Street. Yes, you guessed it, Tom had for many years owned the opposite corner where the bank's parking lot is now located.

Setting up for the first day's business was a hectic affair. All the banks in Houston, knowing Mr. Tom and Ralph Pierce, the new cashier (who had been with the State Banking Department), pitched in and lent all manner of necessary forms and personnel to help the young bank get under way.

It has become customary for members of the banking staff to remember Tom on September 18, the bank's birthday — a framed picture of the bank, a scrapbook of clippings, a watch, etc. A birthday celebration to honor the bank's opening includes the directors and all employees and their wives, husbands or escorts! Such affairs have been held at the Houston Club, The Shamrock, the Houston Country Club, Golfcrest Country Club, etc.

The second opening on December 16 in the new building was well attended and a gala affair. One of the illustrious visitors was the novelist, Garland Roark, whose sea stories remind Mr. Tom of his own adventuresome voyage as a boy. Traditionally, the employees and officers commemorate the opening on December 16 with an informal gathering at Christmas time — in recognition, too, of their Christmas bonus — one month's salary!

The new deposits on the first December 16 added substantially to the original $1,357,000. Today, these deposits total about $22,500,000 in over 15,500 accounts. Capital, surplus and undivided profits have grown from $225,000 to $1,500,000. As to total deposits the East End State Bank ranks ninth among the thirty-one banks in Houston.

In banking, Tom found the same need for working out difficult and sometimes disastrous circumstances as had been true in his construction experiences. Fortunate for the bank that he could apply here the same positive and confident approach. For example in 1947, a $40,000 loan to a millwork company proved a poor investment. Tom himself assumed the defaulted mortgage and set up his own company to carry on, adding additional capital until the amount involved totaled around $120,000. The new company, now known as Constructors, Inc., has branched into other fields and by conscientious application, the deficit has currently been brought down to below $55,000. It is a matter of time, experience and diligence, according to Tom, who is always alert to any opportunity that may have an effect on any one of the four facets of his endeavor — Tellepsen

Construction Company, the East End State Bank, the Church of the Redeemer, and Tom, personally.

Whimsically, Mr. Tom has a bent to carry over from one experience to another some talisman — in the case of banking, it was a grille. The wrought iron gate at the front of the East End State Bank came from the City National Bank when it was remodeled.

"Say," said Tom to Willard Keeland, "if you're discarding that entrance gate, I'd like to have it, and what's more I don't want to pay for it!" And the grille was his.

Then, too, early employees of the East End State Bank remember that the door to the vault was originally in the San Jacinto National Bank and had been found, a bit rusty, in a Westheimer warehouse. How typical of Mr. Tom!

Typical, too, is the gleam in Mr. Tom's eye when he talks about the future of "his" bank. "We have wonderful plans," he says. And that is basic in this man whether it be in building, in banking, in his church: there are always, and will always be wonderful plans.

"Mr. Tom's" Church

"Back of every great movement in history, back of every church building, there is a personality; back of the Church of the Redeemer is Tom Tellepsen," writes the Rev. Gordon M. Reese, who was rector at the Church of the Redeemer from 1936 to 1941. This does not mean that others in the parish, or that the churchmen themselves, had contributed little; on the contrary, there were and are generous, hard-working and consecrated men and women who were invaluable in the growth of the Church of the Redeemer, who gave of themselves as well as their substance. Tom Tellepsen would be the last to minimize their importance. But it so happened that Tom Tellepsen had the vision, the devotion, the drive, the spirit, the financial means and the contacts in business, particularly the construction business, to be in a position to do more and to thus make possible this unusual and beautiful church. It is more than coincidence that during every critical period of the church's history, the name of Tom Tellepsen can be found on the vestry roster and that for the last twenty years, he has been a delegate to the Diocesan Council of the Episcopal Churches of Texas.

In 1920-21 plans were made to build a community church in Eastwood. Mr. William A. Wilson, developer, had specified in laying out the area that a church, and only one, was to be built within the confines of Eastwood. A triangular block, bounded by Eastwood Drive, Telephone Road and Dallas Avenue was designated for the site. It was purchased for $2,000 by a group of Episcopalians headed by the Rt. Rev. Clinton S. Quin, then co-adjutor, and the Rev. Peter Gray Sears, rector of Christ Church in downtown Houston. The Rev. Valentine Lee, who had been assistant minister at

154

St. Paul's Church in Richmond, Virginia, was called to Houston as first rector. A modest rectory was built, mostly of secondhand lumber from Camp Logan, then being dismantled. Some materials were donated by the Wilson Realty Company and others. Bishop Quin and Mr. Sears assisted in raising funds to build a church and Sunday school-recreation building. Tom submitted a bid, but was not low bidder by about two thousand dollars. In his estimate, he had included additional supports to the church structure as he felt the plans were not fully adequate in his respect. After actual construction of the building was begun by Russell Brown, this inadequacy was recognized, and the added expense brought up the total cost.

When Tom and Ingeborg lived on Palmer Street, Mr. and Mrs. Cliff Jones, who lived across the street, had occasionally taken Ingeborg in their horse and buggy down to the First Christian Church. Later, Katjie Tharp, who had become Ingeborg's close friend, taught a Sunday school kindergarten in an abandoned mission on Leeland Avenue and then did the same for Christ Church downtown. She and Ingeborg began taking Howard, and later on, Hortense. The sermons of the Rev. Peter Gray Sears made a deep impression on Ingeborg. He preached "enrichment" by the teachings of Christ and not "containment" — the positive vs. the negative — the kind of spiritual approach Ingeborg had instinctively been searching for all her life.

The Church of the Redeemer was within two blocks of home, and Ingeborg attended from the first. She even taught in the kindergarten. Tom started going to church with his family, and it was he who suggested they study for confirmation and join the church together. According to Tom, from that day to the present, the Church of the Redeemer became "a part of our lives."

Tom and Ingeborg had been seeking a church which would fulfill a longing and an inner searching for a sense of the presence of God, a way of life in assurance of Grace, the adventure and knowledge of learning the deeper truths in and through our Lord, Jesus Christ. To Tom and Ingeborg, Bishop and Mrs. Quin exemplified all of this, and they will never cease thanking God for them and for all clergy who also seek to express in daily life the "whole of man" as Dr. Alexis Carrel wrote in his book *Man, the Unknown.*

The Rev. Valentine Lee stayed four years and he left his little parish well under way. The Rev. William Bratton followed him. Mr. Bratton's father was the Rt. Rev. William Bratton of Mississippi.

Bishop Bratton had interested friends and ex-schoolmates in Houston who were to figure in the well-being of his son's new parish. Through the kindness of S. R. Bertron, President of the Houston Lighting & Power Company, and financier Harry K. Johnson, the site of a camp on the San Jacinto River was offered the parish. The camp comprised ten acres and included a small lake called Lake of the Woods, which was crossed by the Baytown interurban. The site was near Highlands, about twenty miles from Eastwood. They called the camp Camp Bratton.

The rustic beauty of the camp site appealed to Tom, and he threw himself and his irresistible energies into the project. He levelled and sanded the area by the lake; he fenced the property; he built a caretaker's cabin which had all conveniences — all this at his own expense.

Howard was now in his teens and had become an active member of the Young People's Service League and had served as acolyte. The boys, including Howard, Marshall Carlisle, Jack Jacobs, Raymond Buchanan, Carl and Jesse Rogers, Orin and Roland Triay and others, formed a club later to be known as the Log Cabin Club and they decided they would like to have, besides a log cabin, a bath house and bathing pier. They talked to Tom about it. All of these boys had worked for Tom in the summer time, and he knew and liked them.

"Well," he said to them, "you're going to have to work. I'll tell you what to do but you've got to do it right." Eagerly, the boys agreed.

They felled the trees, peeled them and loaded the logs into a two-wheel cart which they took turns in pulling. Tom mixed the mortar and showed the boys how to stack and cement the logs. The floors of the cabin and bath house were concrete, and concrete steps led down to the pier. Piles were cut for the pier and jetted into the sand with a water pump. At the end of the pier they built a diving platform twenty feet high. A raft on pontoons was constructed and anchored out in the lake. A tow rope reached from the raft to the pier so the non-swimmers could get back and forth from deep water. There were even small rowboats.

One summer when the work was at its peak, Tom stayed away from the office for three days and camped on the site for the three nights so that the work might be finished. It was a wonderful experience for the youngsters. They were working together for a worthwhile reason; they learned to be self-reliant and they had fun doing it. It was wholesome recreation. Many of the Eastwood children learned to swim here, as the camp was not exclusively for the children of church members. After a Sunday afternoon swim, there would be picnics and group singing and often evening services.

The mothers and sisters did their bit in planning the picnics:

Ingeborg anxiously approached the cleared place where the barbecue fireplace had been built. Tom was standing arms akimbo, talking to Tom Waldrop and Kenzie Dattner. He scorned an apron.

"Tom," she said, "do you have everything you need for the sauce? There's more butter in the ice box."

Tom grinned at her. "Plenty," and added, "How does it smell? We put some cedar logs in that fire."

Ingeborg regarded the young goat, carefully impaled on the spit. Roast goat was reputed to be wonderful eating, and Tom was master at barbecuing — but somehow she couldn't help but be doubtful — there were a lot of hungry children and adults out there, splashing in the cool water.

"Tom and I were just reminiscing about the building of those six concrete tables." Kenzie Dattner came and stood beside Ingeborg. "Tom insisted on finishing the work at night. Perce was elected to hold the flashlight. We said a doctor should have a steadier hand."

"Well," said Tom Waldrop with conviction, "they couldn't have been any sturdier. They certainly withstood that high water we had last month. You know what this river needs is flood control . . . ." and the three men walked toward the lake, discussing the problem.

Ingeborg picked up a fork and tested the meat. The juice followed the tines of the fork as she withdrew it. "Yes," she thought, "it is almost done — and it does *look* good!"

Suddenly a fireball in a wet bathing suit threw herself towards Ingeborg. "Mother, mother," cried Hortense, "did you see me dive, did you see me dive?"

Calling Tom back to turn the spit, Ingeborg gave a satisfied look at the table spread with the rest of the meal, and hurried down to the lake. Looking out over the water, with the breeze lifting the curls at her forehead, listening to the happy

157

laughter of the swimmers and the people in the boats which were scattered over the small lake like fallen leaves, Ingeborg was very content. "This is wonderful for us all," she thought. "Surely if everyone could experience such comradely fun, could work together so unselfishly as our children and our parish have done — there could be no war and no hate among men, and we would all understand Christ better."

Camp Bratton was, and still is, a very happy memory for countless grown-up children and their parents.

The Rev. Philip Werlein had come to the parish in 1928. Tom was senior warden and wrote the letter accepting Werlein as rector. In him, Tom found a hard-working, aggressive young man intent on furthering the interests of his parish. Plans were presented to the vestry and congregation for a three-story educational building and gymnasium-community hall to be annexed to the present church. There was to be a full basement with rooms in which organizations might meet. A hall with a stage for lectures, programs and plays would be located in the basement under the gymn. There was only one dissenting vote on the vestry. Tom headed the campaign for funds and soon had $40,000 in pledges. The Rice Institute agreed to lend the parish the amount which was needed after $15,000 in cash had been raised. Not only did Tom contribute generously and help to solicit pledges and negotiate the loan, but Tellepsen Construction Company did the work without fee and much of the material was solicited at cost or as donations. Depression put a stumbling block in the way of the program, and it was difficult for the members of the parish to meet their pledges. But together the rector, the people and Tom worked endlessly so that the project might not fail. They could not let it fail. They would not let it fail. Tom supervised the construction. Common labor at fifteen cents an hour (the crafts at forty-five cents) was a minimum wage but it did help get the walls up! Although the third floor of the educational building and the basement rooms were left unfinished, the principal buildings and the tower were built. The cost to the parish was about thirty-seven thousand dollars.

A word about the appearance of the buildings. The exterior resembles Austin stone, but is actually reinforced concrete, poured into forms to give the impression of stone. The tower has intricate fretwork cast in concrete around the openings on the four sides. It has come to be called "Tom's Tower," and Tom and Ingeborg gave the chimes to the church. With a touch of that indescribable whimsy that is almost magical, the tower can be seen over the tops of the trees from Tom's front lawn.

To make way for the new structures, the rectory had to be moved. A lot was purchased four blocks away on Leeland Avenue, and Mr. Werlein, his wife and daughters were literally carried to their new location. Tom installed them on a foundation, added brick veneer, and in general improved and modernized so that it was actually a better house than it had been.

In recognition of his leadership, generosity and devotion to the Church of the Redeemer, the parish planned a surprise for Tom Tellepsen — a thing that is indeed hard to do. In January of 1933, a dinner in his honor was given in the new Sloane Hall. He was tricked into being there on the pretense of a special parish meeting. Lew Matteson who had lived across the street from Tom, was master of ceremonies. Holger Jeppesen, the Rt. Rev. Clinton Quin and the Rev. Philip Werlein spoke on behalf of the congregation. Tom's response was typically from the heart, "I want to thank you all for giving me the pleasure of doing what I have been able to do."

The community hall was dedicated in 1934 to Archdeacon John Sloane, father of Tom's good friend, Dr. P. A. Sloane. Tom composed the dedication. The simple eloquence is reflective of the man who wrote it:

> "Dedicated to the Glory of God and in loving
> memory of our beloved friend and neighbor
> Archdeacon John Sloane. May his spirit ever
> be with us in our endeavor to serve our Master
> and our fellow men."

After Mr. Werlein resigned, the Church of the Redeemer was without a rector for several years. It was during this period that Ed Hail, another dear friend of Tom's, tutored and presented a class of communicants to Bishop Quin for confirmation. This was a service rarely performed by a lay reader. Ed had been Howard's Sunday school teacher, and was Superintendent of the Sunday school for twenty-five years. He and his wife were active in the Church of the Redeemer from the very first Easter Day Service, and Mrs. Hail and Ingeborg worked together in the kindergarten.

The Rev. Gordon M. Reese came to the Church of the Redeemer on the day of the Tellepsens' twenty-fourth wedding anniversary. Reese stayed five years, during which time Tom was to see his daughters married:

The music swelled to a crescendo. Tom felt the collar tighten at his throat. He looked down at Hortense and she smiled at him, with only the tiniest glint in her eyes to indicate that tears might be lurking there.

"She is a beautiful girl," he thought proudly, "and as good as she is lovely." His mind went back many years, and it seemed as if the music he heard came throbbing from the organ in the church at Tvedestrand. The girl at his side was truly the daughter of his bride, and in remembering, Tom was close to tears.

The church was filled to overflowing. How glad he was he had had it painted, and put on a new roof. One could not give away a daughter like this in drab surroundings! As Tom looked out the entry windows, he could see the people standing at the church windows looking in. They crushed behind him too.

"We'll have to think about a new church," he said aloud.

Hortense laughed her crystal and silver laugh. "Now daddy, not right now," she said.

Lorraine was married in 1940 and Tom played his role of proud father with a practiced air: he had done this once before! "I'd hoped we have that new church for you, Lorrainie," he said, "but romance doesn't wait on blueprints. Lorraine hugged him impulsively.

Tom regretted that Camp Bratton had, little by little, lost its popularity. His children were grown and other parents failed to carry on the adult enthusiasm and participation that had made the camp a success. It was finally turned back to the original owner.

Christmas of 1939 proved, however, that Tom was still young in heart. Mr. Reese approached Tom to underwrite the cost of an outdoor pageant on the church grounds. The entire menagerie of Downey Brothers Circus was engaged, including camels, elephants, horses, etc. Tom saw that the special stages were erected, and he took part in the pageant along with Ingeborg and some three hundred

160

members of the church and church school. Music was by the Fogle-West Ensemble. Proceeds of the very successful affair went to charity, and it was a long-remembered experience for all.

Following Reese's departure in 1941, the Rev. Aubrey Maxted served as rector until 1943.

With paternal interest, Bishop Quin had watched over the well-being of the parish of the Church of the Redeemer from the very beginning. Now, in 1945, he recognized the need and sought as rector a man who would be a great leader. He found such a man in the Rev. Thomas R. Harris, who would leave his church in Waukesha, Wisconsin, after twenty-two years. On his initial visit, Dr. Harris stayed with Ingeborg and Tom, and there was immediately established the basis of a great friendship. Between Dr. Harris (whom Mrs. Harris calls *you* Tom) and Tom Tellepsen (whom Mrs. Tellepsen calls *my Tom*) there exists understanding and mutual respect. Dr. Harris has a term for it — *en rapport*.

The following derives from an interview with Dr. Harris:

It was Easter morning. The rain had been falling all night, and the water stood from curb to curb, making the Church of the Redeemer a veritable island. Dr. Harris smiled wanly to himself, "This is how Noah must have felt, watching the waters rise up. Only you couldn't launch an ark in Texas; it's too flat." This was his second Sunday in Houston, his second sermon.

The beautiful Easter music swelled from the organ, and in response, his spirits rose. He walked slowly to face the handful of people. Drab light filtered through the stained glass windows. Casually he noted the wet coats thrown back, but the faces turned to him were intent and he thanked God for their devotion. Tom and Ingeborg sat in their accustomed places on the right (the Epistle side), half way down the aisle.

The service concluded, the members of the congregation having gone their damp way after greeting their new rector, Dr. Harris turned back to the altar. He became aware of a check lying on the collection plate. He looked at it. The check was for $10,000 and a note on the left hand lower corner read "for the new church." It was signed by Tom Tellepsen. In the gray light of the church, Dr. Harris felt a surge of exaltation. Here in a simple gesture — to a stranger in a new land — here

161

indeed was the spirit of Easter: the kindling of hope and enterprise.

From this seed grew the movement that brought into
being the new Church of the Redeemer.

But, first, the rectory on Leeland Avenue was small and
at a distance from the church, and Tom agreed with Dr. Harris
that a rectory on the church grounds would be complementary to
the over-all plant. And, too, the third floor of the educational building and the basement under this building as well as Sloane Hall had
yet to be completed. Tom undertook this in 1945-6. A floor was laid
and walls and ceiling of acoustical tile were installed in the basement
and auditorium which was known as Tellef Hall. Here church services would be held while the old church was being torn down and
the new church constructed.

Mr. Tom built the new rectory for the sale price of the
old — some twelve thousand dollars. The new rectory is conservatively
valued at thirty thousand dollars. It was well built and occupies the
southeast corner of the triangle. Visitors from all over the world have
complimented its design and construction. The exterior walls are of
concrete to match the other buildings and are eleven inches thick.
The interior uses a grooved plywood in all rooms except the kitchen
and baths. An unusual and striking effect is captured by staining in
gold and bronze (the living room) or painting the plywood in different colors. The "house that Tom built" is reminiscent of other
buildings and of Tom's ingenuity! The entrance door is from the
Texas Company; the stairway spindles came from the old courthouse
in Angleton; the carpeting is from The Shamrock; and the roof is
from the bakery of the Fehr Baking Company.

The tiles were hot. The tiles were very hot! Tom
spread them out and considered his problem. Tellepsen Construction Company was in the process of remodeling the Fehr
Baking Company plant, and Tom had begged the old roofing
tiles "for the church." Using them on the rectory roof with its
offsets, meant cutting and fitting them. It was an exacting job.

It was the Fourth of July. Ingeborg was out of town,
and Tom was in one of his moods of restless energy, as was

his wont when a knotty problem presented itself. The holiday gave him a perfect excuse. Not even the union could chide him for doing the work himself.

He climbed up on the roof. It was midday, and he wrapped his hands and arms in newspapers in order to handle the tiles. His knees were similarly swathed. Twice that day Dr. Harris had come by to beg him to desist in the 110° heat. Not until he had accomplished what he had set out to do, would he come down. It was after four o'clock when he went home to shower before having potluck with the Harrises.

"Mr. Tellepsen," Mrs. Harris' voice was anxious, "are you sure you are all right? Let me fill your ice tea glass."

"Thank you." Tom was desperately weary — sapped of all desire even to move. But it was nice to sit quietly in the dining room with the rector and his wife. A breeze from the Gulf had come up with sundown. He was tired, but happy. "You have to know that you can always do it yourself," he thought to himself.

Wealth, social position, fame or fortune will never change Tom Tellepsen. He will always be able to "do it himself." He has that instinctive understanding of greatness that the power God has given man to do, is the basis of life.

The Rev. Gordon Reese recalls a somewhat similar instance. Tom, with only the Negro janitor from the church to help him, installed an attic fan in the old rectory one hot summer day. In Reese's words:

"The terrible heat, the work, the job didn't bother Tom. He wasn't too proud to labor with his hands alongside other workmen. Since that day, I've said to myself many times: 'If the whole country had adopted Tom's attitude towards work, race, color, creed, we would not be beset by labor troubles or difficulties with the race question, and this country would be a much better and happier place in which to live'."

When Tom and Ingeborg built on Park Drive, Eastwood was a coming residential area. Because of port development, the pressure of industrial expansion, many of the older residents have moved away. Not so the Tellepsens. This is their home, their community, their church — here is their heart. From this area, Tom, appointed Senior Warden of the vestry, set out to raise the estimated $250,000 to build a new church. It is 1946, still war time. Pledges are made but the total mounts slowly. Then, upon Tom's advice, an investment is made. A profit of some $44,000 results. Finances are such that steps may now be directed to the actual building. An architect of Tellepsen Construction Company draws the plans — a church without windows to seat, including a balcony, a thousand people!

A church without windows! What a startling proposal this must have been to the building committee. It was a functional idea, true, since the church was to be air conditioned and expanses of glass meant less efficiency of that air conditioning in the summer and loss of heat in the winter. But this was not the main consideration. For many years, Tom had dreamed of a church whose whole perspective would center on a mural at the altar. In his mind's eye the portrayal had slowly taken shape. In the center was Our Lord. About Him are grouped His disciples, only in modern dress as if they came from the ranks of mankind today. Religion to Mr. Tom is a basic philosophy by which you live daily; it lives itself by being a part of daily life. God's teachings through His son are not wholly confined to the Bible; they are standards of behavior, of thinking and acting, that one must follow every breathing moment. Thus the figures and the faces of the disciples are those of people Mr. Tom might know. John Orth, when he painted the mural after Mr. Tom had explained his idea and his dream, chose a farmer, a sailor, a common laborer, an Indian, a minister, an air force officer, a Negro, a white-collar worker, a Latin American, a carpenter, an old man. It took four months to do this mural, and it was sketched, detailed and painted at the Tellepsen Construction Company mill on the acreage behind the office building on Telephone Road. The blue of the background indicates distance and blends into the mottled blue-grays of the ceiling so that there is the impression of being on a hilltop. This is emphasized by the screens at the sides of the chancel, on which are painted trees and foliage. Christ preached out-of-doors in most instances and here, seated in the church, one feels that He is again standing above and before His people, speaking quietly and with confidence. Wherever you sit, His eyes seem to follow you. His eloquent hands, instead of imploring Heaven, are reaching out to the congregation as if truly He included them in His speaking. There is nothing to distract the viewer. The lights, in three coves sweeping

164

the entire length of the auditorium, can be varied in color and intensity. Blues predominate. The lights for the Communion Service can be dimmed by a pedal control at the altar.

In the background, behind the male disciples, are the indistinct faces of women. This is Mr. Tom's thought also. "It is the men," he says "who mostly need religion." It is the maternal influence through which most men find their faith. Mr. and Mrs. Tellepsen gave the mural in memory of their parents, Tora and Tellef Halvorsen and Helge and Ole Hendrick Larsen.

Lectern, pulpit, altar, communion rail were fashioned in the Tellepsen mill. The church organ once was played on state occasions in Governor Ross S. Sterling's home. When the latter was turned over to the Optimist Club for Boys' Harbor, Mr. Tom bought the organ for the church and had it completely renovated. This acquisition is typical of the way Tom has combined economy and sentiment, in instance after instance: such is the source of ingenuity! The pews from the old church are in the balcony; the former altar is in the small chapel beneath the church auditorium. This chapel was dedicated to Kenzie Dattner, a long time worker in the church and many times senior warden, and Tom's dear friend. It is used for small weddings, daily communions, etc., and at all times is open for meditation.

Thought and care have been given to the functioning of a church. The working Sacristy has adequate cabinet and counter areas and a special sink arrangement so that the water which cleanses the vessels used in communion flows directly to the ground. Off the Minister's Sacristy, where garments are carefully closeted and the rector may meditate and rest, are the acolyte room and choir room. One of the hand-made tables from 1506 Palmer Street can be found in the Minister's Sacristy. It was made from scrap lumber in 1912 and is now enameled a dark color; its dowel construction contrasts quaintly with the other more modern furniture.

The entrance hall of the church is wainscoted with Italian marble, and convenient small tables to hold church literature, guest book, etc., are designed and hand-grooved to blend with the decor of the lobby. The doors of the church auditorium are opened in the evening, and by virtue of a small altar light, the mural is visible from the street. Many, many cars slow, or come to a stop before the church every night.

An addition to the church is a gift by the ladies of the auxiliary in honor of Mr. and Mrs. Tellepsen. It is a handsome bronze baptismal font. Here again the installation is such that the water flows directly into the earth.

In the church basement there are rooms for the Boy Scouts (Troop #4), the Girl Scouts and the choir.

The church was engineered and built by Tellepsen Construction Company under Mr. Tom's supervision for approximately $230,000, but is valued at probably twice that amount. The entire plant, which started with an original investment of $27,000 for site, church, recreational building and rectory, is now worth close to a million dollars.

But the value can hardly be expressed in dollars and cents. The Church of the Redeemer is indeed a community center and not for church functions alone. Besides the Scouts, other organizations gather here. The second floor of the educational building now houses a branch of the Houston Public Library. Here can be found other pieces of Mr. Tom's hand-made furniture from the house on Palmer Street. The first floor kindergarten room for neighborhood children is light and airy and a most attractive room. There are dancing classes in Sloane Hall, lectures, book reviews, political meetings, theatricals, films, etc., and the halls and rooms hum with activity. Church dinners, such as at Thanksgiving, are community affairs. The kitchen facilities are adequate to serve five hundred people in Sloane Hall.

Tom attends church regularly. Often when the sermon or his thoughts inspire a desire for solitude, he will leave by the side door of the church.

Tom and Ingeborg have not missed the yearly parish meeting in thirty-five years. It has become the custom that at the conclusion of these meetings, Tom is asked to rise and say a few words. Simply, he expresses his philosophy of religion and of life and thanks God for this church which has meant so much to him and to his family. To his fellow parishioners, his words are a kind of benediction, and the year's interval in their church would not be complete without them.

The church building program being completed, Mr. Tom offered his resignation as Senior Warden. His work was done. But Mr. Tom loves "his" church. Towards it he is paternal and protective. According to Dr. Harris not a day passes but Tom drives slowly by or comes in to wander about. He seems to sense if there is any amiss situation where he might be of help.

From the mountain top in Tvedestrand, the visions he had of praising God and serving mankind are symbolized in this church. In it he humbly offers to his God a measure of the gratitude he feels for His guidance and love throughout his life. There is here, too, a somewhat mystic identification. As lives have been touched and spiritually helped by his church, Mr. Tom feels he has served God as well as man. Through his — Tom Tellepsen's — good works in his church and in his life, are made manifest the will and the power of God. Tom Tellepsen is a true servant of God, and more, he is His disciple.

Mr. Tom's Home

If Mr. Tom's avocado-green Chevrolet were Old Dobbin, with reins slack, it would from habit find its way out the driveway at 4518 Park Drive, to the Tellepsen Construction Company office building at 1710 Telephone Road, down Leeland Avenue to the East End Bank, and over to the intersection of Telephone Road and Eastwood where Mr. Tom glances with affectionate appraisal towards the Church of the Reedemer. This is his life — his home, his work, "his" bank, "his" church.

When they were living on Palmer Street, Tom and Ingeborg had discussed the new home to be built on Park Drive. Tom looked at the pictures Ingeborg showed him in her magazines, and he listened to her request for big windows and a home "that will last the rest of our lives." These desires stemmed from Norway — one an opposite and one a like. As a rule, Norwegian houses had small windows and the larger ones were made up of many small panes. In some way, Ingeborg identified these windows and their restricted vision with the narrow intellectual outlook she had known as a child. To her, wide expanses of glass meant freedom of thought and conscience. Yet all the homes in Norway were well-built and substantial and endured for generations. This, to her, meant stability. Entering the residence at 4518 Park Drive, you recognize the fulfilment of both desires. The windows are large, and, when possible, there are mirrors across from them — "To bring the outside in." The house is certainly well-built and handsome with an air of individuality and old-world charm.

To finance the building of his house, Tom went down to talk to Mr. M. S. Murray at the Lumbermen's National Bank where

168

Tom had been doing his banking. Murray was a bit startled at the elaborate plans Tom showed him with such pride. Tom judged the house would cost around four thousand dollars. Murray tried to discourage Tom on the basis of extravagance, but Tom knew what he wanted. In the end, Murray did help him get his loan from the newly organized Great Southern Life Insurance Company.

Construction of the house was begun in the fall of 1916. Tom did a good deal of the work himself:

It was late, and Tom was impatient. He wanted to get back and finish the forms for the cement urns he was making for the front porch of the new house. Shopping at the Preston Avenue-Milam Street store of Henke & Pillot usually was a pleasant task for Tom, but tonight the list Ingeborg had given him seemed unduly long.

He thrust the sacks hurriedly into the back seat of the Model T and went around front to crank the car. He had stopped very close to the cement wall on top of which the sidewalk led into the store. He was cramped, and as he struggled to put pressure on the crank, the motor sputtered and backfired. The force of the reverse pitched him upward and threw him across the sidewalk.

Stunned, Tom hunched to his knees but his right hand would not support him. He realized that his wrist was broken. The bone protruded unnaturally; the pain was intense.

The policeman who was stationed at the corner pushed aside the curious passers-by who grouped about Tom. "Are you all right, sir? Let me help you. I'll drive you to the hospital."

Tom waved him aside with his good hand. "Its all right, officer, I can drive with my left hand." His shy embarrassment forestalled the man's amazed protests and he let Tom go, steering with his left hand.

At St. Joseph's Hospital the bone was set and the wrist put in a cast. Stay the night? No! There was work to be done. The sling made awkward driving, but Tom got home. He made the six urns, too, all with his left hand. They remained to adorn his home until it was remodeled in 1924, and two now stand in front of the caretaker's house back of the Tellepsen office building. The others are in storage.

169

In the summer of 1923 Ingeborg planned to take the three children to Norway. In secret Tom had decided upon a big surprise. While they were away, he would add another story to the house so that there would be a separate room for each child. After all, Lorraine was five and a young lady!

The night before his family's departure, Tom lay awake thinking of his plans, tantalized by the necessity of keeping them to himself. Suddenly he became aware of soft singing that grew louder until he realized the serenaders were approaching the bedroom windows. He could make out the words "God be with you 'til we meet again." Ingeborg was already alert, slipping from the bed and reaching for her robe. The group of neighbors was led in their singing by Mrs. Hart who lived on the opposite corner across Maplewood. There was talk and laughter, and this episode remains a warm and friendly memory.

Tom lived in the garage while the work on the house was being done, and although during the day he had to be out superintending construction of the Long Reach Wharf on the ship channel, his early morning hours and his evening hours were spent on the house:

One night a stranger appeared in the doorway as Tom worked, fitting cabinets in the remodeled kitchen.

"Yes?" Tom asked.

"I've heard so much about this house," the man replied. "Do you think Mr. Tellepsen would mind if I looked around?"

"Come in," said Tom, "and I'll be glad to show you the place."

The man removed his shoes, as Tom was in his stocking feet. They walked carefully over the gleaming floors and up the stairway to the second floor. He examined all the rooms in detail.

"Old Man Tellepsen certainly has himself a swell home," was his comment, and he went away, unaware that his guide and host was none other than the "old man" himself.

Another incident invites a chuckle and gives substantiation to the statement that painters have an affinity for certain other liquids besides paint. It involves a five-gallon keg of wine Tom had put up from the grapes his family loved to gather every fall on picnics in the woods. It was tasty stuff, and Tom thought he'd successfully camouflaged the keg in the corner of the garage. One night when he came home he found the painters in a merry mood, no painting done —and the keg was empty!

Tom furnished the new rooms. He went to his good friend and former client, Mr. Hugh Waddell, who back in 1917 had helped Ingeborg select her first new furniture — a dining room suite in oak. Pieces of this suite are still in occasional use today!

Tom also had Ingeborg's Hupmobile repainted! He parked it in the driveway before climbing into his own Model T to drive to the railroad station for his returning family. He turned his head in satisfaction to survey his transformation. What would they say!

Tom was bursting with excitement when he drew up to the Union Station. There they were! Howard had grown a foot, he did believe. Hortense tossed her bobbed hair as she threw herself into his arms. Lorraine's cherubic joy brought tears to his eyes. They all talked at once as they drove home, trying to cram into one brief half hour, all their experiences of four months. So absorbed were they that not until the car had stopped behind Ingeborg's in the drive and they had tumbled out, did they realize the changed appearance of their home. Tom will never forget the exclamations of surprise and pleasure - - - it seemed to him as if they literally ran all over the house at one time, up and down, in and out, shouting and calling to each other. It was indeed a very satisfactory surprise.

From his childhood, Tom has loved and appreciated beauty. His mother's deft touches, in an otherwise modest home, her sensitivity to color and angle, these are clearly remembered. They are Tom's birthright. Tom's creativeness is perhaps more evident in the earlier houses he built and in his own home, than today when the bulk of blueprints and the typewritten sheaves of specifications must be closely followed and rarely represent a contractor's own ideas. Yet, as we have seen, a builder must be creative in matching his wits against circumstances — man-made and nature-made. Imagination and ingenuity are the handmaidens of beauty.

The exterior of the house has remained unchanged except for the entrance. The interior is more modern in decor and rooms have been converted or enlarged by removal of partitions, but still the stamp of the unusual remains — a flavor of distant places, the predominance of bronze and brass, of heavy silver and antique glass, of massive hand-carved furniture.

In the landscaping of his yard, Tom has had the opportunity to express his own artistic talent. At one side is a miniature sunken garden surrounded by a luxurious lawn, flowering hedges. The magnolias are full-leafed and the mimosas are unusually beautiful. Later when the corner lot on Maplewood was acquired, he fashioned a pond of boulders and a water wheel that turns as water flows over it into the pond. There are gold fish and lily pads: this for Miller Master Larsen's daughter. Reminiscent also of Tvedestrand, Tom recalled his knack of building boats. For his grandchildren he devised a river steamer, complete with clock motor, paddle wheel and all, to float on the pond in Eastwood.

* * * * * * *

In the early years, Tom worked long hours. Ingeborg knew that darkness did not necessarily mean that Tom would or could be home at any particular time for dinner. She understood. Her old-world background helped her to accept Tom's deep obsession and devotion to his work, to his self-committed, self-dedicated task of accomplishment. "Man is master of his household." So she had been taught.

Ingeborg Tellepsen is a person of great depth of mind and character. The formal teachings of her youth in religious belief and in personal conduct had left her unconvinced, unsatisfied. Always she was seeking for a meaning to life that would find harmony with the assurance of her own instinctively affirmative philosophy.

"Surely there is more to this wondrous bounty of life than gloom and foreboding," and she thought, "Who am I? Why am I? Surely my impulses are for good. I love life so very much; it is so magical. Father in his morning and evening prayers stresses the wickedness of people and the punishment of sin. I cannot understand why fear of the Devil should concern good Christians more than the love of God." These were the adult thoughts of a young Norwegian girl who was to find in the free-thinking atmosphere of America, the inspirational motivation of her life.

In her father's house her scope of reading was limited to the Bible and religious books where the implication "Thou shalt not" was predominant. In her early years in this country she read avidly everything she could put her hands on, even Shakespeare. It

172

was glorious and her agile mind thrived on the stimulation of literature. In Katjie Clicquennoi Tharp, who had married the son of Tom's good friend, George Tharp, she found a kindred spirit. Together they went to lectures, read recommended books and discussed what they had heard and read.

With Katjie, Ingeborg attended old Christ Church in downtown Houston. In the vigorous preaching of the Rev. Peter Gray Sears she found the religious philosophy she could accept with sincerity, enthusiasm and a lifetime of devotion. Looking back, she thoughtfully and humbly reflects that this influence was basic in her adult life; her earnest and impetuous searching was given a point of focus. It was a wonderful discovery to find a church whose interpretations were broad and tolerant and happy. It accepted the things that Ingeborg's conscience had said were beautiful and good. It encouraged her to think, to read, to ask questions and to talk about her innermost thoughts and wonderings, eagerly and openly.

It has often been observed how husband and wife absorb traits and beliefs from one another. As Tom lived his convictions, so in the atmosphere of Ingeborg's intellectual curiosity, he became more articulate in the need of expressing what he thought. Ingeborg, too, on the foundation of Tom's faith and determination, found her attitudes solidifying into confidence and serenity. Throughout the years, any untoward situation was purely temporary. She instilled in the children this same outlook upon the shortcomings of life. Notified of Tom's accident in Mexico, she nevertheless refrained from telling the children. Hortense was a student at the University of Texas and learned of the accident from a solicitous inquiry of her French professor who had read about it in the newspapers. Anxiously she called Ingeborg in Houston. Her mother's answer was what might have been expected: "Daddy will be all right — don't worry."

Ingeborg's studies have taken her into the realm of metaphysics and into the study of comparative religions. She believes in the psycho-somatic benefits of prayer and affirmative thinking. Dr. Glenn Clark is a good friend and stays with the Tellepsens when he is in town to lecture. Both Ingeborg and Tom have attended sessions of the "Camps Farthest Out," sponsored by Dr. Clark all over the world. Here some of the world's leading philosophers and scholars have met to pray, to meditate and to discuss all matter of religious and metaphysical questions concerning Man, his Maker and the universe. Although Tom has not had as much opportunity nor the time to devote to these studies, as has Ingeborg, still he has found these experiences at the "Camps Farthest Out" instructive and inspirational.

Tom and Ingeborg have become very close in a mutual understanding and interpreting of life in its broad and in its personal sense. It is as if they approach this from different directions. Every morning at breakfast they meditate and pray together. Tom will read to Ingeborg. Sometimes he reads from *Weekly Unity,* a publication of the School of Unity; sometimes from Norman Vincent Peale; but his favorite text is a slim volume of poetry and prose entitled *Mightier than Circumstance* by Frank B. Whitney. This book was given Tom one Christmas by Lorraine Sloane, wife of Tom's close friend, Dr. P. A. Sloane. The opening lines encourage the reader to

"Begin the day with friendliness and only friends
    you'll find.
Yes, greet the dawn with happiness. Keep happy
    thoughts in mind."

That Christmas morning will never be forgotten. Ingeborg had been ill but had stoically kept her family from knowing. She had gone through the Christmas Eve festivities as usual. The next morning, as she rested, she asked Tom to read to her. He picked up *Mightier than Circumstance* and as he read, falteringly at first, Tom and Ingeborg were unspeakingly aware of a tremendous and glorifying presence, and Ingeborg's illness seemed to leave her, and she was calm and refreshed. Thus began a wonderful practice — their morning meditation and communion in which Tom finds genuine solace and inspiration. His reading is, to him, a spiritual talisman and a now inseparable part of him. It gives him a reserve of spiritual strength from which he can draw faith and optimism during a business day. He calls it his "bop" which is an affectionate reference to a child's symbol of fulfilled need. As a toddler, Tom Kelly Butler, Tom's eldest grandchild, called his baby pillow a "bop," and without its soft, familiar presence he could not fall asleep.

One custom that would seem to be indicative of Tom's present mode and attitude towards life is the habit of asking to lunch each day two or three associates, from Tellepsen Construction Company, from the bank, etc. Ingeborg plans the menus but never appears; it is strictly Tom's. The talk may be of shop but more frequently travels to relative fields of experience and even philosophy. Thus Tom keeps in touch, not so much with the events of his business interests, but, more important, with personalities and ideas. It may not seem immediately apparent, but in a real way this luncheon hour has a kinship with the morning meditation and renews the spirit and purpose then established.

*   *   *   *   *   *   *

Back in the early days, there was little time for reading or discussion. To Ingeborg fell the task of guiding her children and of disciplining them. The girls cannot remember a single instance of reprimand or punishment by their father. Sometimes they might not see him for several days when work required that he be up at dawn and home past bedtime.

Yet Tom was never too busy not to heed the requests of his children. For instance, the swings had represented an important acquisition to the young Tellepsens:

"Daddy?" Lorraine stood at Tom's elbow, her eyes wide and intent.

Tom turned the pencil in his hand. He had been making a rapid calculation on the corner of the newspaper. He knew that there was something "not right" about that roof plan for the Art Museum wing. He had been uneasy all day.

"What is it, baby?" he asked absent-mindedly.

"Daddy," a wistful note crept into her voice, "could we have a swing?"

Tom grinned and in his mind's eye he saw for a moment a child's swing silhouetted against the waiting skeleton of the Art Museum.

"Of course you can," he said enthusiastically. "I'll have the boys make one up tomorrow."

True to his word, not only a swing, but a complete set of bars, slide, trapeze, etc., was manufactured at the shop and the sturdy pipe legs embedded in boots of concrete.

"Daddy is a perfectionist," said Lorraine in recalling the incident.

175

The swings and other play equipment made the Tellepsen yard the center of neighborhood activity. Everyone was welcome.

Although the children might not see Tom for days at a time, still there was Sunday. Tom devoted Sunday to his family. First they would all go to church and Sunday school together. After services, if they did not have dinner at home, they might go off on a picnic. In either case, when Grace was said, they would all join hands around the circle. This custom began so many years ago they have forgotten just how it started. The casual gesture seemed to cement the emotional bond and bolstered the timid earnestness of the speaker, as they all took turns in asking God's blessing. The custom continues in each of the separate homes today.

After lunch, they might go for a drive, or pick red-berried branches for decoration. They tramped through the woods to harvest wild grapes. Each December they went exploring to cut down a Texas pine for their Christmas tree.

One of Lorraine's first memories is of Sylvan Beach, of being tossed up in Tom's strong arms and falling fearlessly into the yielding embrace of the water. Always, her father's hand was there to help her gain her balance. As the children were not burdened by anxiety and doubt of the future, so they were free of any physical fear. Tom had no such fear and since he treated it so casually, his children did likewise.

Tom was strong and healthy and self-confident. His belief that other people have as much confidence in themselves as he had proved was valid for himself, brought about certain disconcerting moments for his family. Take their individual experiences in learning to drive a car.

This is the episode of the runaway Ford:

Tom had bought the car in 1915, and after Hortense was born, he persuaded Ingeborg to take Katjie downtown to a movie "in my car."

Ingeborg protested. "I can't drive a car."

"There's no trick to it," Tom said. "Just guide the car by turning the steering wheel."

He cranked the car and headed them towards town. Off they went, Katjie clutching her bag in one hand and her hat with the other, and Ingeborg riding high, chin up, looking

176

like she held the mane of a monster. Tom wasn't worried. She'd manage.

There was little traffic, and parking meant just stopping by the curb. The movie over, the two women faced the problem of starting the Ford and disengaging it from the cars ahead and behind it. They found a passer--by who cranked it, backed it out and, who no doubt wholly horrified and unbelieving, watched them start down Leeland Avenue full speed ahead. It must have been a harrowing drive, for Ingeborg said *very* little, but never drove again until Tom bought her the Hupmobile in 1916. An instructor from the agency taught her to drive it.

Tom's technique with the children was quite similar. Howard drove at nine, with some supplemental instruction from John Nelson, superintendent at the Miller Memorial Theater job.

When Hortense reached ten years of age, her father put her in the car and said, "All right, Hortense, I'll start the motor and you drive." She was on her own and recalls she wasn't even sure how to stop! At about the same age, Lorraine was self-taught, too, except that Tom did show her how to shift the gears. She remembers her jerking, jogging journey around Tom's warehouses on Clay Avenue.

"Well," said Tom, "I learned to swim by having to. You can learn to drive the same way," and pausing in recognition of a sudden thought, "You can learn to do a lot of things by having to!"

Tom had complete confidence in Howard, as he had in all his children. When Howard was only sixteen, he drove Tom's car to California on a three-week vacation trip. Along with Herbert Wilbourn and Robert Tracy, he visited Roland and Orin Triay who were spending the summer with their grandparents.

While we're on the subject of driving, let's speak of Tom's reputation for fast driving. The Rev. Mr. Werlein calls Tom a "veritable Jehu" and cites a trip to Austin in two and one half hours. To attend Howard's graduation from Georgia Tech, Tom drove from High Island, Texas, to Atlanta in eighteen hours.

And there were other occasions:

Tom turned his head toward Dr. Harris who sat beside him. They were headed for Waco and an Episcopal Diocesan

177

Conference. The speedometer stood at 80, and Tom had noted Harris' anxious awareness of that fact.

"Are you worried at my driving?" Tom asked.

Dr. Harris glanced quickly at Mrs. Tellepsen, who was dozing unconcernedly in the back seat, and was reassured. "I must confess," he said, "that I, myself, never drive — er, quite this fast."

"Well," said Tom, turning back to the road ahead of him. "What can happen at eighty miles an hour isn't much worse than what could happen at fifty. And I could use the time it takes to drive those thirty miles!"

* * * * * * *

Holidays were bonus days for the children. If no job crisis interfered, daddy would be with them:

It was the Fourth of July. Lorraine was wide awake in a moment, remembering the day. A pleasant chill swept over her, and as quickly her face was flushed with excitement. "The beach! The beach! We're all going to the beach," she sang out as she scampered down the stairs into the kitchen.

"Lorrainie," her mother's voice was softly chiding, "go get dressed. Your clothes are there at the foot of the bed."

Slim's grinning face appeared at the door. "All ready for the baskets, Mrs. Tellepsen," he said. "I've got all the tarps and the cots and some firewood. 'Member last time there warn't a piece of wood worth burning on that beach?"

"That's fine, Slim; here's the hamper and the water. The bedding is in that box there. Oh, did Mr. Tom give you the mosquito netting? I hope there's not an offshore breeze tonight, but we want to be prepared. Howard's going on the truck with you. You'd better get started pretty soon." Slim had been the driver of Tom's first truck, back in 1919, and now was an accepted and welcome companion on all holiday excursions.

This was an annual celebration of the Tellepsens, an overnight trip to Galveston. Slim would stake and support the big tarpaulin to provide shade and to shelter the improvised

178

table. At night cots were put up here and individual tents were brought along for greater privacy and protection against the night air. Tom slept in the open and usually scorned a cot in favor of a bed roll, with a log for his pillow.

The truck was off — coughing its exhaust. Lorraine waved to Howard and raced back into the house to pack her bag. Hortense teased her, "Why do you want to take the shells you got at the beach last time?"

"Sister," Lorraine sighed. How did you explain to an older sister such important facts? "I just want to match them with some new ones — and anyway, it's home to them," and she let it go at that.

Hortense smiled affectionately and continued on her errand. Tom had sent her for the American flag packed with loving care in the cedar chest. She watched him mount it on the elevated pole that pointed out over the front porch, and she noted how the red of the geraniums in Tom's cement urns complemented the stripes in the flag. Father and daughter stood for a moment in respectful silence as the wind spread out the folds of the flag.

Tom put an arm around her shoulder and his voice was mellow with emotion. "It's a wonderful flag, daughter," he said, "and a wonderful country. God has been very good to us."

She patted his hand. Hortense remembered this morning years later when Tom came to her on her wedding day and said gravely, "I think it fitting that we fly the American flag today." After all, on every state and national holiday, Tom proudly put up the flag.

There was a babble of voices. The Waldrops, the Kruses, the Sloanes, the Ferrins had arrived. The caravan was forming — three cars. Ingeborg remembered last minute necessities; some would be forgotten of course. The trip was gay in anticipation of a wonderful holiday.

Slim had found a site for the camp way down West Beach. Already at ten in the morning, there were crowds of picnickers, fishermen, campers. Lorraine couldn't wait to kick off her shoes and dig her toes into the cool sand — what a wonderful, indescribable feeling — like nothing else in the world.

Ingeborg kept an anxious eye in her direction as she took supplies out of the car. Tom had already gone with Slim to see about the seine.

179

"Fish for dinner, mother," Hortense was pulling on her bathing cap. "Did you bring plenty of lemons?" Not heeding the reply, she ran out into the surf, laughing in delight as the water swept up around her knees and she half-stumbled at the impact.

The men had stretched the seine out on the sand. Gently scooping the weighted edge into the water, they picked up the poles at either end and, letting the seine bow slightly with the floats bobbing at the surface, they began to move slowly into deeper water. The first haul was good, and some of the flapping fish caught in the net measured a good twelve inches. They let the crabs scurry back into the water. Lorraine put an iridescent angel fish into her bucket. "I'll build him a castle surrounded by a pool," she cried happily.

It was lunch time and Slim had assembled a table and put out the canvas chairs. No one loitered. The air, the water, the exercise had encouraged jumbo appetites. Each family had brought a covered dish. It was a potpourri of taste and aroma.

Off the shore, a line of shrimp boats paraded up and down in slow but steady pace. The gulls hovered inquiringly, and Howard tossed a crust, and then another. In a moment the vanguard birds had summoned others. They seemed to come from nowhere — gurgling their peculiar, not unpleasant cry — swooping and diving gracefully.

"I don't see how they keep from flying into each other," Hortense mused. Lorraine was laughing at their hurried, clumsy walk. "Like early newsreels in the movies" said Ingeborg.

A nap — or a treasure hunt? Lorraine pondered her choice. A paper sack retrieved from lunch, and off she went to gather oyster, snail and other molluscan shells, tiny petrified sea beans, torn from the disturbed depths of the Gulf, twisted pieces of driftwood. She loved to watch the mollusks that looked like tiny, enclosed fans. They were alive, and when the waves rolled back, would lie exposed. She picked them up and then, one by one, would plant them, watching each turn over on an edge and disappear. It was such fun!

Finally, she wandered back to camp. A terrifying sight met her eyes. Dr. Sloane and Tom Waldrop had Tom flat on the ground and were packing sand on top of him.

Lorraine ran screaming to her mother, resting in the shade of the awning, "Mother, come, they're burying daddy. Hurry! Hurry!"

Ingeborg quieted the frantic child. "Lorrainie," she said, "a jellyfish stung daddy on the side and the sand will help take the sting away." To reassure her, Tom took Lorraine by the hand and led her into the shallow water for a swimming lesson. Soon she tired, and Tom headed out alone into the deeper water. He was a strong swimmer, possessed of great endurance.

That night the moon rose late and seemed to slip out of the pocket of the night, riding the waves for a moment. "There are a million, trillion stars," thought Lorraine and gave up the thankless job of counting them. The breakers had subsided to a fraction of their daytime size, yet left a dribbling line of foam that glistened in the moonlight. The wind and water made a soft duet.

Lorraine stretched sleepily, with the blanket to her chin. She had teased to lie prone upon the sand "like daddy." Towards morning she awoke and felt a strange dampness creeping up her legs. She sat up to find water at her feet; the incoming tide encroached upon the trusting sleepers. She woke Tom, who called the rest, and hastily the men began to move back their encampment.

It was a rather unceremonious way to greet the day, but Slim soon had the coffee pot perking forth invitingly and all agreed that watching the dawn lift the shadows over the water was an experience well worth the early arising. To Tom that awesome moment when daylight stretched the horizon outward over the blue-green of the Gulf had a peculiarly moving significance. It took him back into his own childhood, and for a moment, he was transported in time and space to a mountain ledge in Norway. "How really few of us know the dawn," he thought. "It is God's time of day — it is hope and prayer and thanksgiving."

As much as Tom enjoyed these outings, a great part of his pleasure came from being with his family. He had had repeated tries at hunting and fishing trips. As a bachelor he had spent infrequent holidays fishing in bay waters. Occasionally he went "outside," into the Gulf, to intercept a mackerel run. Mackerel he considers a real delicacy and these occasions reminded him of his boyhood fishing escapades. He tried fishing again in the twenties when Kruse introduced him to his favorite sport — floundering. But Tom was too impatient. He was too busy to sit and do nothing, waiting for a temperamental fish to decide the particular bait Tom had was to his liking! The pall of black mosquitoes that greeted the fishermen made the old saw about "more mosquito bites than fish bites" painfully true in Tom's experiences. Hunting, too, he dubbed a waste of time; there were never any ducks. Only long hours of idleness. Tom wanted action!

* * * * * * *

Ingeborg was determined the children should have every advantage. All three studied piano. Hortense still plays, enjoying in particular her services as accompanist for Sunday school at St. James' Episcopal Church. Howard will probably never forget the recital at the Lamar Hotel at the conclusion of his two years of study. Nor will Tom.

"O.K. Howard," he summed it up, "you're through."

And then there was expression and dancing under Frederick Leon Webster, later to be the first director of the Houston Little Theater:

Ingeborg took her seat in the parents' section of the City Auditorium and spoke in a low voice to Tom.

"I'm more nervous than the girls," and to prove it, she raised an unsteady hand to a damp forehead.

"They'll do fine," Tom was paternally confident.

"You should have seen how they looked at me when I left them. Lorrainie had a tight hold of Hortense's hand and her eyes were full of tears. And Hortense's little mouth was smiling but quivering too!"

The restless audience hushed at the appearance of Mr. Webster at the curtains' parting.

"We'll begin our little program with readings by the older children," he said cheerily. "Now, you go right ahead and applaud and make the youngsters know you like them!"

One by one the tense figures came forward to speak their pieces. Hortense never missed a word; her sweet voice

182

floated shyly into the kindly darkness; the footlights brought small shadows under her eyes. Lorraine, at three, was still too young to take part in this portion of the program, but at intermission Ingeborg hurried backstage to help her into her snowball dress for the winter carnival sequence which included all of the pupils. Ingeborg had made their costumes of white satin trimmed with tiny balls of white fur. The bodice was tight and the brief ballet skirt full and flared. The little caps fit snugly, and fur balls angled from the peak, sometimes falling forward over the eyes. Lorraine impatiently tossed the fringe back off her forehead. "Mommy, I'm scared," she whispered. Ingeborg hugged her, and her smile seemed to reassure the child.

The girls would pull on stage a little red and white sled that Tom had made with great care. It would then become a part of the scenery as they performed their dance with the rest of the group. Another member of the troupe was Catherine Elsbury, now Mrs. A. G. McNeese, Jr. This trio had a picture made, sled and all, and it was published in the *Houston Chronicle*.

It was a memorable experience for the girls, and the sled remained a treasured souvenir for years. Typical of Tom's thoroughness in making anything, the sled was functional, too. On those rare occasions when winter bedded Houston with a soft cover of snow, they took out their sled and managed a bit of sliding on the wet and slick surface of the yard. No magic carpet could have conveyed them to more glamorous places in their imagination than the "sled that daddy made."

* * * * * * *

No discussion of the activities of the Tellepsens as a family group would be complete without reference to the wonderful days of Camp Bratton when Tom and Ingeborg and their children and their neighbors and their children worked and played together. As we have seen in a previous chapter, the Church of the Redeemer was the center not only of their spiritual education but for years, the source of their recreation as well.

* * * * * * *

Of Tom's boyhood friends and acquaintances, five have, quite by chance, visited him in Houston. Publicity on The Shamrock prompted a sixth, Fritz Bech, to write from Copenhagen.

In 1917 Hans Gundersen was first mate on a Norwegian ship which berthed for cargo in Galveston. Tora had given Hans Tom's address. He took the Galveston-Houston interurban and got off at the Eastwood station, some two miles from Tom's home on Park Drive. He asked haltingly of a passer-by if he could direct him to the home of "Mr. Thom Tellefsen." As luck would have it, this passer-by was a brick mason who worked for Tom. It was early evening and Tom was working on his books in the room in his home he used as an office. Looking out, he saw a man pass by the window. He recognized him and ran out the door, calling his name.

Hans had attended the wedding of Tom and Ingeborg in 1912, as had his younger brother, Carl. Carl Gundersen came to the United States and is now Chief Engineer for the firm of Babcock & Wilcox and lives in Wadsworth, Ohio. In 1950 he and his wife visited Houston and called Tom from the Rice Hotel. They met and found much to talk about. Carl jokingly told Tom he would have recognized him by the scar on his right cheek. "We were building a cabin on the mountain behind our house," Carl explained to his wife, "and Tom stumbled and fell against a wood saw. The teeth of the saw clawed his face. But that didn't hold Tom back. He had the strongest arms of any of us."

Tom delighted in showing off his adopted Texas by taking the Gundersens to a county fair at Richmond where Tom bought two calves in the calf scramble; one for the East End State Bank and one for Tellepsen Construction Company. Texas weather treated them, too, to another new experience: a flash flood caught them on their return from Richmond and almost marooned them on South Main Street in a torrent of water.

In 1925, Captain Birger Jorkjend docked his motorship, the *Ferncliff*, at the Long Reach Wharf which Tom had built just two years previously. His cargo was to include the port's one millionth export bale of cotton for the season beginning August 1, 1925. At the moment he was concerned with a more personal matter. Knowing that "Torjus" was in Texas, and he thought in Houston, he referred to the city directory to locate a "Tellepsen" who was married to an "Ingeborg." Their enthusiastic reunion was the first of many such happy evenings together, as Captain Jorkjend made periodic trips to the Orient, carrying Texas cotton. Often the Tellepsens were dinner guests on board his ship.

A charming story was written by still another friend for the *Aftenposten* of Oslo, after he had visited Tom and Ingeborg in

Houston. His name is Captain Harald Blom, who is some six years older than Tom, and who is still, at seventy-four, sailing the seven seas.

Late in 1955, the telephone rang. Tom answered and acknowledged his identity:

"My name is Svendsen," a man's voice explained. "Please excuse my calling, but I promised Haakon Neilsen, Chief Engineer on a Norwegian vessel docked down at the turning basin. He's looking for a contractor by the name of Torjus Halvorsen. I talked to your son, and he thought you might know him."

"Torjus Halvorsen," Tom was puzzled but interested. "No, I don't think I've met him here. Where is he from?"

"A little town in southeast Norway — called Tvedestrand."

Tom was startled and burst out laughing. It had dawned on him. "Yes, I do know the man you're looking for. I'm the man. My name was Torjus Tellefsen; my father's name was Tellef Halvorsen, and I haven't thought of myself as Torjus or heard that name in years and years."

That afternoon Tom and Ingeborg went down to the ship to meet Mr. and Mrs. Neilsen. It was thirty minutes before departure, but long enough to renew an old acquaintance. Neilsen's father had been a customer of Tora's, and Tom well remembered delivering packages to their home.

During their conversation, the Neilsens spoke of Tora and briefly of the silent years when Norway was under Nazi domination. Tom did not hear from his mother from 1942 until 1946, when the occupation was lifted. Her letter indicated prolonged illness. A telegram from Birger announcing her death reached Tom just days before her last letter. Tom was touched by Birger's comment that up to the day she died, Tora daily wore her old-fashioned brooch with Tom's picture in the center.

Today, Ingeborg corresponds in Norwegian with Gunhild Landgang, daughter of favorite Uncle Jörgen. On their trips to Norway, Tom and Ingeborg never failed to visit Gunhild who lives on

185

her mother's farm not far from Tvedestrand. It was of Gunhild that the story is told that Tom refused to see her when she was born "because she is only a girl."

Ingeborg's sister, Louise, still lives in Tvedestrand with her husband and three sons.

Whimsically, reminiscing about his life prompted Tom to follow up a lead to locate kin he believed to be in America. Egild Halvorsen, one of Tellef's older brothers, had settled in Iowa in 1869. Tom now has letters from two cousins, Egild's children — a Mrs. E. M. Mellem of Corpus Christi and Henry Halvorson of Fertile, Iowa. The latter sent Tom, for reproduction, two charming portrait-size copies of old tintypes of Tom's father and his father's mother.

* * * * * *

Mr. Tom has always loved his home. He likes to have friends in. He and Ingeborg would often invite Meg and Kenzie Dattner for a game of bridge. It is true the cards were shuffled, but mostly to emphasize the talking. Few contracts were ever completed; the four would talk and talk and talk. Tom and Kenzie were close and devoted friends. Their talk was of philosophy and religion and no doubt touched on life and death. Kenzie died very unexpectedly. Word reached the vestry meeting where Tom was present. It is a touching tribute to both men that Tom should ask the privilege of saying a prayer and knelt in homage to his friend and God.

Tom's dearest friends have, one by one, departed. Back as far as 1936, Perce Sloane died in Tom's arms. These two had been inseparable for many years. Often Perce would ride with Tom in the evenings when Tom checked his jobs. Sometimes they would talk; more often they rode in silence, needing not a spoken word to communicate their thoughts. In the words of Tom's old acquaintance, Judd Mortimer Lewis, "and one grown friend who knows that keeping still . . . is better than much chattering."

Tom loved home parties. In the late twenties and early thirties some ten couples living in Eastwood and attending the Church of the Redeemer would meet in each other's homes for cards and dancing. Some of these good friends would join Tom and Ingeborg after work and drive to Sylvan Beach or Galveston to swim in the moonlight, and Tom would fry the fish over a driftwood fire — in butter. And they would sing. The Rev. Philip Werlein lead the song with his beautiful tenor voice and Shirley Carlisle's soprano tones would gild the melody with magic. "Like angels singing," thought Tom.

And when there were the well-remembered New Year's Eve parties at the Tellepsens that climaxed with a steak breakfast at a restaurant downtown, with Tom as host.

When Mr. Tom is amused, the wrinkles at the oval of his eyes deepen, the eyes themselves closing to a mere glint, and a smile tilts the corners of his mouth. Tom chuckles in admitting that up until the time he joined the Shrine, he could have been considered a wall flower. He and Andrew Ness would take their wives to dances and stand on the side lines tapping impatient feet, but never venturing out on the dance floor. After he learned to dance, Tom made up for it; he was a favorite partner. When the new Tellepsen Construction Company office building was first constructed, part of the foundation in the back (now offices) had not been walled in and this outdoor dance floor was perfect on summer evening — for square dances. Mr. Tom was in the groove!

A corollary to his natural shyness, Tom warms to the admiring attentions of his daughters' feminine friends and takes great delight in squiring them about the dance floor or having them seek him out for conversation.

* * * * * * *

The Tellepsens follow the old Norwegian custom of observing the family Christmas on Christmas Eve. There are the Joe Kelly Butlers (Hortense): Tom Kelly, 17; Duncan, 14; Merri, 3. There are the Joe Russell Gribbles (Lorraine): Howard, 14; Kruse, 9; Sidney, 8; and Robert, 2. There are the Howard Tellepsens (June Learned): Karen, 14; Howard, Jr., 12; Tom, 8. Generally speaking, all three romances derived from the University of Texas at Austin: June was a Texas "Sweetheart" and a friend of Howard's sisters; Lorraine and Joe were classmates; and Hortense met her Joe at the wedding of a mutual friend!

Although they often gather for other occasions — always Easter Day — Christmas Eve is the most traditional of all. The festive board and the thrilling joy of seeing these wonderful children grow up is a never ending source of thankfulness to God for His goodness. The joining of hands as the Blessing is said by one of the children is always the highlight. After dinner, the doors to the living room are thrown open to reveal the magnificent tree, laden with colorful packages, brought by Santa. Tom distributes them. Hortense will play accompaniment for their favorite Christmas carols and always Tom will read the Christmas story. What treasured memories are these!

*   *   *   *   *   *   *

Perhaps the first community participation by the Tellepsens was back in the days of World War I when two very successful watermelon parties to sponsor the sale of Liberty Loan Bonds were held on the lawn of their Park Drive home. Japanese lanterns swayed daintily, and the piquant remarks of Judd Mortimer Lewis, principal speaker, sparkled as well.

In the early years, Tom worked with the Lions Club. He has been a director of the Y.M.C.A. since 1939, taking part particularly in money-raising campaigns. It is typical of Tom that so many of his own contributions are deliberately cloaked by anonymity. One of the original trustees of the Optimist Club's boys' camp before it was named "Boys' Harbor," it was his encouragement, as well as his thousand dollar check that prompted Don Donahoe, then Optimist President, to go ahead with plans to buy the Governor Sterling Home on Galveston Bay. "A white elephant," others said. Tom had vision. "Go ahead" was his advice, and today "Boys' Harbor" is a going establishment of sixty to seventy underprivileged boys, who find not only education and occupational training, but space and sunlight for growing, and the benediction of sea breezes for sound sleeping.

Tom has on several occasions prompted Tellepsen Construction Company to build at cost, plus one per cent, which is actually an outright contribution since overhead runs close to four per cent. This was true for the Children's Hospital and St. Luke's Hospital in the Texas Medical Center. The two represent an investment of between six and seven million dollars.

In 1945 the Board of Episcopal Churches of Houston set up a committee to find the means of building St. Luke's Hospital. Tom was named a member of this committee. When Tellepsen Construction Company was awarded the contract to build St. Luke's, Tom resigned from the committee. But even then, Tom's participation was not at an end. His parish — the Church of the Redeemer — was given a quota, according to membership, of seventeen thousand dollars. They raised thirty-five thousand.

Tom is today a member of the Episcopal Church Corporation for the Diocese of Texas, a body responsible for the handling of church investments, etc.

In 1951 Tom was surprised to receive the St. Olav medal. This honor is bestowed by the King of Norway on American citizens of Norwegian birth who have given outstanding assistance to Norwegian people residing or visiting in the United States, and whose success is of the kind to reflect credit on the country of their birth.

Tom was a charter member and an officer of the Scandinavian Club of Houston and has served as its president. The club sponsored a Scandinavian Exposition at The Shamrock, which served to acquaint the community with the products and the resources of the Scandinavian countries.

On three occasions, Tellepsen Construction Company has employed young men under the American Scandinavian Foundation trainees program. This Foundation was organized in 1926 and represents Norway, Sweden, Denmark and Iceland. The young men are selected by the national organization and arrangements are made in New York. They apprentice in the capacities for which they are qualified by education and experience. One, a Norwegian, Asbjorn Hagen, eventually trained under Bill Abrams on the railroad bridge across Lake Houston and proved a valuable employee. Now back home, his letters of bridge building in northern Norway bring satisfaction to his Houston tutors and friends. The other two were Chris Christoffersen, from Denmark, and Sigward Soderblom from Sweden.

Tradition provides that whenever Tom is next in Norway, he seek audience with King Haakon VII and acknowledge the St. Olav medal.

But there are no medals for all the kindnesses, the grocery baskets delivered in person, the unsolicited gifts and services to his neighbors, friends and employees. Tom squirms when forced to talk about them. He chooses not to remember yet he gives himself away — literally, too.

There is a lovely book written in Norwegian, with colorful prints of native costumes and scenery. The inscription on the flyleaf is in appreciation - - - "Blessed Mr. Tellepsen and family":
The story goes thus.

When publicity on The Shamrock reached Norway, a Mrs. Kirstin Bodin, a widow, wrote in desperation to Tom.

"My husband," the letter ran, "was a tugboat captain and he moored frequently in Galveston. He bought ten acres of 'orchard land' near Texas City. He paid taxes on it until he died in 1912. I know no more of it. Has the land any value, please? Would you be so good as to look it up for me?"

Tom was so good. The land orcharded salt grass in tangled profusion and was about to be sold for taxes. Tom paid the delinquent taxes and sent the difference between this amount and one thousand dollars (some $700-800) to the owner's widow, who rejoiced, and as she wrote later "bought a stove that needs no kindling." It took a year to clear title as the other heir, a son, was in Korea. Lately Tom was offered $150 for the acreage. He shrugs his shoulders. "It is land," he says, "and may be worth something some day."

The setting sun must brush this bit of nondescript prairie with a gentler light.

When his friends need him, Tom is as near as his telephone. And what is more, he is not content to delegate his help. If at all possible, he will look after the need himself. For instance, a friend called for advice when an unreliable workman had botched the repairing of her front porch steps. Tom took Slim out to the house and himself saw that the work was done properly and would accept not a cent in payment, saying, "You've spent enough on those steps already." Or, when an out-of-town business acquaintance was brought into the hospital for surgery, his wife was made comfortable in the Tellepsen home. How simple to have provided hotel accommodations (and it would have been deductible) but no, Tom and Ingeborg know the heart-warming value of sympathy. This is what makes their kind of philanthropy so different. Dollars build in stone, but human interest builds monuments of the spirit.

To quote an incident from the experiences of the Rev. Gordon Reese: "One day I went into the bank to pay a note which I had taken out for the children's education. I was informed that the note had already been paid. I tried to find out who paid it, but the bank teller told me he was not at liberty to disclose the benefactor; it was a secret, but it had been paid. I then said 'Well, can you shake you head yea or nay?' He decided he could do so. I asked, 'Could one of your board members have paid it?' He nodded in the affirmative. Tom Tellepsen was one of the board members. So I knew it must have been Tom."

There is probably no way short of blackmail, to really gauge the extent of Tom's generosity. It is indicative to say that the maximum amount permitted on the income tax form is by far the lesser figure. To Tom, sharing is a privilege. "In some countries," he says meaningly, "charity is a function of the state, and in these countries America's great opportunities and individual freedoms do not exist."

* * * * * * *

When asked to speak at the Ripley House, Tom complied and in the course of his remarks came to an astonishing conclusion.

"If I would have the chance to be born over again," he said, "I would want to be born poor. I would not want to change one detail of my childhood."

This was not a mere dramatic gesture.

This came from the heart.

Tom has given this idea a great deal of thought. He understands that man needs ever to progress. Without challenge, without sacrifice, even without failure, how can the traits of success — initiative, ingenuity, self-confidence, perseverance — be developed? Character is forged by life situations. To Tom, it is the battle that makes the spoils worth winning.

Because his father had died when Tom was a baby, Tom's youthful environment was modest in material ways. Yet he had love and understanding from his mother; he had incentive and pride in the accomplishments of his boyhood; he had the loyalty and affection of his friends; he had his dreams and visions of a confident future. Through all of this he found the assurance of a philosophy and religious conviction that was to stay with him throughout a vigorous and fruitful life.

"How blessed was my childhood," he says.

Tom has a quaint way of reversing a colloquial phrase. One goes not "back and forth" but "forth and back." How logical this is, and how like Tom Tellepsen. One goes affirmatively forward before it is at all conceivable that one should retrace one's footsteps and go back — for whatever reason.

Tom also acknowledges the validity of the phrase "to give and take." Yet his sense of justice is pretty uncompromising. Being predisposed to give, an unwarranted taking can be the cause of righteous and often vehement anger.

Work is Tom's hobby. His philosophy of work is more than a conscientious application of his high principles. There is an identification here with the purpose and reason for life. The labor of a man — his brain and hand — is to further God's will. Labor is therefore honorable and is the common denominator of mankind. It must therefore be good; it must therefore be right. Only as one adheres to this dictate of goodness and rightness can one man's work, can "one man" in fact, achieve meaning. The stories of his devotion to doing a job well and to his own superlative liking are myriad. There is hardly a page in this book that does not in some way reflect this. The following incident is a good illustration:

When additional plumbing was needed on the second floor of the church's educational building, a professional plumber proposed running the pipe on the outside of the building. Tom decided this would be unattractive, and on impulse, pulled off his coat, and directed a Tellepsen workman to cut an opening in the plaster wall. Through this opening they elevated the pipe, the jagged mesh catching at their clothing. The sleeves of Tom's white dress shirt were torn to fragments; the lacerations bled freely. When Tom stopped, the pipe was in place and his sleeves dyed a damp red.

It is difficult not to expect the same, almost fanatic behavior from others. To Tom, there is little margin for error, but time has tempered temper, and it is a quiet commentary that to those rebuked, there remains no lasting bitterness.

In the early days, Tom's passion for perfection in what he built often meant that at the conclusion of a job, when he was content to step aside and say "It is done well," there was little profit to him. As he grew in experience, he knew better how to estimate the costs, allowing for his self-criticism and high standards. But with the formation of his company and the need to delegate responsibility came the realization that he could not possibly check every job. Yet even today, so inbred is this attitude of conscience that when leaving a social gathering, or coming from a civic meeting, he will say, "Let's drive by and look at the foundation of - - - -" or, "Let's check the job . . . . it's almost on our way." Sometimes, if things are not to please him, Tom will literally wade in and show the workmen what to do. This may be hard on dry cleaning bills and a wife's patience, but is typical of Tom!

If you would ask Tom what period in his construction life he found most exhilarating, the answer might surprise you. Rather than name some major achievement, like The Shamrock or the Melrose Building, he would in all probability refer to the years *circa* 1914-19 when he himself was working the hardest. He would be superintendent, purchasing agent, negotiator, etc. by day and estimator and bookkeeper by night. So eager was he to get on that he might work all night making computations (he had no adding machine) and think nothing of it. It was pleasure to him and not a cause for self-pity or discouragement. At one time he remembers bidding on fifty jobs and not getting one. This love of work and his optimism were godsends, Tom agrees, and without them no real success is possible.

* * * * * * *

There is not one among us who has not pondered the meaning of success, of happiness, the reason and consequence of our being here. Few of us are destined to come to any conclusion. Few of these few who do resolve upon an all-consuming endeavor in life, are privileged to achieve fulfilment. Success lies not merely in the recognition by others, but in a complacency of self — that one has done his best and deserves that recognition. And yet it goes beyond self. The world is divided into many interpretations of the concept of God, and in the earth-bound circle of himself, man must realize that consciousness, the power of thought, of will, of reasoning, of expression come from an Infinite Source. Thus what we think and do must meet a higher scrutiny. Yet conscience is a mirror by which man regards himself in God's sight. The successful man is humble in this knowledge. Success is a crusade of the spirit.

The lad who leaned upon the mountain pedestal above Tvedestrand, watching the Easter sunrise, was to know success. He had the potential then, and through the years, it was nurtured by his working hard and well. He faced the trials of both Nature and Man unflinchingly, and found happiness not in the fruits of labor but in labor itself. He clothed himself in faith in God and belief in self.

193

Ego is the core of all good works — and of religion too; only when blinded by vanity, does ego betray itself.

Tom's is a singular success. He is a simple man still. He rose steadfastly by strict dedication to the task at hand rather than inventive brilliance or the spurred and booted luck that played a spectacular role in the making of most Texas millionaires. He has not chosen to use his wealth to coerce, nor has it been translated into possessions or display of self. He lives today among the friendly walls in the home he built himself. His needs are simple and his luxuries few.

To Tom the measure of success is that he is in a position now to be of service to others when they need him, in ways both big and little, in kindly ways, unheralded and sometimes secret.

Time has a swift current for Tom Tellepsen. Even today he moves resolutely through a full schedule of tasks. Yet there must be times of recognition; life strings these like crystal beads. Looking upward as a building reaches for the blue Texas sky — the glint of metal in the sun, the orchestration of drill and dragline — he must know then that his visions are being realized. Standing in the reverent quiet before the altar of "his" church, the eyes of the central figure assure him that his abiding trust has been rewarded.

The trilogy of Tom Tellepsen is simply stated: "Youth shall dream; man shall labor; faith shall endure."

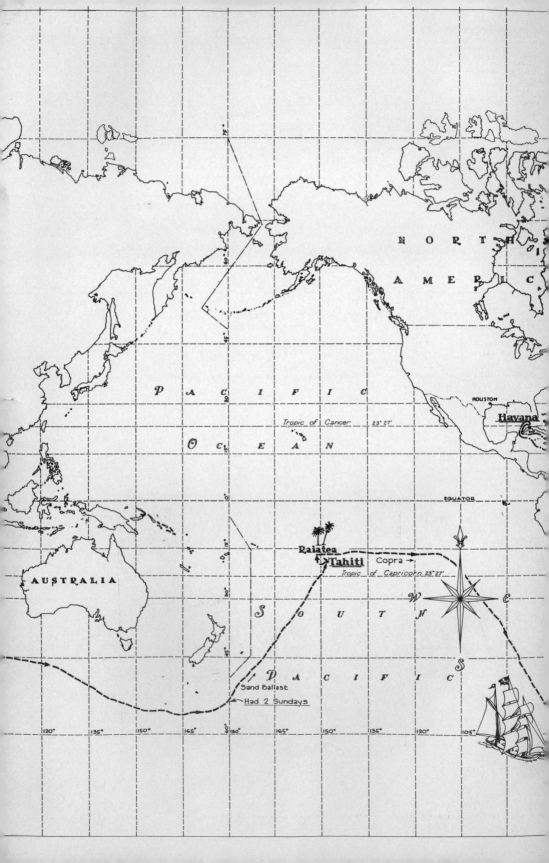